The New Finnish Theatre

The New Finnish Theatre

Jeff Johnson

215 pages $39.95 softcover
34 photos, bibliography, index
ISBN 978-0-7864-4860-9 Ebook ISBN 978-0-7864-5671-0 2010

With its impressive variety of theater, Finland is a superpower of performing arts. Finnish theater, however, is presently a hotbed of cultural debate regarding the artistic quality of its performances. This comprehensive overview of contemporary theater explores many of the most contentious questions concerning applied theater, its devised methods, and the corresponding challenges presented to traditional definitions of theater and related arts. Through interviews with new writers and directors, and first-hand accounts of recent performances, this study attempts to define what it means today to say "Finnish theater." It also addresses issues concerning Finland's emergence as a cultural player within the European Union and implications for its evolving national identity.

Jeff Johnson is a playwright and teacher. Recipient of numerous awards, he is the author of three previous books on theater and cinema.

McFarland

Enclosed please find:

Johnson. **The New Finnish Theatre**

Publication date: June 2010
Price: $39.95

This book is sent to you:

_____ with the compliments of the author/publisher.

_____ for examination.

_____ as your desk copy, with our compliments.

__XX__ for review. We ask that you include our website
address (**www.mcfarlandpub.com**) and our order
line (**800-253-2187**) in any review. **Send one copy**
of your published review, preferably via e-mail as
a PDF file (or a link for online reviews), to
bcox@mcfarlandpub.com. Alternately, publications
and tear sheets can be mailed to Beth Cox,
McFarland, Box 611, Jefferson NC 28640.

www.mcfarlandpub.com
ORDERS 800-253-2187

The New Finnish Theatre

JEFF JOHNSON

Foreword by Hanna-Leena Helavuori

McFarland & Company, Inc., Publishers
Jefferson, North Carolina, and London

Portions of this book were previously published in different form as "Emerging Themes and New Aesthetics in Contemporary Finnish Theatre" in *TheatreForum* no. 24 (2009) and as "The 2007 Baltic Circle International Theatre Festival" in *Western European Stages* vol. 20, no. 1 (Winter 2008).

LIBRARY OF CONGRESS CATALOGUING-IN-PUBLICATION DATA

Johnson, Jeff, 1954–
    The new Finnish theatre / Jeff Johnson ; foreword by Hanna-Leena Helavuori.
        p.   cm.
    Includes bibliographical references and index.

    ISBN 978-0-7864-4860-9
    softcover : 50# alkaline paper ∞

    1. Theater — Finland.   I. Title.
PN2859.F5J64   2010
792.094897 — dc22   2010004219

British Library cataloguing data are available

Front cover: *The Seven Brothers* (photograph by Jyrki Tervo)

Manufactured in the United States of America

McFarland & Company, Inc., Publishers
    Box 611, Jefferson, North Carolina 28640
    www.mcfarlandpub.com

For Pompey Scoot,
who makes The Monster happy

Acknowledgments

Special thanks to Hanna-Leena Helavuori, director of Theatre Museum in Helsinki, who helped in so many ways, but especially in shaping this book, provoking new lines of inquiry, and sharing rounds at Om'pu bar and a serious passion for pizza.

Others who provided invaluable help include Martina Marti for her unwavering confidence, strategic guidance, and hotel rooms in Tampere; Heikki Kujanpää for turning me on to Rytmi bar, which became my base of operations, and for securing a room for me at Villa Kivi; Dan Henriksson for introducing me to the Duck Pond and providing an apartment in the cool Kallio neighborhood, conveniently close to Rytmi and Om'pu.

Thanks to Jukka Hytti, Johanna Hammarberg and Pirkko Koski, who first introduced me to Finnish theatre, and to Laura Antola for her insightful comments.

Thanks also to Bob Von Achen for his essential help polishing this often tricky text.

I would like to thank Dr. Kathy Cobb, provost of the Melbourne Campus of Brevard Community College, for her support and consideration during my research.

As always, thanks to Carla for letting me get away with another one.

Finally, this project could not have been completed without generous financial support from the Finnish Ministry for Foreign Affairs and the Finnish Theatre Information Centre.

Table of Contents

Acknowledgments   v

Foreword by Hanna-Leena Helavuori   1

Preface: Down the Avanto   7

1. Identity Branding, Amateurs and Outlaws   17
2. Inside the Sauna Psyche: Influences and Isolation   36
3. Beyond Nokialandia: The Post-Political Critique of
      Neo-Liberalism   69
4. The Cult of Primitivism: Old Themes, New Forms   107
5. Performing in the Duck Pond: Finland-Swedish Theatre   144

Afterword   184

Works Cited   193

Index   197

Foreword by
Hanna-Leena Helavuori

Finland is the small superpower of performing arts. The variety of theatre performances on offer is impressive. Statistically every other Finn goes to the theatre at least once a year. The total spectator figures add up to around 2.9 million, ranking Finland — a country with a population of 5.2 million — among the top countries in terms of the popularity of theatre. Additionally, there are over 1,000 active amateur theatre companies in Finland, which makes an average of over 10,000 performances annually. A similar level of popularity of theatre in the United States would mean that more than 150 million theatre tickets would be sold.

For many foreigners, watching theatre performances in Finland is a truly overwhelming experience. The audience sits silently. Not the slightest slur is heard. No one voices rampant enthusiasm or utters exaggerated responses. To view a Finnish performance is to listen between the lines, noting subtleties and nuance. In Finnish theatre, the value of the word is high; each is weighty with meaning.

Theater is perhaps the only truly popular form of art in Finland that still matters. Theater here thrives. It has the ability to provoke public debates and stir the consciousness, whether it concerns school shootings, taking care of the elderly, the burnouts, the suicides, the decline of social security, or the increasing commodification of human beings. The themes tend to be rather heavy, even for a country noted for its gloomy songs that echo with carnival laughter.

Theatre artists function as influential debaters. Theater is the watchdog. Do we grasp a reality in the theatre? What are the realities? In what kind of a world do we live? The traditional text-based theatre lives vigorously. In that theatre the focus is on reality, the stories, the mimesis of its plot and characters. Theater is a means of making sense of the world, giving new insights into history; it means recognition in the deepest sense of the word. Theater is like a prehensile organ signaling the reality, or various realities, of its host.

Theater has meant the empowerment of people throughout the nation's history. It has remained essential in Finnish society. It has kept its ethos, its moral presence. While we can claim that Finnish theatre is capable of performing our fears and wishes, we may say that modernism never truly infiltrated the Finnish theatre and drama. That is not to say the haunted image of a standardized drama and its forms still exists, but from these remnants contesting forms of drama do emerge.

A renaissance in Finnish playwriting is underway. And traditionally, the richness of new contemporary domestic plays has been an indicator of the well-being of theatre. The more Finnish plays are performed, the greater the success, which breeds pride and self-satisfaction. While many of us foster belief in the theatre's future, others are less optimistic. Many current theatre practitioners, for instance, have abandoned the young theatre audiences and the challenge to communicate with them by trying to find new ways of performing. If fostering potential theatre audiences fails, the crucial game will be lost. The future of the theatre depends on the big stages of the local municipal theatres. They should be obliged to find new forms and new aesthetics.

There are those who try to find new forms in modernism, attempting to extend the scope of the drama beyond kitchen sinks. Emilia Pöyhönen, for instance, has found a genuinely grotesque, stylized and poetic way of writing. Her recent *The Chosen Ones* (*Valitut*), staged in the repertory of Tampere Worker's Theater, proves that these contesting forms do not have to remain in small houses or experimental venues.

Pirkko Saisio writes plays that treacherously disguise philosophical conversations in human relationships. Works like *Insensitivity* (*Tunnottomuus*), *The Children of Baikal* (*Baikalin lapset*), and *Fever* (*Kuume*) explore difficult themes about people who have lost their moral compass, the political awareness and the mistakes of the young communist generation of the 1970s, and issues relating to the church regarding female priests and the marriage of homosexuals.

Juha Siltanen's *Rage Cabaret* (*Raivokabaree*) mixes the cabaret form and genuine Finnish "goofing art," incorporating a range of different styles, including lyrical monologues, boisterous group singing, comedy sketches, a poor man's ballet, tap dances and quiz shows, infused with the nuances of a comedy act, all poking fun at the audience. "There is some sort of a story, too," Siltanen promises. His performances do not shy away from the politically impudent, offering a neat cocktail blending the political, spiritual and erotic.

In the contemporary documentary theatre the relationship to reality is more immediate than in the traditional drama-based theatre. One could call Leea Klemola's *Kokkola* a documentary partly based on her experiences while traveling in Greenland. The Helsinki Students' Theater's 2008 *Local Council* (*Valtuusto*) is a reenactment based on the minutes of a local council meeting. Katariina Numminen and her Viipuri Artistic Theater (Karjalan Taiteellinen Teatteri) composed a performance based on interviews with refugees from the Karelian region. This hybrid consisted of memories, wartime radio programs and interviews with the evacuees about their experiences. The performance functions as a laboratory for researching memories.

More and more of us consider mainstream theatre to be a categorizing, normative and homogenizing attempt to put all the critical ruptures aside. An increasing hunger exists for more fluid and flexible thinking about theatre and performativity. The contemporary performing arts scene offers interesting alternatives to the realism-dominated paradigms. An interesting renegotiation of relationships between different kinds of theatre or performing arts is ongoing and vital.

On the other hand, the mainstream municipal theatre's traditional educative tasks seem to have ended. It is not difficult to trace an increasing amount of commercialism and celebrity fixation in the theatre. Simultaneously, a newly devised working ethos is finding more footing, and not only in the marginalized theatres. There are genuinely many identities, many performing realities. The performative diversity gives space to new voices. Rather than trying to put labels on this rich growth of various kinds of performances, one just has to be sensitive enough to grasp them.

Perhaps one should use the term performing arts as a kind of umbrella concept that includes various forms of contemporary performing activities: considering traditional theatre and drama or literary text as a starting point is just one reality. Live performance can be considered as a ritual, a game, as therapy, a document ... you name it. All the variations are there. More and more performances deviate from the traditional modernist theatre. They offer new narratives with no theatrical plots. They abandon traditions of linear narrative and use time and duration instead.

Innovative theatre is often created outside the traditional theatre or performance venues. They are performances that live in a no-man's land. What these nomad performances share is a desire to challenge conventional perceptions of performance and reality, of seeing and being seen. They negotiate the traditional status of the text through the fetish of an actor. Aesthetics of minimalism deconstruct the performance into elements. Drama and text-based theatre and traditional authorship have become contested concepts.

There also exists in contemporary Finnish theatre a strong ecological concern. Suddenly, it seems that Finland's performing arts scene has a strong seed of anarchism in it. I would like to call Tuija Kokkonen's recent performance *Mr. Nilson* or *A Performance with an Ocean View* eco-anarchistic in the sense that it depicts some sort of ecotopia. The play is anarchistic in the sense that its performance means freedom, not freedom to enslave the other, not to subjugate the other, not to own or tyrannize the other. Evident in this performance is a lack of hierarchy and a denial of moral and ethical ideals. *A Performance with an Ocean View* took place in a suburb of Helsinki beside an ancient shore of the Yoldia Sea formed after the last ice age. The excursion to this ancient landscape gave the spectators the possibility to mediate with nature, to dwell in time. Wandering clouds or the darkening sky became the silent and slow protagonists.

At the same time as these performances question the people-centered view of the world, they seem to suggest that it is time for us to step aside. This stepping aside means performances allow togetherness without forcing a shared identity. For instance, Kirkkopelto and Alternate Spaces Group's performance *Odradek* could be seen as performative research, questioning the anthropomorphic paradigm. This concept is taken from a short story by Franz Kafka and the odd creature called Odradek. Odradek is something hidden, something useless and marginal. Odradek also dwells in our bodies. It could be interpreted in a Freudian sense as the repressed mind of the oblivion. It is about longing, wishing to be accepted. We are invited to find these Odradeks, see how the Odradeks are functioning in our bodies. We become part of the investigation. This new approach to theatre diminishes the importance of the director; it is more focused on physical exercises, techniques, experiments, emphasizing the elementary and the primitive in the shaping and processing of experience.

This relationship between the audience and the performers, as in a happening or a performance, puts into question the traditional auteur director and all the modernist theatre professions; it means new notions of authorship. It opens space for alternative encounters, different kinds of connections between the performers and the audience. In fact, there is a kind of recklessness and shamelessness, especially among many young female theatre artists who dare to explore new ways of performative research. With innovative companies like The Reality Research Center (Todellisuuden tutkimuskeskus) focusing so intensely on emotions, it is a small wonder that there exists a stunning dose of creative performative madness and unconventional uniqueness in the Finnish theatre. During the same weekend this piece was written it was possible to see Tuire Tuomisto's *The Lonely Rider—A Performance About Depression* (*Yksinäinen ratsastaja—esitys depressiosta*) as part of the new series

"Emotions" at Reality Research Center; a fascinating dramatic staging of Virginia Woolf's *Orlando* by Anna Viitala, a student at the Theatre Academy; Masi Eskolin's *Such As — Supplementary Writings on Good (Sellainen kuin — päällekirjoituksia hyvään)* at Kiasma Theatre; and Kristian Smeds' Ensemble's *Mental Finland* at the Finnish National Theater.

An ardent search is in progress. Unfortunately, these plays have not yet been translated. Yet this work is concrete proof of an emerging polyphonic theatre reality.

To navigate this changing theatrical ground is not an easy task for anyone. But Jeff Johnson has been audacious enough to dive into what he describes as this "avanto" of Finnish contemporary theatre. Avanto (a Finnish word meaning "a hole in the ice") is a good metaphor for this project. As Johnson states, his book is not a comprehensive view on Finnish theatre but is more like an impressionistic fresco or a snapshot. What is so fascinating is that this is not a one-voice presentation. Johnson's "napkin method" has brought together heterogeneous groups of theatre practitioners with contradictory ideas. This book shows astonishing sensibility, a sense for what's at stake in the Finnish theatre scene. Johnson has met many of those reckless artists who are breaking down the conventions. This book gives voice to them.

Of course, a Finnish reader's appetite grows when reading. It is a pity that Johnson missed the genuine vagabond Juha Hurme, the radical Heidi Räsänen, or that he was unable to experience Juha Siltanen's plays, which have been rarely translated. Still, the language barrier is not Johnson's fault.

The right timing is everything, and Johnson began writing about Finnish theatre at a moment of contentious cultural debate regarding the artistic quality of the established theatre institutions. He showed up exactly when discussions about the brand-making of theatres were becoming heated. His visits coincided with a period of renewed interest in theatre. Critics, professionals and the general theatre-going public were abuzz with questions concerning applied theatre and its devised methods and the corresponding aggressive explorations of traditional borderlines between different theatre professions, the traditional division of artistic labor, and the meaning of an emerging class of theatre "precariats" (coming from the words "precarious," referring to the insecurity of part-time and contract work, and "proletariat").

The territorial boundaries between different forms of performing arts are breaking down. We are living in a fascinating rapture zone.

"Don't blame the mirror if your face is crooked." This famous line from Gogol's *The Government Inspector* crossed my mind when reading Johnson's

book. He is not Hlestakov, but his challenging outsider's gaze at another theatre culture brings welcome disturbance and stirs our implicit presumptions.
To the readers who are not familiar with the Finnish theatre, this book provides an arousing voyage into the performative realities of Finland.

Hanna-Leena Helavuori is the director of the Theatre Museum in Helsinki.

Preface: Down the *Avanto*

One night while researching this book I found myself in a bar in a small beach hamlet called Hanko with a napkin full of phone numbers and names I couldn't pronounce. And no cell phone.

I asked a young woman in a kiosk for a calling card. She looked up from texting long enough to tell me she didn't know what I was talking about. Never heard of such a thing. Which made sense, because I hadn't seen a public pay phone since I got off the plane. Finland is the home of Nokia. Everyone has a cell.

"There are more cell phones in Finland than people," she says, texting.

I finally asked the bartender — a hardened post-punk female fluent in studded leather, multiple piercings, spider webs of ink and a multicolored Mohawk, who must have been all of eighteen — if she would not only call one of the numbers but also talk to the person, explain who I was, what I was doing, and ask if the person would talk to me.

Sometimes this method worked; other times, well...

You can tell a lot about a book by what's not in it. Sometimes the bartenders wouldn't make the call. Sometimes people wouldn't answer the phone. Sometimes they talked, sometimes they didn't. Sometimes they showed up, sometimes they missed me. People were out of town, out of the country, at times out of their minds. Some were suspicious. One director said talking to me made her feel like a spy.

But while I was unable to connect with some of the most important figures in Finnish theatre, I did manage to contact many of them. The idea of this book, after all, was not to write about the history of Finnish theatre, or to record the comments of overly familiar figures that have a long track record in the Finnish theatre business. The point was to get an impression of what it means today to say "Finnish theatre." What is the context of the theatre in Finland? Who are the new writers and directors? Are the issues in Finland qualitatively different from other European countries? Are Finnish plays exportable only as exotica, or because of the specificity of their themes? Why are so many of the Finnish dramaturges so interested in exporting, what is driving this nomadic desire, and are simple economic factors decisive?

In the end, my haphazard methodology seemed particularly suited to the spirit of the country. The Finns were mostly humored by my project but also intrigued. They usually shrugged and accepted at face value my operative motif, which I explained by saying, when asked why I had chosen to pursue this project, that I liked to look at things and try new drinks (the girl's famous line from Hemingway's "Hills Like White Elephants"). In comparison, when a German dramaturge from Cologne heard I was writing a book about Finnish theatre, she stared at me for a moment, and then said, "The impertinence!" She laughed, incredulous. I couldn't help but think of Kurtz's dying words, "The horror! The horror!"

But I missed a lot. Intentionally skipping the fifty or so professional theatres around the country in order to focus on the smaller, progressive theatres, I still discounted some important players I would like to have experienced. At the fringe is Reality Research Center (Todellisuuden tutkimuskeskus), which claims in its statement of purpose to "open the channels of communication with local inhabitants about community issues and determine the minimum resources required for a theatre to operate independently"; also Kuriton Company (loosely translated as "Unruly Company"), which bills itself as "a new physical/musical theatre ensemble composed of performers striving to create works that bring together various skills in acting, dance, and music." Other important Finnish language theatres around Helsinki include The Jurkka Theatre (Teatteri Jurkka), the only professional "chamber theatre" in Finland, founded in 1953; and Takomo Theatre (Teatteri Takomo), which translates as Forge Theatre but could also be interpreted as Workshop, founded in 1996 by one of the most prominent theatre directors in Finland, Kristian Smeds. Important theatres outside Helsinki, along with those in Tampere, include the Lovers Theatre (Rakastajat-teatteri) in Pori (a city in western Finland) that performs new Finnish drama and experimental projects; Old Juko Theatre (Teatteri Vanha Juko) in Lahti city center (about 60 miles of Helsinki), founded in 1995, known for its strong commitment to new Finnish writing and provocative political attitude; and Castle Theatre (Linnateatteri), founded in 2003 in Turku, about 100 miles west of Helsinki.

Before I came to Finland I was sure of three things about the country. First, it had won the 2006 Eurovision Song Contest with a band that played heavy death metal and wore monster outfits and dragon masks. Second, script writer and film director Aki Kaurismäki was from Finland. (I'd seen some of his films but all I remembered was how his desperately ironical characters treated suicide as an afterthought.) Third, I knew Finland turned out champion Formula One drivers, but I couldn't pronounce their names.

Even after living for some time in Estonia, a tiny country less than two hours across the Baltic Sea by ferry, I had no clue about Finland. The Estonians liked to claim an affiliation with Finland to separate themselves from their southern (and to some Estonians, culturally coarser) cousins of the Baltics, Latvia and Lithuania. The Estonians were also not shy to express bitterness about their northern neighbor because the Finns had the good fortune not to be occupied by the Soviets during the Cold War and never adequately, in the mind of many Estonians, acknowledged the depth of deprivation visited upon the Estonians by the Soviets.

Otherwise, Finland was just one of those Nordic countries that conjured images of tall blonds, evergreens, reindeer and Santa Claus. (Finnair bills itself as Santa's official airline.)

Then there's swimming in ice.

Alice went down a rabbit hole. The Finns prefer an *avanto*, a hole cut in sea ice that they slip through for a refreshing winter swim before retreating to their saunas, where they heat up over a hundred and fifty degrees, whisk themselves with moistened birch branches while bracing themselves with shots of vodka. This explains their philosophy: if you're suffering from something vodka, tar or trips to the sauna can't cure, it'll probably kill you.

My first glimpse down the *avanto* came while reading *Theatre People—People's Theatre*, one of the few books in 2006 written in English about contemporary Finnish theatre. I came across this striking and revealing passage by Riitta Seppälä, the director of the Finnish Theatre Information Centre: "Hardly anything is known about Finnish theatre outside its national borders, probably because translations and promotional activity have been thin on the ground until recently." After all, "Finnish theatre is relatively young and represents a marginalized language area" (Aaltonen 141).

Seppälä's sentiment might be overstated, but to help rectify this perceived international invisibility, Johanna Hammarberg, the director of the Baltic Circle, and Jukka Hytti, executive producer of the International Theatre Project, in coordination with Pirkko Koski, then the head of the theatre department at the University of Helsinki, approached me in the fall of 2006 to research what is called in Finland "outlaw theatre" in order to introduce Finnish theatre to the Anglo-American community.

I first met Hammarberg in November 2006 while I was speaking at Spēlmaņu Nakts, the international theatre conference in Riga, Latvia, sponsored by the Latvian National Theatre Union. Hammarberg was interested in the research I gathered for my book *The New Theatre of the Baltics: From Soviet to Western Influence in Estonia, Latvia and Lithuania*. She indicated that many of the people involved in Finnish theatre were — surprisingly, to me — unfamiliar with the Baltic theatre (although, as I discovered, they are fairly familiar with Estonian theatre, given Finland's history and proximity to that Baltic country), and that many of the academic and theatre groups were at that time actively working to create networks connecting principals within the Baltic theatre organizations to their counterparts in Finnish theatre. Later, I received an invitation to speak at the 2007 Baltic Circle international theatre conference, scheduled for Helsinki in November. In June of that year I met with all three and, with especial help and interest from Hytti, worked out the initial logistics of my project.

I began my formal research in November 2007 while attending the Baltic Circle Festival. The conference organizers that year promised the event would be a watershed in contemporary Finnish theatre, bringing together an impressive pool of international talent for performances that many Finnish theatre audiences had not experienced.

But I quickly checked the initial impression implied by the organization: that Finland occupied some cultural backwater and had been hermetically sealed off from the international theatre scene, and thus the Baltic Circle was preparing the ground for a seismic renaissance, because the truth, as usual, was more complex.

During the 1960s and early 1970s Finland nurtured healthy avant-garde and performance art movements, including dynamic work from directors like Ralf Långbacka and Kalle Holmberg. The theatre-going public enjoyed theatre standards from the United States and Western Europe, and was exposed to both international classics and various forms of experimentation — including works by Bertolt Brecht, whose plays at that time were considered unorthodox in Finland. But if the 1960s and the first half of the 1970s proved to be a seminal period of radical activity, the late 1970s proved to be a period of creeping ambivalence. Disillusionment with Stalinism and the ensuing crises within the leftist political parties, combined with a general sense of cultural and economic stagnation, settled into the theatre community like a hangover. The new forms seemed shopworn. Of course, this sense of malaise and decadence sparked in response a period that, towards the very end of the decade, produced directors like Jouko Turkka and the first generation of groups bent on renewing theatre language and aesthetics. This energy carried over into the 1980s, creating a period of resurgence inspired by postmodernism that led to a radical interrogation of the nature of theatre, performance space, and gender identities.

Given this rich contemporary background, I could either discount the Baltic Circle's enthusiastic insistence that they were launching a "new direction" in Finnish theatre on a weird allergic reaction to the second millennium, or establish a critical context that took into account the reality of Finland's relative obscurity, irrespective of their well deserved worldwide attention at having won the European song competition.

The Baltic Theatre program that year featured a two-track agenda that highlighted issues particular to Finnish theatre, demarcating not so much a naïve audience as the hesitancy of theatre practitioners to apply new forms, language and techniques to their dramatic productions. On one hand, the program showcased new performances that the organizers described as both "acknowledged and renegade theatre," including performances from Belarus, Latvia, Lithuania, Norway, Poland, Russia, Slovenia and Sweden. On the other, a series of seminars coordinated by the Department of Theatre Research of Helsinki University focused on "New Theatre on the Baltic Shores" and consisted of lectures by visiting scholars from Denmark, Estonia, Latvia, Lithuania and Norway. Peripheral events like performances of contemporary Finnish plays, improvisational theatre and impromptu happenings in venues like Koko Theatre, the Dubrovnik club and Q Theatre complemented the scheduled conference and festival events. (The Q Theatre must be singled out as the primary driving force behind the festival, logistically, practically and spiritually.)

I returned to Helsinki in March 2008, specifically to continue making contacts and to lay the groundwork for my extended summer stay. I had intended that one of my central themes would be the two-tiered system of funding that in essence divided the Finnish theatre community "into two distinct camps" (Ruuskanen 4): those operating within the so-called "theatre law" and those outside the law, known appropriately as "outlaws."

This approach, however, got stickier the more I worked it, and I was soon bogged down in technical minutiae detailing the history of theatre structure. Still, it is instructive to understand at least an outline of the historical development of theatre in Finland because in many ways it bears absolutely no resemblance to theatre organizational principles in other parts of Europe. What makes it especially unique is that its contemporary structure is based in an amateur tradition, not top-down elitism but a grass-roots egalitarian system that mirrors the early Finnish character.

The main practical problem, as I began to investigate different theatres, interview writers and directors and view various performances, was that I could discern little difference — in quality or professionalism — between the permanently subsidized theatres that operate within the guidelines of the "theatre law" and the "discretionary supported" theatre groups — those "outlaws."

So I began to focus less on a certain class of theatre and instead concentrated on the young directors to see if there were common factors connecting the theatres that were taking chances with their performances, those running the risk of alienating their audiences but who refused to compromise their aesthetic values for the sake of box office sales, and those working in more established theatres that the outlaws, for aesthetic or ideological reasons, shunned. I concentrated on the most important Finnish language theatres actively promoting new drama in Helsinki. The most established were three theatres that began as outlaws but which now operate within the theatre law system, although they cleverly manage to maintain their outlaw status: The Group Theatre (Ryhmäteatteri), KOM Theatre (KOM-teatteri), and Q Theatre (Q-teatteri). The other prominent theatre dedicated to new performances operating outside the theatre law — an actual outlaw company — is Koko, located in a former porn cinema near Helsinki center.

I was back in Finland during August 2008, this time at the invitation of the Finnish Theatre Information Centre to attend the Tampere International Theatre Festival, the oldest and the largest professional theatre festival in the Nordic countries, held in the inland city of Tampere. The annual event showcases companies from all over the world, but for me it was a chance to see the best of the new theatre being produced by Finnish writers and directors in the most important theatre hub outside of Helsinki. The timing was perfect because the theme of that year's festival, which also happened to be its fortieth anniversary, was Nordic theatre, so I was able to situate the plays within the context of other Nordic productions. I also had the opportunity to visit the most significant theatre groups in the area, Tampere City Theatre (Tampereen Teatteri) and Tampere Worker's Theatre (Tampereen Työväen Teatteri), as well as some smaller venues like Shipyard Theatre (Teatteri Telakka) and fledgling groups like Theatre Siberia (Teatteri Siperia).

One surprising aspect of my research, which I should have been alerted to beforehand but which was, significantly, as it turns out, never mentioned to me by my Finnish hosts, was the visible (and visceral) cultural split between the Finnish speaking majority and the Swedish speaking minority, called Finland-Swedes. This phenomenon, as much a creation of Finland's past as of its contemporary reality, supports a community of Swedish-Finnish theatres dedicated to preserving Swedish language in a Finnish context.

The more I investigated, the more I began to understand the disproportionate significance of Swedish speaking Finns on the contemporary theatre scene, given the fact that the Finland-Swedes make up less than six percent of the total population. After all, "until 1863 Swedish was the official language of Finland" (Ahlfors 4). During the nineteenth century the prevailing critical opinion of the literati, a class composed mainly of Swedish intellectuals, assumed that "[s]erious theatre could not be performed in the language the public spoke" (8).

Irrespective of Finland's contentious relationship with Russia throughout the nineteenth and twentieth centuries, Sweden remained the dominant minority influence in the culture, and because language is inextricably linked to national identity, theatre became not only a force creating the Finnish national consciousness but also an institution dedicated to the preservation of Swedish for the minority.

To understand the situation of the Finland-Swedish theatres in Finland, I attended the 2009 Hanko Theatre Festival, Finland's largest Swedish language theatre festival. Before and after the festival, with the invaluable help of Dan Henriksson and his team from Klockricke Theatre, I was able to meet many of the most prominent — and promising — figures associated with the Finland-Swedish theatre. As before, with the Finnish theatres, I ignored the most established companies — the Swedish Theatre in Helsinki (Svenska Teatern), Turku Swedish Theatre (Åbo Svenska Teater), and Wasa Theatre (Wasa Teater) in the northern region of Ostrobothnia — and focused instead on the small dynamic community of independent theatres that includes Viirus, Klockrike Theatre (Klcokrike Teatern), Sirius, and Mars Theatre (Teater Mars), along with many other fringe companies actively producing dynamic, challenging work within the Swedish speaking Finnish community.

On my final trip to Finland in 2009, I returned to the Tampere Theatre Festival. The organizers made, in my opinion, a concerted effort to promote theatre as a positive venue for exploring social issues. This was clear from the introduction to the program in remarks by executive director Hanna Rosendahl. "At its best," she writes, "theatre gives commentary on current topics." She cites Lundán's *Unnecessary People*, recycled from 2003 (staged in Swedish at the 2009 Hanko Festival), and Anna Krogerus' *As if for the First Day* (whose *For Sheer Love of Me* was also staged in Swedish at Hanko in 2009) as works that convey "a strong message that finds its way straight to the heart and soul of the audience."

The purplish prose does not diminish the import of her sentiments. The organizers of the festival — which, irrespective of a few quirky shows chosen for diversity and international cachet (including, predictably, old work by Eimuntas Nekrošius and new work by Alvis Hermanis), represent the mainstream of Finnish theatre ideology — focused on issue-oriented plays. They seemed determined to prove that theatre remains a significant force, capable of relevant commentary regarding human welfare and social amelioration.

To be fair, the performances chosen for the Tampere Festival represent the choices of the committee and are selected based not just on the eclectic preferences of the members but also with consideration of the local audience in Tampere and what they will support. The works selected are not necessarily the "best" but are indicative of popular trends, if not always critical consensus.

At the extremes, the two modes can be diametric. Post-dramatic or "performance art" theatre can seem so abstract that the general theatre-going public doesn't relate to it in any meaningful way, and eventually a steady diet of this fare will starve the theatre of its audience. Plays that insist on social relevance — message plays — tend to sacrifice aesthetic values to stress the moral lessons prescribed by the writer. Achieving a balance between what the ancient Longinus, in his formula for ideal art, describes as the ability of theatre to entertain and edify is an elusive task. Hitting that goal, however, obviously separates the good plays from those that receive both critical acclaim and audience appeal — creating, simply, a "hit."

The difficulty is that frequently what the critics admire the audience rejects, and vice versa. This conundrum opens the question of audience reception, which the producers must consider when planning their repertories. Often, the most important factor in what playwrights produce is conditioned by the prevailing concepts, beliefs, expectations and the unspoken, hidden normative ideas among members of the audience as to what constitutes a theatre performance. In their attempt to offer something for everybody, mainstream theatres lean toward a "bread and circus" approach that offers an eclectic mix of serious classic high cultural drama, realistic contemporary plays, light entertaining comedies and musicals. The competition for ticket sales demands that these large houses adhere to that age-old maxim: give the people what they want.

Another aspect of the new situation in Finnish theatre designed into the Tampere Festival program was the desire of the organizers to showcase exportable plays that would appeal to theatre groups in other countries, ideally in large commercial markets in the United States, Britain and Germany. In fact, an organization established in the 1920s and originally tasked with importing foreign plays into Finland, Nordic Drama Corner, has become a sort of cottage industry for exporting Finnish plays for production in other countries. Whether this desire to create a market for Finnish plays threatens the artistic integrity of subsequent work is an issue of some contention. Interestingly, people on both sides of the issue — those like Maria Kilpi who think the marketing ideology does contribute to a decline in the quality of new plays, and those like Niina Bergius, project coordinator for Nordic Drama Corner, who see no effect — both cite Mika Myllyaho's *Panic* as proof of their diametrically opposed positions.

The issue is complex and in the end subjective, a matter of sensibility and interpretation. On the plus side, this desire to transcend national idiosyncrasies forces playwrights to find forms and a theatre language that stretch their style beyond their local experience. The drawback is that the plays intentionally shaped to be a commodity seem generic, formulaic and bourgeois. Plays like Juha Jokela's *The Fundamentalist*, Anna Krogerus' *For Sheer Love of*

In Mika Myllyaho's *Panic*, Jani Volanen, Petteri Summanen and Tommi Korpela play psychically damaged professionals in the "new" Finland. The play explores the downside of Finland's economic boom in the late 1990s, illustrating the machinations of men whose values have been skewed by a corporate mentality, their relationships reduced to marketing strategies and one-upmanship. *Panic* is also a prime example of a new wave of Finnish plays designed to appeal to audiences outside of Finland (photograph by Jyrki Tervo).

Me and Mika Myllyaho's *Chaos*, while anchored in Finnish sensibility, have been open to this charge.

So, two pathologies emerge as theatre in Finland moves beyond its laudable but unsustainable critiques of Nokialandia. First, plays need to continue to be socially relevant, if not strictly utilitarian, but must expand their themes beyond the stress of middle-class materialism and career politics. Second, new plays need to be exportable, nomadic, designed to appeal to audiences outside a particular Nordic chunk of the European Union. Whether these symptoms indicate improvement or decline, a renaissance or decadence, is debatable. That these indicators are real and indicate a tendency in contemporary Finnish theatre is indisputable.

This desire to maintain theatre as a socially relevant force in the indigenous community, and simultaneously to create a theatre that can be exported as a cultural commodity, typifies the often competing, contrary nature of the Finnish people. Until you meet the Finns — those who will actually open up a bit and speak honestly — in English, naturally — you can't imagine how proudly self-deprecating they can be. Their irony — as in Kaurismäki's films — stems from a preservationist's instinct.

Finland is a macho culture dominated by women. Identities — sexual, cultural, geopolitical — are constantly threatened, renegotiated, maintained with a fragile determination and brutal sensitivity, fallout from shoving a primitive soul into the hyper-tech age. It's that rock guitar player in a monster mask calling home on his cell phone.

Finland exists like an exclusive club where the Lutherans have been displaced by karaoke.

In Finland they speak a mysterious language, share impenetrable inside jokes, their aloofness the only sane response to a world outside their borders that, in the minds of many Finns, has clearly gone mad.

On stage, the actors famously shout and get naked.

Without question, Finnish theatre lacks exposure in the so-called Western European countries, especially in Britain and the United States. As recently as 2007, the Lit Moon theatre in Santa Barbara, California, billed its presentation of four plays by Finnish writers as "a truly historic event: the first repertory of contemporary Finnish plays ever staged in the United States, and marks the first time a Finnish director has been invited to direct a play for a professional American company." Simply put: The American and Western European theatre communities have had very little exposure to the thriving theatre scene in Finland.

So, given the context, this book is designed not as a definitive exposé on the history of Finnish theatre but more as a remedy to this perceived lack of recognition, a study not necessarily focusing as I first intended on "outlaw" theatres but finally highlighting the theatres considered by people in the business to be the most dynamic and exportable, representing the current situation of "new" Finnish theatre.

1

Identity Branding, Amateurs and Outlaws

Depending on the sources and their various perspectives, the Finns historically have either nurtured or resented a so-called identity crisis. Dan Lago, author of the 2004 book *On the Viking Trail: Travels in Scandinavian America*, suggests that the political dominance of Sweden and Russia caused the Finns to be "confused for eight hundred years" (243).

Lago also promotes the stereotype of Finns as "working class, struggling in a bleak economy, taking simple pleasures like fishing and drinking" (242). And while these stereotypes can be reductive and simplistic, many historians affirm them. J.V. Snellman, the famous philosopher of the Finnish nationalist movement, identified general traits and ideologies in the nineteenth century that continue to define the Finnish national character. Nationalism, liberalism and socialism, for instance, along with the influence of the Lutheran Church, are acknowledged as consistent common factors in the majority of Finland's civic since the 1880s.

David Kirby, in his 2006 study *A Concise History of Finland*, cites Finland's status as a frontier country as the prime factor contributing to a national character that he describes as contrary and dualistic, if not clinically schizophrenic. The task of civilizing and harnessing natural resources demanded respect for the law, civil cooperation and obedience to the institutions created to maintain order. At the same time, the wild environment and inherent anarchy in any frontier region fostered lawlessness, radical individuality, rebelliousness, a mistrust of outsiders and defiance of authority (Kirby).

Folklorist Lauri Honko notes that the idea of an identity crisis has been hard-wired into the Finnish psyche since the Treaty of Hamin in 1809, which dissolved the seven hundred year old alliance between Sweden and Finland and established instead a cultural bond with Russia. Even so, the repudiation of political ties to Sweden did not erase the cultural connections. "The educated, Swedish-speaking minority had to decide whether to turn towards Russian culture or to identify themselves with the language and underdeveloped culture of the majority. They chose the latter course even though it entailed a dramatic change of language and the difficult task of building a new identity."

In his 1999 essay "History and National Identity," Anthony Upton writes that "a nation is an abstract concept built upon a foundation of fact" (153). He also acknowledges that creating a national character, stemming from nineteenth century Romanticism, is "built around a manufactured national image" (162). Upton notes that even given "the use of history to create and validate a national identity" (154), in the case of Finland "language alone was not enough to create a movement and an ideology that the masses could relate to" (156). But the history of Finland and of being "Finnish" is inextricably linked to Finland's relationship with Sweden and Russia. "Even before the modern concept of nationhood had been formulated, the Swedish kingdom, of which Finland was then a part, had resorted to history to assert a Swedish identity" (155). Upton concedes, "The question of the relationship between the Finnish people and Russia is an essential element of the national image" (161). But after Russia took control of Finland from Sweden, the Finns began to assert their autonomy by retaining Swedish laws and customs. The native Finns were suspicious and prejudiced against the Russians, considering them culturally inferior to the Swedes. (The Finland-Swedes joke that during this period the Swedish elite "gave" the Finns their independence and civic culture as a response to Russian aggression.)

Identity building in Finland lasted well into the twentieth century, and the influence of Swedish theatre on Finnish culture cannot be overstated. Finland-Swedish cultural heritage, however, does not necessarily complicate Finnish identity today except as a subtext that will be explored in another chapter.

But even discounting the importance of the Finland-Swedish issue, especially as it relates to the Finnish resistance to Russian hegemony, the question of an identity "crisis" seems more acute in Helsinki than in other areas of Finland. This ambiguity is to some degree attributable to the capital's cosmopolitan status and international character, plus the fact that for much of its history Helsinki has shared its linguistic cultural heritage among speakers of Swedish, Russian and Finnish. As Bengt Ahlfors, one of Finland's most famous contemporary playwrights, notes, "Helsinki was a multicultural city long before the concept was invented and made into a problem" (4).

The current notion of a Finnish identity crisis is, on one hand, more existential than post-colonial. According to journalist and historian Jeroen Bult, writing in 2006, Finland's unique geopolitical position even after the Cold

War contributes to Finland's reluctance "to shrug off its familiar cocoon of neutrality... Finland is in the midst of an identity crisis as it looks for a new role in a world that has changed considerably since the implosion of the Soviet Empire in 1991." Bult argues that Finland's situation vis-à-vis its sense of an intrinsic national identity was accelerated when it joined the European Union in 1994 and NATO's Partnership for Peace program in 1997, strategic decisions after the collapse of the Soviet Union that nullified Finland's long-standing policy of non-alignment.

It could be argued that theatre's role in defining contemporary Finnish national identity involves an aesthetical diffidence. The Finns tend to regard their acting style as less refined than the more genteel, polished and subtle style of the Scandinavian model that for years was accepted as a sign of high culture, especially during the formative period when Finland was developing its own cultural voice. This does not mean that Finns in general consider their theatre inferior, but there is evidence of a willful rejection of the Scandinavian theatre style.

In an attempt to define the new Finnish image, cultural mavens and savvy politicians attuned to the tourism industry began a self-conscious program to create a "new brand" for Finland. In an August 2009 article in the *Helsinki Times*, historian Jason Lavery discusses this program, introduced by Foreign Minister Alexander Stubb in 2008. The idea is to develop entrepreneurship within the cultural sphere, financed by the Ministry of Education, the Ministry of Trade and Commerce, and other private partners to increase the value of culture along with other exports like the forest industry and information technology. By tapping into the business of culture, the government hopes to create a more visible brand of what it means to be Finnish. Lavery cynically notes that "national identities are constantly being redefined, not by committees, but by nations themselves" (2). He points out the historically dualistic nature of Finnish national identity, at one moment "perpetuating the myth that Finland is inaccessible to foreigners" and the next rejecting Finnish exceptionalism and asserting that Finland, "according to many, [is] 'the most American country in Europe.'"

Part of this effort to create a "new brand" for Finnish culture is a concerted effort on the part of theatre organizations in Finland to produce a batch of plays in translation specifically designed for performances in markets outside of Finland. The demand for Finnish plays abroad has certainly increased during the last ten years. Much of the success of this program can be attributed to several factors, including an increased focus on training drama translators, the increased activity of playwrights to create new original texts, and the efforts of drama agencies working through the Theatre Information Centre to network with foreign theatres.

The practice of exporting a manufactured brand using dramatic works in translation is problematic. The question is whether plays are written specifically to be exported. If so, does this self-consciousness on the part of the playwright affect the quality of the work, its sense of being from a specific place as opposed to being nomadic? Is seeing a play through the eyes of another culture an end in itself, or is this compulsion to export based on economic factors? Should there be a clearer distinction between what the playwrights create and what the promoters market? Do the promoters, working with translators, adapt texts to fit a targeted audience? Is this ambiguity of intent between the original work and the translation always an issue? Do themes of plays in translation always become dissociated from a particular cultural context? Or is Finland a special case, where the localized humor and the Finnish world view are too difficult to convey to another culture?

The answers are complex. Many writers instinctively deny they are producing plays specifically for production abroad. They tend to fault the translators or marketing "gate keepers" for re-contextualizing their work, a process that — often inadvertently — creates commodities, plays as interchangeable as SIM cards, in which a perceived virtue — accessibility — becomes a fatal critical liability.

In "Targeting in Drama Translation: Laura Ruohonen's Plays in English Translation," Sirkku Aaltonen from the University of Vaasa suggests "that targeting a particular audience as part of a specific theatre praxis decides the way this dramatic or theatrical is conveyed in translation." As evidence he cites various translations of Laura Ruohonen's plays for Anglo-American markets. One of her plays, *Olga*, described in promotional material as her "breakthrough play," is a prime example of both the virtues and drawbacks of a Finnish play that has been successfully exported.

In its original form, *Olga* was staged in 1995 at the Finnish National Theatre and directed by Ruohonen. An English translation was subsequently performed at the Traverse Theatre in Edinburgh, Scotland, in December 2001, directed by Lynne Parker.

The pretext of the play involves an improbable mismatch between Olga, a shrewd elderly woman living by herself in a tenement flat, and Rundis, a young petty thief who befriends Olga while robbing her. Olga and Rundis are two scroungy characters surviving on their wits; they are marginalized but likeable because they demand authenticity in a world of frauds and injustices. The key to the comedy lies not only in the incongruous romance between the two misfits, but also in the gender role reversals. Olga is a dominant, independent woman, not inclined to hysteria. Rundis is a weak, sentimental bird watcher. Evidence of Pinteresque absurdity permeates the play, but the story of Olga and Rundis never seems derivative and the humor is original.

Rundis contradicts common male stereotypes. In the opening scene, he is shown being carried home on the back of his girlfriend. When Olga first meets Rundis, she mistakes him for the new cleaning lady. Instead of engaging in typical male pastimes involving sports, he is a bird watcher, intrigued by a rare "bearded tit" (an actual bird that even in translation cleverly plays on the gender-bending that pervades the action). He is ineffectual, incompetent, and bitterly disaffected. In contrast, Olga is a tough survivor who sticks to her values even as her family and acquaintances have abandoned her to a welfare system that instead of protecting her leaves her vulnerable to unscrupulous opportunists who constantly prey on her. She is also an idealist, so she is constantly disappointed by the nature of the people who surround her, even as she befriends the nihilistic Rundis.

When Olga, for instance, tells Rundis, "We've got to stop the world from turning ugly," Rundis responds: "You gotta get used to it." A force of chaos in the world, Rundis is attracted to the levelheaded serenity Olga has managed to create in her life. Inversely, Olga thrives on the unpredictable energy of her young quasi-lover. Given the differences between their situations — her age and idealism, his youth and disillusionment — their affair is doomed. But what they share — beyond obviously being marginalized by society — is an intimacy that transcends their poverty, a faith in each other that shames the cynics around them.

Olga was well received in translation. Writing about the performance at the Traverse Theatre in Edinburgh, critics praised Ruohonen's lean style. In *The Guardian*, Elisabeth Mahoney notes approvingly her use of "slight, picaresque scenes with an emphasis on eccentric details." For *The Scotsman*, Joyce McMillan highlights Ruohonen's ability to create a "profound sense of wit and lightness." These comments, as astute and accurate as they certainly are, might be more accurately attributed to Lynne Parker's directing than to qualities inherent in the script (especially given the hesitancy of Finnish critics to use terms like "slight" or "lightness" when describing Finnish theatre).

More illustrative of and pertinent to the issue of branding and exporting Finnish culture are comments by the same critics implying that *Olga* reveals cultural truths about Finland that seem instead to reinforce stereotypes about the country. Mahoney discerns "a dark, brooding image of Finnish culture, of absent men who have drunk themselves to death, and of the women left behind, directionless, unable to communicate, aggressively defensive." McMillan explains that Olga and Rundis "are linked, in a deeply Nordic way, by a feeling for the landscape around them — the trees, birds, berries that represent the life force, increasingly threatened by environmental change and loss." Mahoney even finds "Ruohonen's vision, its otherness, deeply relevant in a Scottish context."

The implication is that a properly translated Finnish play marketed for export can reveal insight into both the character of the Finnish people and the culture of the country into which it is exported.

Aaltonen explains this phenomenon by what he calls "targeting." To target "a particular audience in a particular location at a particular point in time" translators employ a "strategy" that "may then omit, add and reshuffle the lines of the new source text" that "draws attention to the linguistic and cultural difference of the text from texts in the target culture." Aaltonen identifies omissions in *Olga* that "included non-realist non-verbal inserts, that is, stage directions but also short scenes, which may have been seen as a digression from the main story."

Mahoney's finding in the play a theme "deeply relevant in a Scottish context" might well be a response calculated by the targeting of the translator, the producers and the theatre practitioners colluding against the original intent of the script. Aaltonen considers this specific targeting as a potential threat to what he calls "faithfulness" even while he is aware that "faithfulness is read differently in different cultures." Acknowledging that the "precision of targeting can vary from a loose spatial and temporal socio-cultural frame to a specific concept in a concrete physical location at a precise time of the day," Aaltonen argues that the "more closely a text can be targeted at a stage performance, the further away the translation strategy moves from the 'faithfulness' ideal of literary translation."

The detrimental effects of targeting are most evident in plays emerging into the mainstream — especially those promoted by the Nordic Drama Corner — that critique, in a fairly consistent realistic mode, the neo-liberalism that threatens the welfare state in twenty-first century Finland. The focus on social commentary, coupled with the preferred style of psychological realism, remains popular with the mainstream theatres and their audiences. But many critics and promotional agents consider plays depicting the impact of social policies on ordinary people, presented in a realistic fashion, particularly suitable for marketing to theatres outside of Finland. Plays of this type are not necessarily inferior to more experimental styles, but by emphasizing theme over style, the playwrights are clearly not challenging the language of theatre or taking chances with the shape of their performances. By privileging issues over aesthetics in a familiar dramatic context, they are, in a sense, playing safe. This trend is evident in a slew of new works translated into English and specifically targeted for marketing outside of the Finnish theatre network.

Like *Olga*, a few targeted Finnish plays — including works by Juha Jokela, Anna Krogerus, and Mika Myllyaho — have met with success abroad. Other plays that received positive critical responses in Finland have been less successful as exports. Plays by Arto Salminen and Pasi Lampela, for example, follow the typical formula for viability — they are critical of the new social model and are couched in predictable social realism — but ironically their chance of being marketed abroad might actually have been hurt by the sort of targeting Aaltonen has identified.

Salminen's *Stockroom* (*Varasto*), adopted from his novel of the same title, is a humorless imitation of so-called "kitchen-sink drama," popular in England in the 1950s, the most famous example being John Osborne's 1956 play *Look Back in Anger*. *Stockroom* seems all the more like a transplanted work from post–World War II England in its British English translation by Eva Buchwald, replete with rough slang, Anglicized working class allusions, and grimy, despicable characters trapped in a claustrophobic, loveless world of Malthusian madness.

Set in the basement stockroom of a painting and decorating outlet, Raddish and Rollinson (their Anglicized names) are low-paid workers in a dead-end job. When not filling orders for supplies, they spend their time idly chatting about sex and throwing darts at a board decorated with pornographic images of women. Raddish supplements his income by stealing goods from the warehouse and delivering them to Broadbent, an unreformed Soviet who admires Brezhnev and believes the "Soviet Union exists in every western company today." His philosophy is dialectically opposed to that of Raddish's employer, Elmwood, who espouses Calvinist virtues like thrift, sobriety, hard work and personal sacrifice. Elmwood explains that he "skimped on everything, absolutely everything," and attributes his success in business to a belief that "the world rewarded those who bothered to try." Meanwhile, Karita, a promiscuous sales assistant, discovers she is pregnant and forces Raddish into a facsimile of marriage by threatening to turn him in for stealing from the company. When the owner accuses the stockroom staff of theft, Raddish turns in his co-worker, proving the owner's observation that Raddish is, after all, just the kind of person made to "survive this harsh world."

The promotional material for *Stockroom* describes the play as "a darkly humorous study of the strategies for survival at the bottom of the economic ladder." That is certainly true. But one of the major problems with the play in translation is that while it presents a plausible portrait of the poverty-stricken pockets of a post-industrial England in decline, the image of contemporary Finland seems unrecognizable. The world of *Stockroom* is a dystopia without a single redeeming quality. Communal ties have been decimated by Darwinian capitalism. Relationships are based on blackmail, responsibility is enforced by extortion, and instant gratification produces only addiction, dissatisfaction and jealousy. Everyone preaches the apocalypse, and everyone has a pet scapegoat. The business class blames generous state benefits, like child benefits and unemployment compensation. The workers blame the business class, imagining how they "glow and rub their hands with delight at the sight of all the poverty and misery they've achieved." The criminals are nihilists, the beneficiaries of a dysfunctional capitalist model.

At best, society has been reduced to a Manichean nightmare of vicious competition between the criminality of exploitative, dehumanizing corporations and a Russian-style mafia. As Broadbent explains, justifying his thievery, "nowadays it's all about survival, which means dough and power." In Broadbent's view, the middle classes are self-defeating dupes, having "made virtue their standard to the point where it's become a vice." Elmwood, representing the businessman's perspective, is a bitter self-righteous prig, complaining about paying wages and maternity benefits, "all the bloody costs of employment," and if he makes any profit — "a meager penny or two" — he has to "fork out sixty percent tax on it."

At worst, the youth have simply succumbed to anomie and apathy, with no ambition, no sense of community values, fatally marginalized. As Raddish's supervisor puts it, the nation is plagued by "half a million citizens sitting on their sofas picking their noses." The parents have lost faith not only in their children but in the system. The supervisor complains that "there'll be no new jobs created except in home-brewing and drug trafficking." The education system offers "pint-of-lager training courses" and women are ineffectual whiners suffering from "mould allergies" and "the menopause."

The play also suffers from structural problems. Instead of a dramatic critique of social inequities, the failure of the welfare state or the immorality inherent in skewed corporate ethics, the play presents a series of diatribes against straw men set up conveniently to represent abstract targets of resentment. When the characters are not trading abusive remarks and scatological insults, the dialogue is unnaturally polemical. The arguments are vicious, often irrational and based on stereotypes — the slut, the sexist pig, the mafia fatalist, the evil businessman — that ring hollow. More problematic, the anticapitalist rants are delivered by particularly despicable characters. Not one character functions as a normative value against which the others might be judged. No one respects anyone, or acts out of any humanist impulse. Salminen's vision is so hopeless, his characters so unredeemable, the realistic slice of life advanced in the play is reduced, by its caricatures, to farce.

A more anodyne work, and to some degree less "targeted" in translation, is Lampela's *Westend* (titled in English), which had its premiere in 2005. The promotional material for the play describes it as "a powerful depiction of twenty-first century Finland, where people's internal conflicts are suppressed behind a hard exterior." The theme certainly intends to debunk the myth that money can buy happiness, to puncture the bubble in which the privileged ensconce themselves away from the unpleasant intrusions that disrupt the illusion of sanctity and success wealth supposedly provides.

The play deals with a family at the exact opposite end of the social scale from *Stockroom*. The story takes place in an area that resembles the exclusive Baltic Sea neighborhood of Espoo, about nine miles outside of Helsinki, home to many of the executives who have profited from Finland's high-tech industries. Tommi is a self-made entrepreneur whose company is about to be bought out for a huge sum of money that will cap his life's ambition: to become enormously wealthy and to prove that he can compete — and win — against the "fucking little princes who jump from the halls of the Helsinki School of Economics straight into their father's firms." His wife Anita, an alcoholic lawyer who comes from "respectable, old family money," has found her life, after years of psychoanalysis, marriage and motherhood, empty and meaningless. Their daughter Elena is a disaffected young woman studying for her law entrance exam, as equally exasperated by her parents' materialism as with boyfriends who "always came so quickly I was never satisfied."

Tommi is a product of a working class family whose Calvinist work ethic drove him to "kill my old man, kill him with money" in order "to buy the world's approval." Part of his drive to succeed included infiltrating Anita's family, representing a distinctive class based on money and privilege, and then earning a place at the table — "those nightmarish dinners in that goddamned haunted house" — by marrying Anita. "I've conquered you," he tells Anita. "I've conquered your entire venerable family." While the audience can only speculate on why Anita married Tommi, Anita was never anything for Tommi but a step on his way up the social ladder. Though his daughter remains emotionally distant, he admires her for being "strong-willed," the one virtue he believes to be the key to his success. In his hubris, he still believes he is pursuing — and achieving — the dream of materialistic success. "I'll make a lot more money," he brags to Anita. "I can do whatever I want." He sees his accumulation of wealth in religious terms — "like being born again" — and as an existential victory, boasting, "No one's ever going to fuck with me again." Blinded by envy and a pathological need to beat the competition — more to settle his vendetta against entitlement than any sense of professional accomplishment — Tommi simply accepts his wife's debilities and his daughter's estrangement as collateral damage in pursuit of his goals.

Anita's dissatisfaction stems from her early marriage and motherhood. She complains, "I was twenty-two when I had Elena." She suspects that "somebody somewhere was playing a really dirty game with our dreams and used all of that rock-n-roll and sex and freedom stuff to make shitloads of money." Her nightmare is that she is experiencing "the slow death of a marriage brought down by the drudgery of everyday life," a situation she hopes to escape, but she frames her intent in vague utterances like "I have to get out of here" and "I want to feel like I'm alive" while remaining psychically paralyzed. She resents having played the traditional role of older sister, taking care of her ill mother, "that half-crazed vulture." She is left wallowing in a shallow cynicism, bitter about the choices that led her from one comfortable life to another, as if some cosmic conspiracy were to blame for her sense of emptiness. In a perfunctory non sequitur, she describes Finland as "a Promised Land for Americaworshipping [*sic*]." Just as she refuses to accept responsibility for the mess she's made of her life, she suggests that outside forces have been arrayed against "our young Finnish maiden" in order to subject the country "to the predatory needs of Uncle Sam and NATO." This critique, disguised as an attempt to insult Tommi and his belief in the new American business model adopted by Finland, seems as gratuitous as the news of the murders committed by children of Elena's peers, and exemplifies the polemical style of the performance, which ultimately diminishes the integrity of the action, no matter how accurate her assessment.

The catalyst designed to set off the drama in this toxic family arena is Anita's brother Henri, who drops in after ten years absence. An itinerant, promiscuous bohemian (presumably funded by his family's fortune), Henri made his name in Finland as a photographer. But he has come to visit his sister to announce that he has given up his profession because, as he tells Elena, "what I really need is to be saved from myself." He likens his years of drifting from city to city, from woman to woman, living a cavalier life among people who are "trying to be trendy, but at the same time they're living in fear," to a "half-read book." The result of his romantic rambling is a "disease more deadly than AIDS: massive, massive boredom." Anita, in one of her more prescient observations, dismisses Henri's sophomoric ennui as "reverse narcissism." For Elena, Henri is a potential white knight who can rescue her from her life of privileged dissatisfaction. She first tries to seduce him, but when he resists her advances, she simply demands that he take her away from her family. Instead, Henri decides to move in, providing, the audience assumes from his point of view, a sense of stability — especially after the deal that would have created Tommi's fortune falls through. Having leveraged his assets, Tommi is left with his business ruined, deep in personal debt, his life in shambles. In Henri's vision, the crisis will allow the family to "find each other in a totally new way," but given his anxiety about events in the world outside of his control — he tells Elena, "Anything can happen, at any moment" — his decision to stay seems as much a retreat from the world as Anita's alcoholism, Elena's misguided sexual experimentation, and Tommi's pathological need to dominate his business competitors.

One of the most egregious but, in the context of the play, underutilized of these unpredictable intrusions is the news that "Elena's old classmates, in fact, these infamous children of good families — went and slaughtered an entire family!" The family's awareness of this inexplicable violence by people like themselves barely scratches the surface of their protective veneer. Their reaction might suggest callousness bred from aloofness and insularity, but for this information to be injected into the story, and not have any consequences beyond passing references that contribute nothing to the immediate action, points out a dramatic weakness in the play: the audience hears more than it sees. In theatre, this reliance on explication — the lengthy character analyses, the self-justifications, the speechifying — enervates whatever dramatic is tension created by the narrative arc.

The themes of these plays both identify and criticize this new brand, illustrating the impact the high-tech, Anglo-American style of capitalism has had on the nature of the traditional Finnish family, while elucidating the emerging national character associated with Finnish identity.

Dennis and Elsa Carroll write in "Contemporary Finnish Theatre: National Myths and Beyond," "Myths of national character do not always constitute reliable guides to a country's artistic expression, but in Finland they give some insight into the great importance theatre has in the lives of many Finns and into the dominant tone of Finnish performance" (35). These critics locate the dominant mode of expression in Finnish theatre in "the motifs of harshness and deprivation in [Finland's] national history" (36). Finnish theatre and television critic Matti Linnavuori has defined Finnish theatre as creating "amusing ways of telling why self-destructiveness and violence flourish in Finnish reality" and claims it is a place where "mythical Finnish rage [is] channeled into poetic everyday tales."

If it is true that the traditional form of Finnish theatre derives from its mythical or actual national character, then to divest oneself of this dominant mode and appropriate a counter-intuitive style is an act of chauvinistic suicide. But this desire to escape the heavy, Nordic melodramatic Finnish tradition and seek out new forms of expression illustrates how this identity crisis is rooted to a certain degree in the changing aesthetics of contemporary Finnish theatre.

The idea of a "national character" is, of course, problematic, especially in heavily populated countries integrated through years of post-imperialistic immigration and globalization such as France, Germany, Great Britain and the United States. What might once have been construed as a national character becomes a chauvinistic caricature, like The Marlboro Man, Inspector Clouseau or James Bond, characters hardly representative of any real individuals living and working in their respective countries. But even given this caveat, in nations with relatively smaller and more homogenous populations, like Finland, a national character is easier to accept. The issue crops up often, usually in the foreign press to provide a context for a foreign audience unfamiliar with Finland's culture, history or geopolitical situation. As late as 2008, discussing a showing of new art from Finland, Ken Johnson in the *New York Times* writes about "this cool-hot dichotomy [that] reflects a split between the flinty and the mystical in the Finnish sensibility."

The conflict between identity and expression can also be explained in terms of Finland's isolation, or perhaps more accurately, the sense of being insulated, as if there were little interest in the rest of Europe as to what might be happening in Finnish theatre, what contributions Finnish theatre could make to the greater theatre scene throughout Euro Land, and, conversely, how little interest exists on the part of the Finns regarding what might be happening outside their homeland.

Norway had Ibsen. Sweden had Strindberg. Finland had... Aleksis Kivi?

As in many northern European countries, even though there is no evidence of any direct links, some historians like to trace Finnish theatre back to village cultures, shamanistic rituals and pagan folklore. And like other emerging nations affiliated with the Hanseatic League (including Estonia, Latvia and Lithuania), according to this convenient narrative, these ancient forms of cultural expression eventually evolved into theatre performances and became associated with national identity, playing a definitive role in developing Finland's ethnic distinction.

The simple model implies that ever since nomadic hunters first settled the land and forced the indigenous Lapps to the north, the Finnish language has remained distinctive and vital, a linguistic curiosity which fell especially under threat during the thirteenth century when Sweden controlled the area, and again after the Napoleonic Wars when Finland was annexed by Russia.

More recent events are easier to qualify. Ever since the first request by Pekka Kumpulainen of the Peasant Estate in the Finnish Diet in 1872 for government subsidies to support the Finnish-speaking theatre on equal terms with the Swedish-speaking theatres, and again in 1902 when the Fennomans rejected Russian control and "redefined the concept of the nation to privilege themselves" (64), the idea of a national network of repertory theatres sponsored by the state to promote cultural and national identity was firmly established in the community of Finnish theatre professionals and patrons.

In spite of these foreign occupations, Finland remained a fiercely autonomous region until it declared independence in 1917. Consequently, during a period of fervid nationalism in the early nineteenth century, Finland was determined to distinguish itself from the two dominant forces in its history, Sweden and Russia. The urge to realize their own culture led some Finnish nationalist poets to create a canon of traditional folk stories many scholars dismiss as inventions, "what William Wilson has called 'an imagined heroic past'" (Wilmer and Koski, *Dynamic* 17). The most famous example, perhaps, is Elias Lönnrot's collection of poetry compiled from Finnish and Karelian folklore, *Kalevala*, the Finnish national epic. Even so, the Finnish language — and the preserved folklore, no matter how specious — provided the basis for a distinct cultural identity that survived various annexations and subjugations and which, during the "National Awakening" of the nineteenth century, served as a unifying factor in Finland's independence.

Consistent with its early geo-political dominance by Sweden and Russia, the emerging modern theatre in the independent nation of Finland (beginning in 1919, after civil war established the republic) exhibits little of the influence of its Scandic-Russo past. But unlike its Baltic neighbors, whose modern dramaturgical aesthetics were shaped mainly by the French/German conventions of the well-made play, boulevard theatre and melodrama, Finland's theatre, because as a phenomenon it developed late as a national literary form, developed a non-professional, raw, earthy style, a product of amateur theatres entertaining the working populations of small rural areas. Later, this amateur-based theatre incorporated some influences from the Lutheran tradition — especially moral introspection and psychological realism — as well as some of the subtle naturalness and simplicity required by the new theatre introduced by Ibsen, but for the most part the style of the typical Finnish theatre remained much less refined than its Scandic and Germanic neighbors.

The Fennomanic desire for independence, along with the hybrid styles of the early Finnish theatre, produced a catalog of national protagonists. S.E. Wilmer and Pirkko Koski, in their *The Dynamic World of Finnish Theatre*, have identified three types: mythical, historical and peasant, all played like instruments in the symphonic quest for political, geographical and cultural independence. Congenital with the creation and propagation of these symbolic characters was the establishment of a national Finnish-language theatre. In the mid-nineteenth century, the culturally dominant Swedes considered the Finnish language an inferior medium for artistic expression, and in the late nineteenth century Russification programs imposed Czarist censorship on the Finns.

The results of these linguistic-cultural clashes were predictable: first, in response to the Swedes, the Finns established a national theatre in 1872 and performed plays in Finnish at the Arkadia theatre (originals as well as translations), and the efforts of the Russians to limit Finnish autonomy only provoked a backlash and defiance that ultimately led to the establishment of what has been described as "a cultural fortress" (61) in the center of Helsinki. "Finnish theatre's special place in the heart of the population can be explained by the fact that the birth of Finnish-language theatre in the 19th century was part of the construction of a national identity" (Seppälä 9).

Finland's unique history of amateur theatre cannot be stressed enough in understanding the popularity of contemporary theatre in Finland. (In 2008, in a country with a population of 5.3 million, the total number of theatre spectators recorded in Finland was 3.9 million, including visitors to free theatre groups, summer theatres, and the regional operas.)

The amateur theatre in the nineteenth century had a strong educational role. Theatre was a tool used to refine the coarseness of aspiring intellectuals hoping to shed their rural manners. By the beginning of the twentieth century, the theatre played a decisive role in organizing and promoting various political, educational and cultural causes, including workers' rights, youth movements, and women's issues. While the amateur theatres of this period were active in worthy civic responsibilities, theatres were also developing commercial interest; i.e., they became businesses interested in turning a profit. Because the workers' theatres had a huge loyal following already, they were well positioned to pursue a capitalist venture. The local workers' associations built their own assembly houses, which functioned as community centers, complete with libraries, restaurants, orchestras — and they hired theatre directors to stage performances. These establishments became the local seat of both cultural and political power; they also created an infrastructure that theatres could naturally use.

Before the Civil War of 1918, theatres were divided along political lines. The Reds used theatre to promote their Socialist sympathies, the Whites and their German allies to sell their nationalist agenda. Independent workers' theatres produced plays advancing the Socialist ideals of the Reds, while theatres like the National were associated with the Whites and the bourgeoisie. It was not coincidental that plays like Maria Jotuni's *The Golden Calf* (*Kultainen vasikka*), a drawing room satire staged in 1914 about middle-class life, premiered at the National. Basically, the split was between the workers' theatres and the bourgeois non-political theatres, which played out, literally, on the political stage. Though many of the people active in the workers' party decided to join the conflict, some supporting the Whites, others the Reds, others were active in the civil administration, and a few managed to remain neutral. Many actors were killed, others went into exile, and several were condemned to prison camps.

After the war, the struggle between socialist movements and the bourgeois theatres played out much like the rest of society, split along political lines. Upton writes, "The divisive legacy of the 1918 Civil War was an operative factor in Finland's interwar politics at least as important as any underlying tendency to coalesce around the democratic center" (163). As a result of this political division, the towns created a double theatre system. Because the workers' theatres were the leading theatres in most cities after the Civil War, they were the dominant force when the local rural communities and towns founded new permanent city theatres. The workers' theatres can be compared to the popular people's theatres, even though they were not agit-prop theatres. The most popular repertoire was naturally all sorts of popular folk plays, comedies and operetta sing-alongs.

For a brief period after the war, the socialist workers' theatres tried to establish themselves as institutions promoting class struggle, and their media supporters scorned the actors that had sided with the Whites. Radical elements within the workers' theatre movement tried as late as the early 1920s to continue the revolution by staging plays that dramatized the civil war from the Reds' point of view. Meanwhile, the theatres supporting the social democrats refused to organize. This conflict led to an artistic schism between the two theatres, with the workers' theatres supporting political action and the social democrats focusing on a more popular repertoire of canonized classics. When the government moved to censor and even criminalize these renegade theatres, and with no massive popular support, the movement quickly died. Even so, less radicalized drama like Hella Wuolijoki's *Law and Order* (*Laki ja Jarjestys*), a romantic view of the Reds espousing radical socialist ideology was staged in 1933 at Koitto Theatre, a decidedly leftist repertory. But even these politically engaged, independent theatres were not immune to middle-class appropriation. Koitto, for instance, merged with the subsidized Folk Theatre in 1933 (Wilmer, Introduction to *Law and Order* 221).

Once the conflicts, both the actual war and the partisan wrangling that followed, had been resolved, the established workers' theaters were able to challenge the bourgeois non-socialist theatres. The greatest unifying factor aligning all the different theatre groups in Finland was the bottom-line of box-office success. What evolved from this double theatre system was the obligation on the part of both the national parliament the municipal authorities to provide subsidies to both the workers' theatre and the non-socialist theatre. The fact that the workers' theatres managed to garner state support on a par with the professional theatres testifies to the powerful influence of amateur theatres that persists in contemporary Finnish theatre and explains the antagonism between the local rural culture and the urban (Helsinki) culture (Mikko-Olavi Seppälä).

Especially traumatic, as it was for most of northern Europe, was the period between 1938 and 1945. These years include the Winter War of 1939–1940, when the Soviets invaded; the Continuation War of 1941 to 1944, when the Finns fought alongside the Germans against the Soviet forces; and the War of Lapland, when the Finns fought the Germans to repel them from the country. During this time, the schism between the two camps — the workers' theatres and the civic theatres — were united for the common good, even setting up theatre performances near the front lines to boost the morale of the troops.

While history tends to render these conflicts in abstract theoretical modes, theatre is singularly capable of portraying the raw human dimension during these brutal, confusing years. Upholding the Lutheran tradition, twentieth century Finnish theatre is rich with dramatic chronicles that demonstrate the character, irony and resolve of the people that lived through the wars and, in doing so, forged the issue-oriented direction of Finnish theatre still in vogue today.

Upton suggests that after 1948, "the emergent Finnish welfare state [...] developed into the current consumer society" (162). This embrace of the consumerist model, no matter how tempered by Socialist principles, has led politically to "a successful coalescence round the moderate centre of politics" (162). This consensus, however, does not explain the schism between those audiences that prefer (and insist on) a traditional, realist, popular, issue-oriented theatre and those that embrace the more experimental theatre associated with the avant-garde. Part of this cultural conflict can be traced to an ingrained provincialism in Finland that pits the uninitiated, often rural population against the intellectual, urbane elitists. After all, a crucial factor in the historical development of the Finnish theatre was the relative poverty of the country and the cultural homogeneity of its inhabitants.

In a letter to the *Helsinki News*, for instance, published August 2, 2009, a reader expressed utter disdain for the kind of theatre being produced in Helsinki. The reader argued that the cosmopolitan, elitist style popular even at the Finnish National Theatre had nothing to do with the lives of ordinary people. The reader's argument focused on the fact that the people producing current theatre were creating performances aimed at other elites educated at the Theatre Academy, creating a hermetic, incestuous community who were using taxpayer money to promote their private agendas. The reader also complained that many of the productions insulted the very citizenry that provided the tax money to fund the artists' educations and their productions. The reader suggested that the National Theatre and the other city theatres participating in this charade be blown up (Kelloniemi).

The reader's complaint, while illustrating how difficult it is to determine a "national character" or a "Finnish sensibility," might also explain the uneasiness felt by some mainstream audiences regarding experimental theatre and their preference for traditional, realistic, issue-oriented theatre.

While the divide between the country and the city is an undeniable reality in Finland, some of the old-school actors and activists in Helsinki nostalgically recall a city split along social and political lines. This cosmopolitan division between the Socialists and the bourgeoisie has been exacerbated by gentrification typical of many urban areas undergoing "rehabilitation." And even if this identification is not so much a reality as a nostalgic indulgence, the passions run deep, and they tend to leech into theatre allegiance based on political alignment. Anna Veijalainen, artistic director of the decidedly progressive Koko Theatre, jokes that her theatre is located on the "wrong" side of the bridge, meaning it sits on the south side of Töölö Bay, which not only divides the city geographically but politically as well. A few blocks away on the north side of the bridge is Hakaniemi Square, home of the Social Democratic party. The hub of the area is Rytmi Bar, a hotspot for students, bohemians, artists, actors and film makers, and where every year a march celebrating the workers and communist sympathizers is organized. Veijalainen's side of the bay, to her chagrin, hosts the central tourist areas, the main shopping promenade, chain restaurants and hotels, and that bastion of institutionalized theatre, the National.

For years, the National Theatre has served as a convenient scapegoat for disaffected patrons, maligned not only by populists but also by a more elite theatre community whose taste runs counter to the prevailing aesthetic of the mainstream press and popular culture. Yet historically, to fulfill a desire on the part of the government in its attempt to promote a civic society, the venerable theatre house has been instrumental in establishing the statewide funding system that supports a network of theatres throughout the country. The initiative for subsidizing theatres began when touring companies regularly set out from the National to bring culture to the provinces, and it quickly developed into a grass-roots movement.

To facilitate access to theatre, local groups were formed and evolved into city theatres. These establishments continued the tradition of amateur theatre and were closely aligned with workers' theatres. After "the workers' theatres were amalgamated with bourgeois theatres into municipal theatres" (Wilmer, *Dynamic* 29), the groundwork for government subsidized theatres was firmly ingrained in the national civic conscience. The amalgamation of amateur, worker and bourgeois theatres was codified in the Theatres and Orchestras Act of 1993, which guaranteed state support for theatres. The act set the shares for subsidies from state and local councils, but for the majority of theatres, the municipal support is larger than the state contribution. After 1993, "theatres were more often classified according to the state system: the 'state theatres' having special status... and the 'outlawed theatres' with discretionary state support" (129).

Funding for "state theatres" has always been based on a complex formula, but along with the established national and municipal theatres the subsidies also cover "independent companies, dance theatres, and puppet theatres, which were founded in the 1970s and '80s to challenge institutional theatres" (Seppälä 10).

The Theatre and Orchestra Act, according to which established professional theatres receive funding from the state, was enacted towards the end of the recession
in 1994. It was intended to secure the preservation of the country's theatre network, but it... could not be re-extended to cover new groups, so they were left
on the margins, reliant on scarce and discretionary state funding, individual production grants and personal stipends [Ruuskanen 4].

The theatre law, created to secure a dynamic network of theatre troupes, has
succeeded in the eyes of the outlaws only in producing mediocrity. With
guaranteed funding, most of the repertory city theatres continue to compromise (in the eyes of their critics) their artistic integrity, creating "safe" productions to please their conservative constituencies. "Many new performances
... are, with regards to topic and expression, the kind of thing that institutional theatres, who are under pressure to see a healthy return on ticket sales,
would not dare to risk" (4).

According to Erik Söderblom, director and former professor in the Acting Academy at Helsinki University, the big stages were trapped by their need
for audiences, so they had to sacrifice their aesthetics to survive. Most of the
city theatres throughout the country specialized in mass-market entertainment to attract large audiences. Referring to the popularity of American musicals, Söderblom quips, "The most important question on a job application
was: Can you perform in musicals?"

Traditionally, theatres operating within the Finnish "law" were guaranteed funding and were expected to satisfy the expectations of their subscrib-
ing audiences, but "their crowd-pleasing repertoires had no appeal for
innovative young artists" (4). Most young theatre professionals prefer to operate outside the "law" because it reinforces conformity and promotes what
some call bourgeois aesthetics. They are convinced that "new kinds of performances require a production system that is different and more flexible than
that of institutional theatres" (4). Even so, these "outlaws" operate under a
constant financial stress, receiving "less than half of the wages recommended
by the applicable labor agreement" (4).

Ironically, this labor agreement facet of theatre law might help the large
theatres regain their artistic integrity. Because the big theatres operating within
the theatre law are funded according to how many people they employ, and
with many people retiring, they will soon begin hiring some of the new talent now performing within independent groups. This natural cycle of new
hiring should enliven the productions at the major houses. Still, according to
Söderblom, what is needed most is "visionary leadership" among the top echelon of the state theatres.

As of 2008, the "law" supported 46 drama theatres throughout the country, while it excluded nearly 50 independent theatre groups, "but the situation

is in constant flux" (4). Only twenty-seven of these groups received discretionary funding for independent groups. State subsidies formed 25 percent of their total income, the local council's support was 18 percent and the self-generated income was 57 percent. Most of these groups depend on project-based financing and grants. The result is that many of these theatre companies operating without the safety of subsidies provided under the "law," but which have opted to establish risky experimental venues, do not even have a home-based venue. Of course, almost by definition, the majority of outlaws do not want a permanent site, seeking a performance space only when they are creating new productions.

Many independent companies still feel constrained by the bureaucratic encumbrance and aesthetic control of local municipalities and opt to create performances without worrying about conforming to the requirements inherent in state regulations. The former groups are subject to review and approval by various bureaucracies, and they have a more rigid operational structure. The outlaws have more freedom both organizationally and artistically, but they suffer from precarious funding. Yet, because some of the most innovative theatres in Helsinki are operating within the "law," the demarcation between outlaw and subsidized theatre in Finland is murky.

Most of the outlaws "are usually young people who have been unable to realize their own artistic vision in existing theatres or who have not been able to secure work from the professional field" (10). Outlaws operate with "more flexible decision-making because they are not under the Local Government Act" (Wilmer, *Dynamic* 131). Even so, these "outlaws" do not necessarily exist without any state support, and their funding is not contingent on popular consensus, political correctness, ideological expectations or committee censure. In fact, "state-aid to 23 of these kinds of groups was 930,000 euros in 2004, which made 23 percent of their total income" (147).

The establishment of "outlaw" theatres — whether legitimately renegade or merely alternative (i.e., not guaranteed state subsidies but well-established by subscription or private financing) — reflects two constants in twentieth century Finnish culture: a sense of regional, sectarian or factional connections and, paradoxically, an intense collective chauvinism. This fealty to the idea of being Finnish stems from Finnish modern history. The period is a catalog of social disruptions, years during which the Finns struggled to maintain their unique cultural identity while suffering debilitating geo-political upheavals. Events threatened not only to destabilize Finnish national integrity, but also imperiled its very ontological foundation and existential freedom.

2

Inside the Sauna Psyche:
Influences and Isolation

Four plays published in English document the Finnish postwar era. They offer the Anglo-American audience a clear view of the particular contradictions, moral ambiguities and necessary choices the Finns were forced to negotiate to survive what Steve Wilmer and Pirkko Koski describe as "this post–Nietzschean world of godless and mindless destruction" (Wilmer, Foreword, *Stages of Chaos: The Drama of Post-war Finland* 8).

Veijo Meri's *Private Jokinen's Wedding Leave* (*Sotamies Jokisen vihkiloma*) manages to combine straightforward "kitchen sink" dramatic structure with an absurd series of events that established a narrative tradition in Finnish theatre for a generation. Audiences were quick to identify with the ironical treatment of personal misery and privation in the guise of a national effigy. They also connected with the recurring existential themes of Finns fighting wars, killing and being killed in order to retain both their individuality and an abstract state entity. The play also underscored the powerful role of women in Finnish society.

Alpo Jokinen, granted a wedding leave from the front, returns to civilian life to find a wife. The world of men, highlighted in war, is chaotic and gritty, dangerous and ridiculous. But in the civilian world men are no less ineffectual, comical and slatternly. The women Jokinen meets treat men as if they are children in need of supervision. Most consider marriage an opportunity for a pension. After encountering a series of candidates more concerned with the contractual benefits of marriage than any sense of mutual respect and affection, Jokinen's own motives reflect his desperate self-interest. One woman, trying to coax her friend to marry him, points out that if he returns to the front without a marriage certificate, "they'll say he's a deserter and shoot him" (Meri 102).

The women are portrayed as caricatures: tough-minded, no-nonsense practical Finnish women who view marriage as a business deal from which they expect a good return on their investment. When Jokinen expresses doubt that one of his intended will not show up for the ceremony, she dispels his suspicion by claiming, "You don't know me. I'll walk through a snowdrift in high heels" (105). She sums up her philosophy by telling him, "No matter how much you love a man, you've got to keep him under your thumb" (119). In the end, he instinctively chooses a naïve governess who accepts their marriage as inevitable, an event that was destined to occur without making much difference in her life one way or another. Recovering from a war wound in the hospital, Jokinen tells the girl she will soon become accustomed to being called mistress, and she says, "I'm used to it already" (150).

Private Jokinen's Wedding Leave both parodies and praises the typical Finnish spirit of stoicism and determined resolve, celebrating the skill of ordinary people to survive extraordinary circumstances. The play promotes a stereotype that finds its roots in the historical character of the Finnish capacity not only for surviving in an inhospitable, isolated and harsh climate but also for carving out an advanced, progressive, stimulating and creative culture. *Burnt Orange* (*Poltettu oranssi*) by Eeva-Liisa Manner, on the other hand, demonstrates how this need for an indomitable strength to persevere does not come naturally to everyone, and how often this otherwise admirable trait is not acquired or maintained without cost to the psyche and spirit. Even though the play is set outside of Finland, in a small unidentified town in Austria or Germany, its theme is particularly apt for the situation of Finland during the twentieth century, when social and political strife was duplicated in the personal histories of families trying to cope with the wrenching social upheavals caused by wars, tension with the Soviets, and the post–Cold War capitalist model that threatened the welfare state on which so many families had come to depend.

Marina, a young woman suffering delusions and various psychological disorders, is sent to a doctor for treatment. But after confessing her desire for the doctor, and then being rejected by him, she regresses further into madness and in the end is sent to an asylum. Underlying the narrative is the implicit sense of angst prevalent throughout Europe before World War I. Her father refers to Marina as Cassandra, suggesting that maybe her condition is a natural response to the fact that "the whole world really is in danger" (Manner 178). He confesses, in a rare moment of sympathy and understanding, that his daughter is suffering "the grief of the whole of creation. We're heading for such dark times" (182). Marina intimates the same general anxiety when she tells the doctor, "We're all in great danger" (187).

Ostensibly a critique of Freudian psychology and its incapacity to explain the poetic eccentricities of those more sensitive to the everyday terror of existence, the play also assaults the vulgar pieties of the middle-class, "which rigidly enforces conservative sexual mores on women" (Wilmer, Introduction to *Burnt Orange* 155). It highlights the muteness of Finnish families, their hesitation to discuss the hidden unmentionable dramas beneath the polished veneer of respectable neighbors. The following exchange between the doctor and Marina is instructive:

> DOCTOR: Many jaded bourgeois daughters despise what they've been taught, and particularly the manners. There's nothing specially personal about that. It's your class you ought to despise.
>
> MARINA: Are the other classes better then?
>
> DOCTOR: No. The peasants are greedy, stupid and treacherous. The educated are stuck-up, hidebound and stereotyped [Manner 202].

Finally, the doctor suggests she "shouldn't adhere to a class that wrongs others" (203). Clearly, this passage is more polemical than the rest of the rather poetic text. And it was the poetic style, combined with the hallucinatory scenes and downbeat ending, which established "Burnt Orange" as a model for a more subjective, impressionistic theatre, even if its structure remained faithful to the well-made play. Its themes, however, condemning middle-class certitudes and the soul-sapping price of conformity, fit nicely into the general ideology of leftist Finnish theatre in the 1960s.

The dual themes of social upheaval and war affecting dysfunctional families continue in both Jussi Kylätasku's *Oven* (*Uuni*) and Vesa Tapio Valo's *The Boys* (*Pojat*). A radio play, *The Oven* is described by Wilmer as "an allegorical comment on the effect of war on two generations" (Introduction to *The Oven* 249). Having converted his home-heating stove into a unit burning so hot it turns the kitchen into an odd sort of sauna, a father and his son end up sitting on a bench and reminiscing about their troubled family past. The action implies that the mother, mysteriously absent, has been walled-up in the oven by the father and is being burned alive as the two men get drunk and talk over old times; ironically, the warmth of the fire prompts a fragile reconciliation between the men, as the father laments how, though he fought bravely against the Soviets in the Karelia, his valor was in vain because the Finns ultimately lost the region. As he recounts the fighting to his son, he recalls setting fire to a house where later a body was found bolted into an oven, the victim presumed to have been burned alive.

Kylätasku's text suggests that the acrimony pitting the mother and father against each other stems from the deprivations of the war and the father's sense of guilt at having lost the territory he had sworn to defend. As a result of the unfilled lives led by his parents and their competition for the affections of the child, the son, having suffered a loveless childhood, has become an overly educated office worker divorced from his roots in the country. His father resorts to the only method he knows to reclaim the boy and to prove that he is, after all, his father's son. In a typically ambiguous understatement, the father tells the son, "It's homemakers like her that we have to thank for whatever this country is today" (Kylätasku 264).

Valo's *The Boys* also depicts Finland during the Continuation War, but whereas *The Oven* concentrates on the aftermath of that conflict for later generations, *The Boys* focuses on the immediate effects of war on the children whose absentee fathers, in this strange case, are replaced by German soldiers. In the war, the Finns did not consider the Germans allies, but they welcomed their assistance in the fight against the Soviets. The presence of the Germans was not so much feared as conditionally welcomed. Nevertheless, having German soldiers garrisoned in the northern city of Oulu created myriad social disruptions and difficulties for the citizens trying to affect normalcy during a desperate period.

A sprawling epic adopted from several novels by Paavo Rintala, the piece was first released as a film; the stage version appeared in 1990. The social issues are by now familiar to Finnish theatre audiences. The play "pokes fun at pomposity and religiosity ... [and] gung-ho patriotism is exposed as hypocritical" (Wilmer, Introduction to *The Boys* 280). But beyond recounting the boy's adventures — an archetypal coming of age story — the difficulties of the double-casting and the dramaturgical logistics of staging what is in essence a "memory play" initiated a new appreciation for experimental theatre that inspired many young directors to take chances with asymmetrical narratives, scene juxtapositions and anachronistic naturalism.

The flavor of mainstream contemporary Finnish theatre is evident in a separate collection of plays published in English, all written by playwrights born between 1957 and 1970, titled *Humour and Humanity*. Because "[m]arginal language areas have usually great difficulties in selling their texts to foreign theatres, especially in gaining acceptance on the Anglo-American stage" (Aaltonen 148), this edition of translations represents only a tiny fraction of scripts written for the stage by Finnish playwrights. According to the editors, these plays are not representative of the avant-garde in Finnish theatre but instead "exhibit a somewhat conventional European dramaturgy ... linear, logical and mainly chronological" (Wilmer, *Humour* 11). They reflect "the uncertainty and changing values coinciding with social, political and economic changes at the beginning of the twenty-first century" (9).

Border Crossing (Punahukka) by Kari Hotakainen explicitly addresses how Finland's relationship with Russia evolved after the collapse of the Soviet Union in the early 1990s. But its main thesis dovetails with another, more oblique theme: one character's paradoxical crisis of faith in a country where eighty-six percent of the population professes to be Evangelical Lutherans but "half of all young men under the age of 35 are indifferent to religion" (Korpela). At the core of the play is a rather conventional look at unconventional relationships that explore new moral paradigms for Finns created by the dissolution of the Soviet Empire. Though the characters transcend their functions and become individualized despite their being reduced to types, they illustrate the economic symbiosis between Finland and Russia that flourished during the Soviet era but collapsed with the demise of the Soviet economic system.

The story involves two brothers, Pekka and Seppo, "taking advantage of a country that had been in chaos" (Hotakainen 23) by smuggling precious religious icons from Russia, hidden inside *matushka* dolls, to sell in Finland, financing their "health-farm weekends ... trips to Crete, shoes, dresses ... and other worldly things" (23). Their operation is interrupted when Pekka supposedly experiences a religious awakening, mixing new-age spiritualism with old-fashioned self-abasement and asceticism. As atonement for what he perceives as acts of injustice in his past, he renounces their smuggling enterprise, giving away a shipment of icons worth 3,000 euros and inviting his half-sister Katja, an unemployed Russian lab technician turned prostitute, to live with him and his wife Elina, who has just petitioned to adopt an orphaned child. What follows is a comedy of errors in which Pekka's conversion undermines the aspirations of his brother, his wife, his sister-in-law and his mother.

The theme concerns the brothers' guilt for their black market instincts, inherited from their spiritually corrupt father. While Seppo, in a genuine attempt to amend his ways, decides to invest in a restoration business (the metaphor obvious) and to sponsor a needy child in Russia, Pekka's expiation illustrates the old maxim about people who, seeing the light of Christian redemption, are blinded by it. His shallow, convenient religious conversion illustrates the fragility of personal values in the cut-throat capitalism inherent in the post–cold war socio-economic environment. In a final honest epiphany, he sums up his character: "a guy name Pekka who messes up things, who fights with priest ... who hides money, who smuggles icons..." (97–98).

In the end, human values triumph over market demands. Pekka's boorish intransigence and self-righteousness paradoxically lead to happiness and self-fulfillment for those whose lives have been so disrupted by his actions. His wife leaves him but remains his friend and sexual companion, Seppo and Katja become partners in the restoration business and solidify Seppo's commitment to his Russian ward, and the brothers' mother is reconciled with her wayward children and the women in their lives.

As in *Border Crossing*, themes of existential authenticity and the impact of bottom-line business ethics on humanistic values also inform both *Mobile*

Selling out: (left to right) Tommi Raitolehto, Miia Selin and Samuli Muje in Mika Myllyaho's *Mobile Horror*. The young entrepreneurs negotiate in a society where values are dictated by materialism and acquisitions have become the measure of success. The corresponding loss of spiritual values jeopardizes their ability to empathize and communicate honestly (photograph by Ari Ijäs).

Horror by Juha Jokela and *Panic (Paniikki)* by Mika Myllyaho. The plays illustrate the downside of an economic boom, reminiscent of Finland's recovery after the collapse of the Soviet market in the early 1990s when "Finland advanced rapidly into an information society, being at the forefront of computer and mobile phone technology, the spread of the internet, and advances in education" (Wilmer, *Humour* 9). Along with the opportunities for monetary wealth, which too often create a society where values are dictated by materialism and acquisitions become the measure of success, the corresponding loss in spiritual values jeopardizes the ability to empathize and communicate honestly.

In *Mobile Horror*, three entrepreneurs whose "mobile phone entertainment company" (Jokela 115) has been bought by a conglomerate are tasked with creating ever-new products or risk losing their jobs. Terhi, the senior partner recovering from industry burnout and still fragile from her breakdown, tries introducing Gandhian principles into the company's new product development. Seppo, the cynical marketing director, mocks her initiative until, in a perverse epiphany, he realizes that even the noble values of Gandhi can be co-opted and reduced to "product policy" (145). Mikke, the idiosyncratic graphic designer, is addicted to vulgar murder-mystery novels but manages to translate Gandhi's principles into saleable images composed of cheap sentimentality and titillating violence.

The attempt to reconcile Terhi's idealism with Seppo's ruthless marketing instincts, packaged by Mikke's perverted imagination, proves too stressful for the partners. The new products venture collapses and the trio loses faith in both their personal integrity and professional ethics. Ironically, just as the team realizes a rare moment of authenticity, when, in Terhi's words, she confesses that she has no illusions that "mobile phone entertainment can help anyone or make the world a better place" (186), the CEO actually approves their newest product, Mobile Love, a pastiche of treacle and "love stories, happy endings ... a little drop of eroticism" (192). They forsake their attempts to "bring some meaning to this emptiness" (186), concluding that "false enthusiasm is better than depressing reality" (189). Compromising their attempts to humanize their industry, they sell out for job security and "counting your chickens" (197). Having sacrificed their integrity at the altar of the market economy, their redeeming product Mobile Love has become a "Mobile Lie" (196). Their fall — in biblical terms — from human grace into soulless corporate depravity is complete.

Panic involves another trio representing the business caste populating contemporary Finland: Leo, an engineer; Joni, a journalist; and Max, a graphic designer. The men, all spiritually damaged by the pressures of Darwinian capitalism, suffer from the perceived irreconcilability between business ethics and humanistic values. Obsessed with their careers, their ambition acerbated by narcissism, they have become divorced from their essential Other: Woman.

The men inhabit solipsistic worlds, suspicious of intimacy. Joni, a television personality who hosts a show called *Alter Ego*, "fell in love with himself a bit too much" (Myllyaho 391). His notion of a relationship is limited to a "game" (361). He reduces women to "tits and ass" (361). He projects a media-created reality: distant, cool and superficial. His brother Max, a fastidious bachelor with a pathological fear of closed spaces — even his own bathroom — refuses to admit he actually loved a woman named Heidi, yet ever since she left him he has withdrawn into his apartment where he claims to be "trying to process my emotions" (376). He pathetically hopes his cerebral response to passion will protect him from the pain of human engagement. His defense is penetrated when Leo, an old friend, arrives drunk at his apartment. He is upset by his situation with his partner Mari, who has given him an ultimatum: commit to their relationship or call it off.

Leo's predicament initiates a soul-searching session among the three men, revealing that what they had come to perceive as strengths — Leo's resistance to commitment, Joni's promiscuity, Max's agoraphobic retreat — are actually signs of weakness, the machinations of men whose values have been skewed by a corporate mentality that reduces relationships to marketing strategies and one-upmanship. The men discover that their machismo posturing and need to succeed in their careers have left them empty and unfulfilled, trapped in a classic conundrum: "women are both the source of and the salvation to the troubles of these insecure and disoriented men" (Wilmer, *Humour* 326). As to whether the men can act on their "new perspectives" (Myllyaho 393), the playwright is ambiguous. Leo will "ask Mari what she thinks about love" (393), Joni is "thinking about" (394) a sexual friend as a potential steady partner, and Max decides "one day, I might walk down to that kiosk to pick up a few things" (394). Their individual recoveries seem, at best, tentative.

The indictments in *Panic* also expose issues of "gender identity and sexuality" (Wilmer 10) that inform *Queen C. (Kuningatar K.)* by Laura Ruohonen. On the surface, it is an historical piece about Queen Christina, the eccentric teenage heir to the Swedish kingdom who reigned during the tumultuous post–Reformation period, including the time of the Thirty Years War. Queen Christina was an unconventional intellectual during a time when Stockholm was one of the intellectual centers of Europe.

But the play uses historical circumstances mainly to frame contemporary feminist issues in Finland, especially "the role and purpose of the female in society" (10). In Ruohonen's version, Christina rejects the ideal of "womanhood" imposed on her by society. She disdains her expected royal obligation "to mate, give birth and die" (413), choosing instead, according to her confidant and court philosopher Rene Descartes, to be a gender-neutral creature who "rides, swash-buckles, swears a lot, sleeps little and badly, walks around in men's clothes" (413). Her decision leads Descartes to wonder "at what point does the woman cease to be female" (413).

Although Ruohonen's focus is on "the significance of gender, in the natural sciences, history and philosophy" (Hyvärinen 26), the play presents its subject obliquely. It derives much of its power by investing in symbolism, especially the use of a huge mysterious eel, a "mythical well-cleanser" (26) at the center of the play. Comparing herself to the eel, Christina marvels at the piscatorial fact that when the males swim into fresh water, "they too become female" (403). The huge mysterious eel at the center of the play looks at her "without any preconceived ideas, with the kind of look that left us both unconquerable and free" (418). Those around her interpret her intellectual rigor as petulance, her promiscuity as childish curiosity, her pride royal ambition. But Christina refuses to marry, reigns on her own terms, and abdicates as a supreme exercise in free will. In her actions she represents for Ruohonen "a modern rebel who does not accept the role of a woman, mother, female ruler which is offered to her, but shamelessly builds a new identity by break-ing the boundaries of gender status" (402). Ruohonen's philosophy, which has been described as "feminist humanism" (Hyvärinen 25), is steeped in ideas more forcefully espoused by Mary Wollstonecraft and other feminist polemicists who followed her, and the issues of stereotypical expectations of women in contemporary society seem dated.

In fact, women in Finland enjoy a prominence and equality that women in many other countries — even the first-world industrialized West — do not. As Pirkko Koski and Steve Wilmer note in the Foreword to *Portraits of Cour-age: Plays by Finnish Women*:

> At the turn of the century, the political power of Finnish women changed overnight. From being a conservative country in which females were subjected to their fathers and their husbands under Lutheran doctrine and state laws, Finland ... became the first country in Europe to introduce universal suffrage [Wilmer, *Portraits* 1].

Critics agree that during the early part of the twentieth century, "some of the most successful Finnish playwrights were women" (Wilmer, *Dynamic* 48). But as Koski and Wilmer point out, "the social transformation moved more slowly and the roles that women played in their public and private lives evolved over a longer period" (1). The strength of Ruohonen's play owes more to the vivid and metaphorical presentation of her fictionalized Christina than to its socio-political themes, though issues of feminine identity and gender roles are still evolving and do make for potent themes in contemporary Finnish theatre.

Along with the anomie created by bottom-line marketing philosophy and feminine issues of gender identity, another theme of contemporary Finnish drama concerns social problems inherent in the capitalist model affecting "the marginalized in society, those who live in the borderlands of bankruptcy, sub-stance abuse, and psychiatric disorder" (Wilmer, *Humour* 10). Reko Lundán's play *Can You Hear the Howling?* (*Teillä ei ollut nimi ä*) addresses "a number of social issues that became increasingly problematic during the years of reces-sion in the 1990s in Finland" (203).

Risto, a career soldier living in a small town in southern Finland, is a single parent whose twins, Aki and Liisa, must negotiate relationships, school, money problems and the women who casually drift in and out of the house. A hard-drinking ladies' man, Risto is frequently away on assignments, leav-ing his children to fend for themselves. He is not abusive or exceptionally selfish, and he genuinely has their welfare in mind. Because the time of the play shifts between events during 1981 to 1987 and 2001, the children, born in 1969, are portrayed first as tweens and then as young adults.

Without the benefit of a traditionally stable home-life, Liisa is forced to assume the role of mother to Aki. While he deals with the normal stresses of being an adolescent boy with absent parents, she struggles to resist her smoldering Electra complex when confronting the various women in Risto's life. Given their circumstances, the children are well adjusted, mature and responsible. Their estranged mother, a deadbeat alcoholic, lives in squalor a hundred kilometers away in Helsinki, and though the children harbor resentment for being abandoned, they stay in touch and visit occasionally.

One night Risto meets Jutta, a designer living with her mother, Irma. The children become fond of this new mother figure, and over the objections of Irma, Jutta and Risto marry. Unbeknownst to Risto and the children, Jutta has a history of mental illness and drug addiction, and soon she reverts to her destructive behavior, manipulating the family, suffering hallucinations and mania. After several provocations by Jutta and machinations by Irma — including accusing Risto of abusing Liisa — Aki discovers that she has been hiding their mother's letters to them, and he attacks her. The final scene takes place in the "present day" (Lundán 317) when the children visit a domesticated Risto and a pacified Jutta living a quiet life of resignation, their marriage reduced, in Jutta's words, to "the way it is: I sit on the sofa, he sits in the sauna" (318).

Of the plays in *Humour and Humanity*, Lundán's is the most prosaic. Instead of using irony, metaphor or physicality to render his vision, Lundán creates a piece of straight social realism (the genre preferred by KOM Theatre, where Lundán apprenticed), relying on elements from the so-called "kitchen sink" genre instead of the poetic ambiguities inherent in the more experimental modes of contemporary theatre. The action is delivered in a naturalistic style. The dialogue frequently devolves into squabbles and tedious exposition, creating an insidious, claustrophobic environment simmering with mundane treachery and ordinary evil. The play is a portrait of dead-end lives, of a dysfunctional family trying to subsist within a society where the social safety nets have either broken down or do not exist.

What *Can You Hear the Howling?* shares with the other plays in the collection is the role of a female as both a dynamic and destructive force in the public and private arenas of Finnish society: the workplace, the family, the social milieu of the dating scene. Like Katja in *Border Crossing*, Terhi in *Mobile Horror*, Mari and Heidi in *Panic*, and even the willful Christina in *Queen C.*, Jutta is another woman who is "both the source of and the salvation to the troubles of these insecure and disoriented men who are struggling to find their way" (Wilmer 326).

A weakness of issues-oriented plays is that they tend to be preachy and pedantic, and in Finnish theatre this tendency exemplifies both the strength and weakness of contemporary productions. Historically, Finnish theatre has been associated with reform groups, various worker's party movements and women's rights issues. In the Foreword to *Portraits of Courage: Plays by Finnish Women*, Koski and Wilmer credit theatre with transforming the political status of women during the suffrage movement in the early 1900s. "The theatre helped to question and redefine these roles, and female playwrights provided insight into the difficulties that confronted women in the patriarchal Finnish society" (1).

Although the profile of KOM theatre has changed dramatically since the radicalism of the 1970s, in a 1978 profile of KOM Theatre, Dennis and Elsa Carroll identify KOM as one of the truly committed and politicized venues operating in Finland. "During the 1950s a direct examination of political and social questions no longer occurred in the theatre" (Carroll, "KOM-teatteri" 377), but it is generally acknowledged that "labor and youth club movements early in the [twentieth] century had strongly associated themselves with Finnish-language theatre" (378). (KOM Theatre was instrumental during the 1970s in resurrecting a Communist alternative to "more apolitical theatre groups" [378]).

Although Finland is not notorious for its politically engaged theatre, it has some tradition of using theatre as a weapon. In the early years when Finland was struggling for its independence and cultural identity, productions performed in Finnish criticizing bourgeois theatre were essentially directed at Swedish-language theatre. During the party-politicized theatre of the 1970s, radical performances sought a direct examination of political and social questions. Regardless of the era or the intention, these sorts of proselytizing performances associated with anti-bourgeois theatre — especially in a text-based Lutheran context — too often privilege the "message" at the expense of aesthetic values. Even today, Finnish theatre — with its roots in traditional Lutheran pulpit pounding (i.e., sermonizing on morality) — continues to sacrifice performance values for the righteousness of the lesson. On the other hand, radical staging can alienate audiences, which, according to the Carrolls, happened when during the 1950s the experimental theatres in Finland abandoned their social polemics and veered into a "somewhat abstract no-man's-land" (377) associated with Absurdism.

This was the case in the neighboring Baltics during the 1990s. In Estonia, Latvia and Lithuania, theatre was religiously associated with political resistance. Basically, it emerged during the years of occupation as a vehicle of propaganda and resistance to the Soviet occupation. But it was transformed after independence into a theatre of entertainment in search of social relevance. This phenomenon of swinging from a politically dedicated theatre to one of pure cultural appeal tends to result in a decadent aesthetic experience, creating beautiful but superficial presentations mired in the subjective vision of the director without any redeeming social relevance. For the Baltic countries, as now with the Finns, creating art that does not regress into solipsistic curios is crucial for maintaining the social viability of theatre.

The problem facing the young directors today in Finland is how to marry new forms of theatre with relevant social content.

More recently, many progressive writers explain this "crisis" politically as stemming from dissatisfaction with the new constitution of 2000. According to its critics, the new government, heavily invested in promoting privatization, pays mere lip-service to social welfare while slashing services and protections for the disadvantaged, including cuts in education and health care. These critics object to the government's reform policies that in practice threaten traditional Finnish socialism and favor the Anglo-American socio-economic model based on market economies.

Much of the discontent within the leftist camp also centers on Finland's decision to join the European Union, which promotes international cooperation, global markets, and European integration. Traditional unionists, agrarians and various old style communist sympathizers as well as enlightened progressives tend to resist globalization, fearing that a faceless bureaucracy in Brussels might usurp Finnish self-determination. The issues, mainly disputes regarding earnings-related benefits, unemployment compensation, expenditure deficits and related topics are technical and complex. But as social critics, the writers and directors of the progressive theatres are eager to address these subjects in humanistic terms. They consider political engagement a proper if not obligatory role for theatre, keeping its status relevant and viable in contemporary affairs.

The approach to political questions these days is different from the activism invigorated during the 1960s and 1970s. Finnish theatre then was a hotbed of political dissent, especially for the leftists and communists threatened by what they perceived as Finland's drift away from socialism, its nascent embrace of the Western capitalist system, and its eventual integration with the European Union. The mode of political theatre in Finland today is, in common parlance, more carrot than stick, more seductive than polemical. Gone are the imperative harangues from the soapbox, the instigative appeals for direct action, along with the in-your-face shock performances attributed (spuriously) to the worst excesses of Antonin Artaud's *Theatre of Cruelty*, including assaults on audience members, as well as disgusting displays of spitting, urinating and self-abasement popularized by militants eager to freak out the bourgeoisie. But disregarding the most extreme histrionics of those belligerent spectacles, the two-pronged attack on conventional mores — blending declarative content with aggressive forms — continues to underscore the current dilemma facing the Finnish theatre community: i.e., what exactly are the defining themes unique to the contemporary Finnish experience, and is there an authentic Finnish aesthetic model to express them?

Of the dozen or so small, innovative non–Swedish speaking theatres in Helsinki, the most established are Group Theatre, KOM, Q Theatre and Koko. Since their inceptions, these theatres have conscientiously avoided slipping into decadence, shunning performances that simply reduce a theatrical performance to just another form of popular culture; they all invest in theatre as a forum for social criticism. But those involved with these companies also understand that the relevance of theatre rests not just on its ethicality but also on its aesthetic values, and it is this concern with form, with presentation, that sparks the most lively discussions among artistic directors. Significantly, it is their focus on the dramatic mode of expression that illustrates the so-called identity crisis more than any of the political or social issues the new Finnish theatres purport to address.

Yet young Finnish writers, directors and actors continue to hunger for, and be receptive to, outside influences, especially developments in the Baltics, Berlin, London and Moscow. They are equally eager to export their theatre, keen to show off a new generation that has clearly moved away from the parochial model of psychological realism — identified as the staple, in style and substance, of Finnish theatre for years — toward a more experimental hybrid style.

As for Scandinavian influences beyond the traditional Swedish model, Karen Vedel, a Danish scholar of theatre and dance, suggests that space, place and body could serve as a possible focus in the Finnish search for modes of recovery. According to Vedel, much of the new Danish theatre is collaborative, creating a hybrid of inter-cultural and international influences incorporating dance, video and installations to challenge the nature of theatricality. A performance, she suggests, involves the intention of the actor as perceived by the audience and a space that by its design is set apart from the everyday. To break this model, new works by Danish performers tend to put the negotiation between the audience and the performers in play, especially the power relationship established by the producers (actors) and consumers (audience) and the game rules that maintain the reality of a performance.

She cites as a good example of this iconoclastic mode the production of *Silk and Knife* by Jiri Kylián at the Royal Danish Theatre. Before the show begins, the audience is led on a forty-five minute tour inside the tunnels beneath the theatre, then through the labyrinthine halls of the building, finally crossing the stage before taking their seats. The idea, according to Vedel, is for the audience to experience a "crossing of borders" by which the "illusion is broken down between what is the product and what is the audience." Vedel also identifies *The Black Rose Trick Hotel* by Signa Sørensen as a "performance installation" that transformed an abandoned Malmö warehouse into a theatrical public event by inviting an audience to spend up to 10 days nonstop among some 50 Swedish, Danish and German actors who assumed the roles of various denizens of the "hotel." The installation subverts both the idea of performance space and the comfortable passive receptive position normally and comfortably assumed by an audience; the spectators become co-performers, collaborating in the production as the line between reality and performance is constantly threatened.

As for Baltic influences, the Finns have taken critical note of several productions by directors in Riga, Latvia, that have challenged the unifying boundaries between spectator space and performance space. An early example exploring this issue was Andrejs Jarovojs's *This Is Riga Calling*, a performance that was basically a three-hour bus trip around Riga, a sort of mystery tour that stopped at different spots around the city where performers presented improvisational pieces. The participants were never quite sure if the citizens on the street were part of the performance or were actually ordinary pedestrians. In Alvis Hermanis's *The City*, the audience was invited to the New Riga Theater, where Hermanis met them, and then they walked along a city boulevard where, as in Jarovojs's *This Is Riga Calling*, performers mixed with pedestrians while using the city space for improvisation. At the end of the walk, the audience was led into a real apartment — the neighbors unaware that their building had been turned into a performance space — where actors combined real living space with performance values, a process Latvian critic Valda Čakare calls an "exercise in conversion."

Movements in Estonian theatre, too, impact new Finnish theatre. Works by directors like Tiit Ojasoo, Mart Kivastik and Andrus Kivirähk suggest a new sense of engagement that, contrary to recent practice, confronts not only the nation's Soviet past but also its new nationalism, a trend contradicted by Finnish reticence to investigate both its past relationship with the Soviets and the current tensions with Russia provoked by Vladimir Putin. Some Estonian critics — Anneli Saro, for one — suggest that this honesty — that is, a willingness to confront issues that until lately have been considered taboo, at least for the contemporary writers, directors and audiences — is a result of Estonia's focus on training new writers, guaranteeing fresh material and perspectives instead of relying on the standard theatre fare reworked by directors desperate to be considered new.

As in Finland, many of the subjects involving Soviet crimes and Estonian chauvinism were marginalized after independence; the focus then was on Anglo-American topics and productions. Now, audiences and theatre groups are once again interested in regional and national Estonian themes as well as international trends. Saro points to three specific examples of what, she claims, represent a recovery of traditional Estonian approaches to performance art: a return to traditional narrative structures, reinterpretations of cultural history, and new versions of the history of the Soviet years.

Writers like Kivastik and Kivirähk are now less reluctant to write about the Soviet experience, which, it must be stressed, is a new development in Estonian theatre and is still a topic most Finnish writers — with a few rare exceptions like Sofi Oksanen and Kristian Smeds — shy away from. Spearheading this resurgence of political theatre, returning, as it were, to a theatre of engagement indicative of the theatre of resistance during the Soviet occupation, Ojasoo uses ironic nationalism in *Hot Estonian Guys* to achieve what Saro describes as "documentary cabaret." Ojasoo toys with the cliché of beefy Estonian studs hoping to revitalize the national Estonian spirit and culture by impregnating as many women as possible. The acting is stylized to create an ironic distance between the technique and the effect, but it also celebrates while critiquing the reemerging phenomenon of Estonian nationalistic tendencies prevalent in the current socio-cultural sphere.

Garnering the most attention from the Finns are recent developments in Lithuanian theatre, especially the recent movement away from the metaphorical theatre of Eimuntas Nekrošius through the transitional theatre of Oskaras Koršunovas to the post-modern work of Gintaras Varnas. The career arc of these three directors accurately reflects the political and social reality in Lithuanian society during the years from the 1970s to the first decade of the twenty first century.

Edgaras Klivis, a scholar of theatre research at Vytautas Magnus University in Kaunas, Lithuania, suggests that the experimental style of the "new" Lithuanian theatre was a direct response to Soviet sanctioned social realism. Based in theories of mimesis, the Marxist totalitarian logic was simple: if reality is a picture, and you control the picture, you control reality. In the 1970s, this use of mimesis was still the operating principle behind the Soviet's use of realism as a political tool for social control. To counter the colonizing effect of social realism, some artists and theatre directors — Nekrošius, for one — rejected the genre and chose a metaphorical theatre, a dangerous tendency in the eyes of Soviet authorities. Metaphor, which operates by creating new truths from a clash of seemingly familiar images brought together in unexpected ways, destroys the ordinary, the expected. Metaphor threatens social control. But throughout the 1990s, as politics changed, metaphor as a weapon had no target. The theatre of Nekrošius became aesthetically interesting, but it no longer had the social relevance it wielded during the Soviet occupation.

According to Klivis, the theatre of Koršunovas represented a transition away from the impotence implied in the late stages of the theatre of metaphor practiced by Nekrošius. Because there was no longer an "enemy," metaphorical theatre seemed distant, irrelevant, isolated and elitist to the younger generation. It became narcissistic, a vehicle conveying only the abstract fantasies of the directors, themes disconnected from life. In response, Koršunovas returned to the mimetic, but infused it with irony. His stylized realism represented a new, anti-elitist attack on the consumer-based capitalist model. Koršunovas' approach led to another mode, exemplified by Varnas, in which the director uses the traditional ideas of theatre — psychology, narrative, dramatic situations — but by rethinking and recasting the older mimetic approaches, he exposes the destabilized meanings contained within them.

While these influences from its neighbors situate Finnish theatre at the outer edges of the contemporary Baltic sphere, Outi Lahtinen, scholar of theatre research at University of Tampere, notes that early Finnish drama was also generally discounted in the Hanseatic zone. Lahtinen cites KOM Theatre, which has a rich tradition of providing a space to develop and advance new work, as perhaps one of the most important players helping to remedy this situation. KOM created a program called KOMtext (KOMteksti), dedicated to developing new writing by Finnish writers. One successful product of KOM's program is Laura Ruohonen, who has created several plays focusing on dynamic roles for women and whose plays continue to be translated and performed throughout Europe. Her success also illustrates that historically Finnish theatre was, and for the most part, still is actor-driven.

Although popular theatre in Finland is influenced by the "art theatre" that defines Berlin, it is also shaped by programs from the Anglo-American bloc, including both realistic genres and more stylized work, along with the standard fare of satirical sit-coms and reality shows that makes British and American television so popular. Still relevant too are British playwrights like Tom Stoppard, Harold Pinter, Sarah Kane and Mark Ravenhill. Anna Veijalainen, artistic director at Koko Theatre, cites Kane as one of her "foreign inspirations" (Maukola 22) and has staged *Cleansed* and *Blasted*. "Kane's language is unbelievably fine," Veijalainen says. "It is authentic and, in all its horror, poetic and captivating" (22).

Finnish directors (like artistic directors throughout the Baltics) also acknowledge an affinity with Irish theatre, finding in the works of Martin McDonagh, Conor McPherson and Geraldine Aron depictions of small community life that generate universal appeal. The audiences in Finland identify with the Irish, seeing their own situation reflected in their history as much as in their contemporary situation. Both Finland and Ireland have been marginalized nations that gained independence relatively late in modern history. Both have struggled to maintain a national identity while being overshadowed by more dominant forces. Like the Irish, the Finns confront a newly transient population, job mobility, and economic uncertainty brought on by globalization. Theatre can act as a counterforce to these perceived threats, not just by maintaining nostalgia for a simpler romantic view of one's history and place in the world but also as an antidote to the complexities of contemporary life. In Ireland, "Theatres are increasingly being seen as a resource that residents of a locality may use to resist certain aspects of globalisation" (Lonergan), and a parallel movement is evident in Finland, indicated by the commercial success of Irish plays throughout the Nordic region.

Of all the artists in the contemporary Western canon, the most significant are the Germans Peter Stein and Frank Castorf, and American Robert Wilson. Stein, whose shifting aesthetics makes him hard to categorize, is also emulated across the continent. While his early faith in the text was often criticized by so-called "strong" directors who use the text only as a point of departure for their own metaphorical interpretations, Stein was considered radical for his rejection of multi-media spectacles. He focused instead on character and dramatic intensity. Though he later began to dispense with text, often initiating extreme rewrites, it is his elaborate use of space and visuals, along with his collaborative approach to performances that has had the most impact on young Finnish directors. Wilson's signature — using three-dimensional performance space, combining eclectic art forms, including video, installations, exotic staging, dance and operatic effects into the theatrical experience — pervades productions throughout Europe; his influence is endemic. The deconstructionist technique of Castorf is equally influential. His meta-theatrical games, anti-empathetic mode, rejection of narrative logic, and integration of extreme personal quirkiness and self-referential pastiches into his post-dramatic, overly stylized performances permeate the styles of young directors throughout Europe. Early on, Wilson's work "confused audiences, shocked them out of their lethargy [...] put emphasis on spectacle and disjointedness instead of narrative continuity [... his] theatre spectacles quote history out of context to shatter conventional narrative" (Arens 15). Productions as disparate in style as Kristian Smeds' *The Unkown Soldier*, Esa Leskinen's *Satan Comes to Moscow*, Pekka Milonoff's *Towards* and Heikki Kujanpää's *Birth of a Salesman* clearly and distinctly bear the indelible thumbprints of Stein, Castorf and Wilson.

In Finland, one artist attuned to trends in both exploring performance space and testing the boundaries between performance and actuality is Eero-Tapio Vuori. His works "challenge the spectator to consider how performance differs from the reality" (Silde 14). In a piece similar to the experiments of Jarovojs and Hermanis, Vuori conceived *Helsinki by Night*, mischievously billed in the 2005 Baltic Circle program as a "late night bus ride through Helsinki, booked for foreign festival guests."

Actually, the tour group was unknowingly submitting to a performance piece that, while taking place on a sightseeing bus, was designed as "a mobile documentation." The idea, according to Reality Research Center (Todellisuuden tutkimuskeskus), the creative team behind the exercise, is to riff off "surprising commentary and events that alter the participants' view of the city" in order to create a bizarre experiment to alter the pre-determined perceptions of the participants, e.g., that they were on an actual "tour" and were being presented with an unfiltered experience. Reality Research Center, listed by *Finnish Theatre* magazine as "among the most visible challengers and developers of the new Finnish theatre aesthetic" (Ruuskanen 11), explains that the parameters of its "rapid documentation with mobile devices" were constrained only "by dark November night and the limited memory of the video cards" while they "set out to capture fragments and feelings raised by the performance [...] and published them using the video-blog platform developed by HP and Virtaamo."

Vuori's mystery tour, where reality and theatre are mixed, is especially successful with foreigners because it plays within an unfamiliar landscape, but the effect is even more pronounced when the tour involves local audiences because the landscape, composed of familiar streets and neighborhoods of Helsinki, is de-familiarized by the tour guide's incongruous observations and improvised, often intentionally provocative commentary. The result is phenomenological: to recast the familiar as something startling and strange in an effort to force the subject to reconsider the possibilities of her environment. The intention is to examine the traditional sightseeing experience, for both natives and tourists, in order to create a new experience, not just by giving familiar objects a new context but also by incorporating randomness and unexpected variables into the journey.

Vuori's work resembles other experimental plays popularized in London and New York. In David Rosenberg's *Contains Violence*, for instance, audiences on the terrace of the Lyric Theatre in London spy on people across the road, watching them through binoculars as if they are living private lives, listening to their dialogue as if eavesdropping. In Paul Walker's 2007 *Ladies and Gents*, performed inside the Bethesda bathroom stalls in New York City's Central Park by the Irish Art Center, the audience is divided into two groups, one directed to the men's room and one to the ladies' room. With a nod to *Rashomon*, the two groups watch fragments of the central story (selling sex), then trade places and hear another fragment. The truth of "what happened" is left up to the viewer.

(Too frequently, these exercises play out more like gimmickry than innovative theatre. At the extreme end of this trend toward blurring if not entirely erasing the boundaries between performance and actuality are plays like *Etiquette*, created by Silvia Mercuriali and Anthony Hampton under the artistic brand Rotozaza and played at Edinburgh in 2007. In this piece, audience members become actors following a recorded script.)

Another influential writer who has worked with Realty Research Center is Maria Kilpi. Part of her appeal is that even in her experimental work, she manages to keep herself grounded in the fundamentals of theatre. Productions like *With Love from Pori* manage to avoid the pitfalls of gimmicky art by focusing on the human element inherent in an intimate dramatic performance. The piece, developed in collaboration with Lovers Theatre (Rakastajat-teatteri) includes historical sources, interviews and a mixed media presentation that crosses genres and opens possibilities to free theatre from its grounding in straight dramatic narrative.

Her interest in formalism is most evident in her final project as a 2007 graduate of the Theatre Academy in Helsinki. Kilpi describes the piece, titled *Epilogue (Epilogi)*, as a "performance without performers." The work is divided into two parts. In the first half, as the audience sits in the center area of a black box theatre, abstract scenes created by sound and light are played around and through them. One of the most interesting ploys for Kilpi was gauging the audience's response when, near the end of the first half of the performance, the lights were suddenly directed at the audience, randomly connecting some members, isolating others. The play of lights added a weird element of exhibitionism and voyeurism to the audience's experience. Because no one in the crowd was alerted to this aspect of the performance, they simply reacted, unsure how to relate to the lighting strategy. Some liked being exposed and played along; others resented being spotlighted and felt violated. The lights were randomly programmed, so it was only a matter of pure chance that certain people were hit with the light while others were left in darkness. The exercise, spontaneously creating performers and observers, interrogates the very nature of the producer/consumer dichotomy and questions how audience expectations can be created by post-dramatic situations.

Kilpi's intent was to use non-representational concrete sounds and visuals to provoke a response from those exposed to the images. The process resembles a psychotherapist passively showing Rorschach patterns from which the patient creates meaning. The signifiers — Kilpi's sound and light patterns — are neutral and arbitrary. The viewer imbues the images with significant context, revealing motives necessarily unique.

In the second half of the performance, the audience watches a bank of TV monitors while a selected group of Kilpi's friends sit around them typing random messages on laptops. In this exercise, there are no visuals. The performance is essentially reduced to pure text, but without any logical design or dramatic structure, no narrative arc or meaningful context. After twenty minutes, a slide show begins, composed of photographs of her friends and personal archives. Then the theatre doors are opened, the actors thank the audience, but the slide show continues and there are no other adjustments made to the studio lighting or instructions from the personnel.

The audience is left to decide how to conclude the performance, wondering if this is just another facet of the show or is actually the end. They are forced to their own context. Kilpi describes this situation as "dramatic structure without contents." As in the first half of the performance, her desire was to remove any symbolic meanings and supply only concrete circumstances that the audience must come to terms with outside of their expectation or conditioned responses. The result illustrates the human paradox: we live in a community of private meanings while only sharing public space.

Given her interest in formalism and her work with Reality Research Center, it seems surprising that her most acclaimed work is a rather traditional, straightforward one act drama titled *Sore Spot* (*Harmin paikka*) which

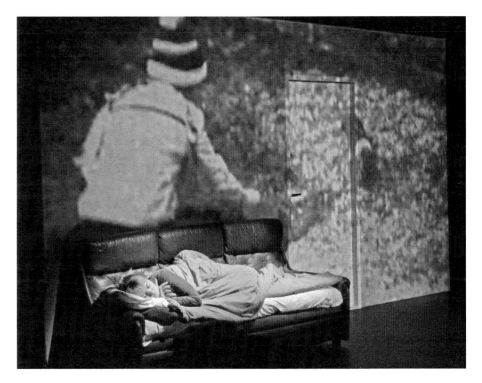

Emilia Sinisalo in Maria Kilpi's *Sore Spot*. A young woman's Christmas visit to her grandmother turns into a poetic encounter rich with existential implications. The projected video images never seem intrusive or superficial; they are smartly integrated with the action to illuminate the deep, almost Jungian connections between the two women (photograph by Vertti Teräsvuori).

won the 2007 Stückemarket prize in Berlin and has been translated into several languages. Developed at the National Theatre in Helsinki and directed by Minna Nurmelin at the 2009 Tampere festival, the play is a study of contrasts. It presents the ordinary circumstances of a young woman's Christmas visit to her grandmother as a poetic encounter rife with existential implications. While exposing the irreparable rifts between youth and age, hope and despair, impatience and resignation, the play underscores the common humanity connecting the two women in an intimate bond that transcends the particular experiences that separate them.

The set reinforces this paradoxical theme of separation and connection shared by the women. The stage is split between the grandmother's bedroom and the couch where Laura sets up camp. A fallen tree stage right divides the cozy interior from the harsh winter outside the stark apartment. A streaming video of home movies projects images of childhood memories on the walls behind the bed and couch. When the house lights go down, the video images stop and two stark spotlights illuminate the women, each isolated in her private space — the grandmother on her bed, Laura on the couch: different women mirroring each other, the older representing what the other will become, the younger what the other was.

They awkwardly work around each other's idiosyncrasies. They puncture the swelling silences with talk about the weather. The grandmother avoids the past. Laura avoids the present. When they visit the graveyard where the grandfather is buried, the grandmother lights a votive candle, but Laura is distracted and uninterested. She tries to create a sense of significance by constantly videotaping their activities, but her actions betray her false enthusiasm, like a tourist taking obligatory snapshots to remember an otherwise unremarkable summer vacation.

The style is unusual in its minimalism and lack of irony, given the vogue for postmodern saturation and pyrotechnic media spectacles. In a time where extravaganza, elaborate metaphors and pretentiousness trump the quiet steady depiction of the complexity of human emotions, *Sore Spot* seems all the more radical in its simplicity. The play is static, often lifeless. The projected video images never seem intrusive or superficial; they are smartly integrated with the action and work nicely to illuminate the deep, almost Jungian connections between the two women. But one of the main strengths of the play lies in how Kilpi manages to keep the story particularly Finnish — evoking memories of traditional songs, the green marmalade candy — but also universal, presenting the loneliness of old age, the importance of youth, and the dilemma of communicating across the great generational divide common to all cultures.

Achieving this effective, straightforward style of virtuous simplicity seems even more impressive considering Kilpi had originally envisioned a non-text based piece composed of post-dramatic fragments in random sequences.

"At the academy, it was trendy to write in this style," she says. "Everyone wanted to experiment with fragmented narratives. I wanted to create performance art in this postmodern mode."

In her early drafts she studiously resisted text and plot. But the more she worked the individual scenes, the more she understood the need for some unifying structure. This led to an interest in associative narrative. She also began to develop autobiographical material, which in turn led to an interest in the possibilities of documentary styles. Meanwhile, she had composed a prose piece about her grandmother that she began to fictionalize, maintaining the essential truth of the various episodes from her memories while working them into dramatic situations.

With encouragement from Katariina Numminen, her teacher at the time, she decided to investigate how she might use plot elements to organize the sequences, but in an alternative fashion, not strictly according to the Aristotelian unities.

Kilpi admits that at the time she was actively shaping the play, looking for a unifying structure — essentially, a plot — that would not stifle the freedom of narrative she considered key to the success of the play, she began reading the late British playwright and Nobel winner Harold Pinter. (Traces of Pinter are fairly obvious in *Sore Spot*, albeit in an original, not derivative fashion.) Pinter, at first, seems an odd — even counter-intuitive — choice as a model for investigating plot as a unifying feature in a play. But for Kilpi, his subtle plot graphs complemented her desire for a loose structure that still managed to maintain the associative integrity of the scenes without locking the sequence into a firm Freitag model.

To facilitate this loose structure, she utilized a series of actions that, by repetition, become metaphorical. Waiting for a bus, for instance, either to arrive or leave, and the time spent walking to and from the bus stop, and the waiting itself, creates what Kilpi calls the "ritual of the ordinary." (Think of T. S. Eliot's devastating line from *Prufrock*: "I have measured out my life in coffee spoons.") Ironically, Kilpi's initial resistance to formal narrative structure yielded to the necessity of organizing principles, and the result is a playful blend of imagistic poetry and psychological drama that seems neither frumpy nor trendy.

Another playwright enjoying a critical reputation for writing social commentary but whose style stands in stark contrast to Kilpi's is Anna Krogerus. In 2006 she was awarded the Finnish Critics' Association Award for her play *For Sheer Love of Me* (*Rakkaudesta minuun*). The play premiered at the National, directed by Irene Aho. In promotional material provided by the

Nordic Drama Center, *For Sheer Love of Me* is depicted as "a subtle, perceptive, compassionate and at times humorous examination of the processes of alienation and estrangement in a family."

The action is meant to capture a pre-teen's perspective while she is invisible in the eyes of her parents, who are more invested in their trendy professions — the father a version of Dr. Phil, the mother an interior designer — than in the well being of their daughter. They are serial narcissists, their distorted sense of sexuality as much a self-reflection as their occupations. The father's ego is mirrored in his television personality, the mother's in her projected self-exposure. Self-obsessed, they miss the central tragedy: the end of their daughter's childhood.

Less a dramatic peek into the lives of a contemporary Finnish family than a cultural commodity as generic — and exportable — as any realistic, Eurocentric, made-for-television sitcom, the play is an excellent example of the pitfalls of many of the Nordic Drama Corner projects, an organization dedicated to marketing what it describes as "Finnish plays for the world stage."

The play is a typical text-based talk-a-thon, more argued than visually rendered, the dialogue brisk if mundane. More serious than the structure, however, is the impression the play creates regarding the current state of the Finnish family unit. Aside from the fact that none of the characters is necessarily likeable, the situations are petty and predictable. The original script centers on Sylvia Jalovaara, the ten-year-old daughter of Tea, an interior designer, and Lauri, a pop-psychologist with a television talk show. Krogerus intended to portray the daughter's suffering from the indifference of her narcissistic parents, but Sylvia's plight seems less a by-product of her parents' self-interest than her own lack of imagination.

Tea plays a batty Mary Tyler Moore, updated to act out repressive impulses toward self-destruction and hysteria. Lauri, Tea's Dick Van Dyke counterpart, is an opportunist and a realist more threatened by bi-sexuality than adultery. Their young neighbor, Saana, a university student, is a convenient foil onto whom the others can project their desires. Krogerus' attempt to add a level of tragedy by having Tea acknowledge naming her daughter after the American poet and suicide Sylvia Plath (a phrase from Plath's poem "Tulips" is also quoted in the title), and then in the last act having the mother lying as if dead on the floor of her living room with the oven door open, only reinforces the weakness of the dramatic situation. Krogerus' play is a good example of how difficult it can be to write about empty lives without having the characters' emptiness drain the play of its intensity.

As a portrait of contemporary Finland, the representation seems trendy beyond reality. The motivation for Saana to show up one afternoon is to have her neighbors sign a petition to prevent pollution in the Baltic Sea. When

Sylvia discovers Saana has a dog — the pet she craves but which her parents deny her — Saana agrees to let Sylvia care for the dog while Saana is away. Due to Sylvia's carelessness — flirting with boys from her school — the dog is hit and killed by a car. Sylvia tries to cover up her misdeed by hiding the dog in another neighbor's attic. Meanwhile, the two women become "cunt cousins," Sylvia's term for "two women [...] fucking the same person." Tea initiates an affair with Saana's boyfriend but is devastated when he does not reciprocate her passion. Saana, more out of revenge than lust, seduces Lauri, but that affair is equally unsatisfactory.

In a disturbing scene, Sylvia, confused and frightened by her first menstrual period and having never discussed menstruation with her mother, walks in on her father and Saana having sex on the living room couch. In another scene, she comes home to find her mother passed out on the floor, drunk, with the oven door open, reminiscent of Sylvia Plath's suicide. The death of Saana's dog becomes a symbol for the absence of commitment, compassion, understanding, empathy or kindness in the couple's lives, as well as for the damage human carelessness can cause.

Krogerus is popular in critical circles. Her next play, *As If for the First Day* (*Kuin ensimmäistä päivää*), received the 2009 Savonia literary award. The theme of this play deals with working conditions in a home for the elderly where nurses are hired without permanent contracts. The stress of the job, combined with the apprehension of working without job security — a new and socially disruptive concept in Finland — undermines the faith of both patients and nurses in the welfare state.

Like *For Sheer Love of Me*, this play is also dialogue-driven, relying on explication and characters discussing their motives while much of the dramatic action occurs offstage. It is seeded with hot button issues — ageism, sexism, racism, anti-immigration bigotry, inequities in the workplace, exploitation of women, the plight of single mothers — but it is so overloaded with social problems that the play tends to collapse from its own weight. The legitimate concerns raised by Krogerus seem less dramatic than perfunctory.

These observations are conditioned and qualified by the fact that they are based mainly on readings of scripts in translation as opposed to performances in the original language. Hanna-Leena Helavuori, director of Theatre Museum in Helsinki, points out discrepancies that illustrate Aaltonen's thesis about Finnish plays becoming distorted or corrupted in translation, especially when "targeted" for specific markets:

> Krogerus's plays have a huge theatrical potential, which the director Irene Aho was able to realize in her staging of *For the Sheer Love of Myself* at the Finnish National Theatre and *As If for the First Day* at Kajaani City Theatre. Her plays are ironic, black comedies that use naivety as a conscious strategy.

In a bad interpretation this all can look like stereotypes and as such uninteresting.

Performances also vary depending on directors, actors, performance space, etc., but if the playwright's intent is compromised, as is the case often in translation, the result cannot be salvaged or corrected by a nifty production.

The story focuses on Ritva, a fifty-year-old nurse's aide. She spends her life dutifully working at the nursing home, sincerely caring for the elderly on her ward, but her compassion masks the loneliness and emptiness of her life. While complaining of her work load and the cuts being enacted by anonymous bureaucrats more interested in the bottom line than the welfare of the patients, she easily plays the martyr, sacrificing her personal life to cover for her coworkers.

The central tragic element in the plot deals with Ritva's mentally disabled son, who lives in a group home and feels abandoned by his mother; she seldom has a chance to visit because of her heavy work schedule. When, in the first act, Ritva warns the staff at the group home not to let her son play in the river, the outcome is clear: on the day Ritva finally drops all pretense of civility and lets fly with a scathing speech condemning the ethics of the committee in charge of regulating expenditures — and assuring that she will lose her job — the home calls to tell her that her son has drowned.

As If for the First Day is a prime example of the difficulty playwrights face trying to create plays that promote social concerns at the expense of dramatic action. Most indicative of this syndrome is the scene in which Ritva delivers her monologue haranguing the oversight committee; the speech is a lengthy diatribe that denounces the inequities of the system, but in performance it sounds, at best, like a self-righteous screed, and at worst like a position paper prepared by a politician.

The final scene is even more problematic. As if unable to dramatically conclude the story, Krogerus tags on a sophomoric Epilogue in which the actor playing Ritva addresses the audience. She delivers a series of rhetorical questions and superficially philosophical musings, admitting that she cannot say what happened to Ritva (because, she says, she is not the actual person but only an actor) but that she longs for a "world where I wouldn't feel so lost and worthless." She concludes, not by invoking cosmic *aporia* but with dramatic impotence: "I just wanted to tell you this. I don't know why. Somehow it felt important."

According to the promotional literature for the play, the members of the jury that awarded Krogerus the Savonia literary award celebrated her focus on "social maladies," but the committee but was especially impressed by her role as one of the "defenders of women and others who are underprivileged."

Women's issues are certainly a priority in the new theatre of Finland. But while playwrights like Krogerus writing in the realist mode and Kilpi in her more poetic style address women's issues in their work, their approach, couched in dramatic action, explores the subject through sequential narratives involving identifiable characters working through social interaction.

At the fringe theatres, the playwrights take a more radical approach. The action often involves performances dealing with gender construction, identity politics and the fluidity of social assumptions. Miira Sippola from Mill Theatre (Myllyteatteri) employs the techniques of Tadashi Suzuki to explore physical forms of emotional expression. In 2008 Mill Theatre pitched a "theatre tent" in a park and held a nine-day tragedy contest. Sippola's piece was titled *Lot's Wife* but was designed around the form of the classic play *Medea*, allowing Sippola to connect several ancient myths of tragic (and some might say heroic) women to events in the contemporary world while reconsidering and reshaping classic forms. Pauliina Hulkko designs extremely stylized performances in a classic postmodern assault on elitism and conventional, reassuring narratives. In *Amoralia*, produced in 2003 at the Kiasma Theatre in the Museum of Contemporary Art, she connects medieval religious texts with pop songs, poetry with polka, mixing polyglot dialogue with haunting, nonverbal situations. The actors, half-naked and painted like harlequins out of a Toulouse-Lautrec nightmare, assume grotesque poses that mock pretension with pretense, character with caricature.

The importance of Juha-Pekka Hotinen in the dramaturgy curriculum at the Theatre Academy and his impact on a whole generation of young writers and directors cannot be overstated. Hotinen questioned conventional approaches to dramaturgy by focusing on how old forms could be recycled and reworked to create new forms of popular political and social theatre. In contrast to the tradition of an *auteur* director or the dominance of a writer in the realization of a performance, Hotinen emphasized the director's curriculum developed by Maarit Ruikka, which stressed co-operation between the playwright and the director, so that the production evolves through a truly ensemble creative process.

Hotinen's influence, direct and indirect, is evident in much of the new work emerging at both the fringe theatres and the more established houses in Finland.

One of Hotinen's former students is Kristian Smeds, the most recognized Finnish playwright outside of Finland. Best known for his blockbuster *The Unknown Soldier* (*Tuntematon sotilas*), which ran over 120 times on the main stage of the Finnish National Theatre since its premier in 2007, Smeds has been a fixture in Finnish theatre since founding and directing the Forge Theatre (Teatteri Takomo) in Helsinki in 1996. After leaving Forge, he became the director of a theatre in a small town in northern Finland, where he could work away from the influences of a cosmopolitan environment like Helsinki. Next, to further distance himself from the common experiences and historical contexts of Finnish society, he went into a more traditional exile, freelancing for three years in the Baltic States. He finally returned to Helsinki to form the Smeds' Ensemble.

Of the valuable tools Smeds learned from Hotinen, the most noticeable might be the ability to see and understand dramaturgical structures, to read and interpret plays analytically. Under Hotinen's tutelage, the Theatre Academy stressed integration of disciplines. As Smeds explains, "When I was a student, you could choose from the specializations writing, directing or acting. What was special, however, was that all of these specializations worked closely together. [...] I chose writing, but we were required to act and direct our pieces and those of others. [...] I know a lot of colleagues who — like me — were able to easily make the leap from writing to directing [...] based on this experience" (qtd. in Kuyl).

Some of the more innovative performances feature the experimental work of Katariina Numminen, Milja Sarkola, and productions associated with Sometimes Foggy (Avoittain Sumua). Other important artists include Juha Hurme, the director of Hunger Theatre (Nälkäteatteri), who focuses on his own dramaturgy as well as re-thinking Finnish classics; Esa Kirkkopelto, a philosopher and Professor of Artistic Research at the Theatre Academy in Helsinki who works with an experimental theatre-laboratory called In Alternate Spaces, a part of Hunger Theatre; and Milja Sarkola, the director at Forge Theatre, whose works, including *Mail to Eva Dahlgren*, explore metatheatrical implications of performances and audience reception theories.

The output by these performers demands to be taken seriously. Other work, however, while engaging, often expects too much of itself. For instance, the publicity flyer for Aune Kallinen's *Life Like* (*Toden näköinen*), performed at Kiasma in 2009, reads like a paean to Heidegger. According to the literature, *Life Like* (the pun is obvious)

> is based on shared, although at times incomprehensible, reality. It introduces the possible and impossible political dimensions of the personal, questions the notion of an individual and wonders where I end and You begin. It focuses on a shared, political view and serves for a meaningful way of being in the world. The aim is [...] to marvel at ourselves as humans.

Often, by the very nature of this type of work, the performance is more interesting than the theories on which the work is based.

One of the most documented performances to come out of Kiasma — which has in many ways assumed the role of ground zero for staging avant-garde work, especially that which promotes feminist performance perspectives — was

Catchment Area — Memos of Freedom (*Valuma-alue — muistioita vapaudesta*) by playwright and director Tuija Kokkonen. The work is so multi-faceted that a synopsis doesn't do it justice or even begin to capture its complexity, but its significance cannot be discounted. *Catchment Area* marked a defining moment in post-modern, post-dramatic investigation into political and ideological themes in contemporary performance. The performance, in three parts, was presented in Kiasma between 1998 and 2003. The work is a deconstruction of Shakespeare's *Hamlet*, but the original play is merely a pretense for an exploration of the new paradigms of "performativity" (Sutinen 28) and "the gendered and hierarchical world of theatre" (31).

Memo I opens with Hamlet and Ophelia trying out new methods of presenting theatre productions. Their intention is to reinvigorate a decadent theatre that in their view has become repetitive to the point of meaninglessness. In this sense, the premise of the performance is a critique of the contemporaneous situation in Finnish theatre, which many critics and producers considered stagnant, irrelevant and corrupt. "In 'Memo I,' repetition is presented as an obstacle to the renewal of theatre" (33). In *Memo II*, Hamlet and Ophelia have left the building and abandoned the performance, leaving the minor characters behind to play for the audience. In addition to the three characters, a videotape of Hamlet and Ophelia recording songs and traveling around Helsinki plays non-stop throughout the performance. "'Memo II' is anti-theatre in the sense that it is not dominated by psychologizing, historicity, realism or naturalism" (37). In *Memo III*, the audience is met in the lobby of the museum and given written instructions, an audiotape and headphones. The audience members play the audiotape consisting of fragments of the former two performances while watching three video projections — two showing scenes from the previous performances and another of the cast performing in actors' wigs. "In 'Memo III,' relinquishment and passing become naturalized as parts of the essence of the performance and the possibility of something new" (40).

Hanna-Leena Helavuori describes *Catchment Area* as a "strategy of resistance" (66), describing the play as a statement against assimilation into any categorical identification with institutional theatre productions.

> Kokkonen examines strong gendered agency, the closed structure of Aristotelian drama and its powerful agent/subject. Kokkonen opens up hierarchic oppositions by taking up a position between them, in an intermediate space that allows the emergence of third concepts [66].

For the younger, more radical Finnish directors bent on challenging the nature of theatre, this self-reflexive interrogation of randomness, ambiguity and contingency in performances generates a lot of interest. The idea is to explore the relationship of performance and reality and blur the line between actor and audience. The problem is that artists must inevitably confront what Frank Kermode calls the "inescapable element of the counterfeit" (236). Exploring the imposition of form onto reality invites a Kantian metaphysics that even in praxis is endlessly speculative and can express only the tautological "dissidence between the inherited forms and our own reality" (221).

The trend in Finnish theatre has been moving for several years not only toward metaphorical and physical theatre, but also, according to Mika Myllyaho, artistic director at The Group Theatre, toward a mixed-media incorporating video, dance, cross-genre elements and self-referential devices indicative of the influence of both the "strong" Lithuanian directors and the theatrical experiments originating in Berlin. Myllyaho suggests that the way forward, to keep theatre dynamic, is to find new forms of expression for traditional themes. But he downplays the clamor by critics for anything "new," and he is not so concerned with form. "The themes are universal," he says, "so you can mix form as you need to." He feels comfortable "breaking the frame" because the plot arcs remain necessarily classical. Myllyaho is a firm believer in the uniqueness of the theatre experience, and is confident that finding "new forms for old themes" will assure a strong audience for theatre performances regardless of new fads in electronic entertainment. "Don't fight the new media," he says. "Incorporate it."

With few exceptions, most Finnish playwrights still find it difficult to have their works translated and performed abroad, mainly because of the tendency of writers to focus on parochial issues that could be obscure to foreign audiences. One major exception is Juha Jokela's *Mobile Horror*, a play that, according to Outi Lahtinen, put Finnish theatre on the international map. The play involves three entrepreneurs whose mobile phone company has been bought by a conglomerate; they are tasked with creating ever-new products or risk losing their jobs. Relationships are reduced to marketing strategies and one-upmanship, and their new products venture collapses with a loss of faith in both their personal integrity and professional ethics. The success of the play is based on particularly universal themes — relationships reduced to marketing strategies, spiritual values sacrificed for the sake of profit — that resonate with audiences throughout the developed world.

But this kind of easily exportable play is rare in Finland.

Pirkko Koski, a former professor of theatre research at University of Helsinki, notes other reasons for the lack of exportable Finnish theatre. Koski likens Finland to its neighboring Baltic nations: a diminutive country with a limited social milieu. How to transpose social situations accurately from one culture to another is an issue that confronts any translator. For countries like Finland, the problem seems more acute. According to Koski, constructing cultural images from a small society like Finland's requires that the material be relevant in other contexts, especially in the Anglo-American social framework. Ironically, the smaller the country, the more esoteric, exotic and obscure the material.

Mobile Horror is a play that taps into the collective imagination of anyone from a culture caught up in the soul-sapping demands of dog-eat-dog capitalism, and is therefore immediately accessible to multi-cultural audiences. A more delicate play like *Border Crossing* by Kari Hotakainen, which addresses Finland's relationship with Russia after the collapse of the Soviet Union in the early 1990s, is harder to transpose accurately into a different cultural context. The ostensible subject of the play is the subtle and essential relationship the Finns shared with the Soviets during the Cold War, and it is the esoteric and personal metaphorical layers of meaning such a special relationship entails that exemplifies the difficulties faced by translators of many Finnish plays.

As Koski explains, the original Finnish title of *Border Crossing* is *Punahukka*, which means, literally, red wolf, but which also means a disease in which the red blood cells break down and the victims exhibit red spots on their skin. The original title further implies a political and existential threat from the Soviets — the red wolf — during that period of history. The translated title *Border Crossing* was an attempt by the translator (S. E. Wilmer) to focus on the ordinary idea of the commerce between two countries, in this case Russia and Finland, but also the more universal notion of the main character making changes — border crossings — in his personal life. Much of the richness of the play is literally lost in translation.

Maria Kilpi's *Sore Spot* is another good example of the difficulty in rendering the nuance of Finnish into English. The Finnish title *Harmin paikka* implies an ambiguity nearly impossible to capture with an English transliteration. Harmin is a noun meaning a trifle, something not serious enough to worry about. Paikka means place. So the literal translation is *A Place to Worry*. You would use the phrase if you spilt milk on your blouse, but you might also use it cynically if you uttered it in a real crisis. Then again, in a real crisis, you might use it ironically with a certain intonation to imply the complete hopelessness and despair of the situation. *Sore Spot*, given the rich ambiguity of the Finnish expression, seems too pedestrian and specific to render the effect Kilpi's original title is meant to convey. The title also implies an esoteric historical reference the Finnish would be quick to acknowledge but which would be lost on average viewers from outside of the country. The sore spot for the grandmother is the fact that she had to move from the Karelia and essentially became a refuge after the territory was lost to the Soviet Union.

Heikki Kujanpää, a director, playwright, actor and one of the original founders of Q Theatre, suggests that the isolation of Finnish theatre is intrinsic. In his view, Finns in general are not curious about outside cultures, and plays from other countries do not especially interest the average Finnish theatre audience. This apathy regarding foreign performances causes the institutional theatres to be overly cautious in selecting which plays to perform. Because the Finnish theatre has its roots in a fairly rigid Lutheran tradition, the typical plays rely on text more than visuals, and the mainstream houses are reluctant to experiment for fear of alienating their audiences.

Kujanpää admits that the influx of foreign influences since the mid–1990s has had a positive influence on Finnish theatre, especially the work from their nearby neighbors in the Baltics. In his appreciation of Baltic theatre, his metaphors are precise. He compares Lithuanian theatre to a cathedral, partly because of its Catholic tradition and the reverence most Lithuanian theatre audiences exhibit toward their art, but also because the themes are usually weighted with a spiritual significance elevating them out of the mundane into the mythological. He likens Latvian theatre to a house, as the themes are more localized and focused on the lives of ordinary people, though the Latvian writers are famous for their romantic depictions of relationships that often mask the honest critique contemporary social situations demand. Estonian theatre, for Kujanpää, is a cloud, since the Estonian writers and directors tend to use a lighter touch than either the Lithuanians or Latvians. They are free to question and play around with the form of drama, and their structures do not necessarily adhere to what he calls the Anglo-American rules.

In general, all of the principals involved in contemporary Finnish theatre agree that the majority of Finnish theatre-goers prefer traditional text-based dramas firmly grounded in Lutheran ethics, psychological realism and stories of ordinary life. They also agree that this sensibility is ripe for aesthetical rehabilitation.

Exemplifying how the Finns feel that they are indeed behind the curve when it comes to employing more exciting and experimental forms of theatre art, Finnish actor and translator Jussi Lehtonen — who collaborated with Pauliina Hulkko in *Amoralia* — recalls his experience studying in Vilnius, Lithuania, with Grabstaitė Vesta, actor, choreographer, director, and teacher of the physical theatre methods according to Oleg Kiseliov and Suzuki. As a Finn training in Lithuania, he confirms the role of the director as *auteur* and the dominance of physicality and metaphor in the theatre that contrasts significantly with typical narrative-based Finnish productions. The new Lithuanian theatre directors tend to treat all text as subtext, all language as metaphor, an approach that the Finns, with their tradition of revering the text, have only recently began to adopt. His study in Lithuania, so foreign to his schooling in Finland, underscores how institutionalized traditional methods remain in the acting curricula in Finland and how the resistance to new methods seems ingrained in mainstream Finnish theatre.

The unreformed socialists still prefer realism. The self-referential game-playing constructs of postmodernism echo the abstract, solipsistic aestheticism of the twentieth century Modernists, and the responses of the reformers to these art theatre performances resemble the Marxist critique of Modernism. At risk of simplifying the discourse, one critique situates the argument pragmatically, positing the difference between private and public interests, with the Modernists' decidedly interior studies stressing individuality and psychology, which is set against realists that prefer a turn outward toward communal values. No question but that art after World War II "contextualized the Cold War's bruising esthetic and political battles — they often coincided — over art's promise and possibilities in the rapidly realigning postwar world" (Katz 83). Georg Lukács states the issue succinctly: "The great lesson to be learnt [...] is precisely the extent to which a great realist literature can fructifyingly educate the people and transform public opinion" (215). Lukács objected to "reactionary obscurantism which finally twisted itself into the diabolical grimace of the Fascist abomination" (217).

Making the leap from obscurantism to Fascism is problematic and a symptom of Lukács apologist's agenda, but the leftist distrust of Modernist tendencies does persist in Finland, even in the post-radical years after the heyday of activism in the 1960s and '70s. If anything, the accusation of Modernism playing into the hands of reactionary capitalist interests has become more pronounced. Serge Guilbaut, in his 1983 study of post–World War II art, *How New York Stole the Idea of Modern Art,* suggests that abstract works create "'an art of obliteration, an art of erasure'" (qtd. in Sandler 67). Similarly subversive, postmodernist strategies, instead of depicting life in order to ameliorate it, question the difference between fiction and reality. Destabilizing truth, reality, performance and authenticity can, in the Marxist critique, challenge dominant ideologies and expose pernicious imperialistic power structures that become reified as moral values. In doing so, art can reassume the role of edification in the Marxist-realist critique. But too often, and this seems to be the contemporary objection to the current postmodern theatre, the interrogating performances are refined out of relevance, the metaphors so exotic and irrelevant outside of the artist's vision, the play becomes meaningless except as an ephemeral aesthetic experience.

Theoretical, abstruse, intellectualized, poetic, aggressively self-referential: the formula guarantees alienation, whether that is the desired effect or not. As a result, performance art remains peripheral in Finland, mainly because Finnish audiences and state sponsored city theatres resist more diverse and experimental forms of theatrical performance. The general public prefers the tried-and-true formulaic warhorses of psychological realism, musicals, comedies and family dramas. This resistance has helped foster the myth of a generic Finnish character as well as a generic "Finnish" dramatic mode — stereotypes alternative theatres continue to challenge.

Finnish Theatre optimistically announced in 2004 that a new crop of writers was breaking ground because their work was socially engaged, as if a revival of political relevance was an avant-garde breakthrough. More significantly, the magazine interpreted this trend as an improvement over the anemic theatre of the recent past. "The plays deal boldly with contemporary issues such as immigration, the rural margins of the EU, terrorism, and the effects of the stress of working life on ordinary people" (Kurki 2). Curiously, this declaration, along with the accompanying observation that the "realistic theatre tradition has been successfully broken by the young generation's experimental productions" (2), highlights the fact that Finnish theatre tradition is based in realism, even as theatres from the National to KOM, from the outlying city center theatres to Q Theatre, continue to experiment, but cautiously, mainly at the edges of psychological realism.

Most of the established directors continue to use theatre as a vehicle to critique current events, to investigate the human situation and, even as it galvanizes a newly emergent Finnish national character, to maintain social relevance. But others are more focused on reforming their aesthetics. Their work tends to question the nature of theatre, challenge the ideas of performance space, and interrogate the correlation (and collaboration) between audience and actors. They employ metaphoric physicality, ironically reworking the mimetic tradition by recycling ritualistic dance and musical styles into traditional dramatic narratives.

Given their penchant for fresh forms and edgy material, the vanguard of young directors in Helsinki evinces a concerted movement away from typical psychological realism, experimenting with more oblique, elliptical and surreal theatrical possibilities. As noted by the Carrolls, "this utilization of a form of realism cannot be regarded as a return to theatrical conservatism [...] it is part of a conscious attempt [...] to instill radical content into the consciousness of a bourgeois public tired of stylistic presentational" ("KOM-teatteri" 386).

The ground, in other words, is fertile for a new approach that meshes socially conscious themes with experimental aesthetics, achieved without abandoning the principles of either. These new Finnish directors, and the theatres that support them, demonstrate a focused desire to revitalize social relevance in the Finnish theatre while exploring inventive and original contemporary performances.

3

Beyond Nokialandia — The Post-Political Critique of Neo-Liberalism

The oldest independent professional theatre in Finland, The Group Theatre (Ryhmäteatteri), has been an innovative presence since its inception in 1968, when a collective of young artists decided to create a space for performances that challenged the prevailing sensibility of theatre-going audiences. Instead of the standard fare of comedies, musicals and drawing room dramas, usually based on German or Swedish standards, The Group wanted a space for Finnish artists to stage classics free from the trappings of state-run repertory theatres. The company first performed in temporary premises in various venues around the city. During the early 1980s, The Group became the hub of contemporary Finnish drama, a true actors' theatre, offering an antidote to the director-as-auteur approach that had become fashionable then. When the company moved to its present location in 1982, renovating a former cinema in the Kallio suburb just outside the city center, the name Ryhmäteatteri was adopted.

While The Group Theatre's early reputation was established by touring and presenting classics, visiting schools and prisons around Finland, today it sets itself apart from other production companies, especially by its summer theatre performances on the island of Suomenlinna, an island suburb of Helsinki. But in addition to staging celebrated performances in Suomenlinna, The Group's artistic directors Mika Myllyaho and Esa Leskinen have also managed to keep the main stage productions in the Kallio space at the cutting edge of Finnish theatre.

According to Myllyaho, after 2004 the principals at The Group became interested in new forms of expression that challenge the idea of theatre. He cites as a main influence the work of directors in Berlin, especially Frank Castorf. These plays tend to be illogical, reject linear narrative and conclusive interpretations, and represent a skeptical attitude toward psychological interpretations. Just as Castorf subjected Shakespeare, Hauptmann and Dostoyevsky (among others) to radical re-workings — featuring potato salad food fights, urinating in buckets, improvised speeches, slapstick, anachronistic music and spliced film clips — Leskinen and Myllyaho have also experimented with devaluing meaning through provocative theatrical techniques, fragmenting texts and inserting associational material, videos and intentional disruptions into their productions.

But for all its emphasis on new forms of expression and flirting with the avant-garde, Myllyaho, perhaps best known for *Panic* after it was translated into English and successfully toured internationally, paradoxically prefers plays that maintain a social consciousness and a relevancy to the Finnish situation. His attitude is not jingoistic, but he insists that for theatre in Finland to remain locally relevant it must address local issues. Myllyaho resists directing (or producing) imports, and when he has — he cites Martin McDonagh's *The Lieutenant of Inishmore* as a good example — he deleted the local allusions, inside jokes, personal references particular to Ireland (with McDonagh's permission, Myllyaho is quick to point out) and sought instead to highlight the general interest themes that would appeal to and have the most impact on the lives of the Finnish audience.

Like the actors and directors who formed other progressive theatres in the wake of The Group, embracing and refining its vision of artistic independence and innovation — especially KOM and Q — Myllyaho insists that the work staged at The Group promotes social consciousness, creating a dialogue regarding the current political realities in Finland. He has, as noted above, directed imports, but mainly, he says, for entertainment value. Even then he chooses plays with themes that transcend local issues, which comment on the lives of ordinary people and focus on the human elements common to all cultures.

Echoing Kujanpää, Myllyaho describes contemporary Finland as stable but fragile, its traditional social safety network threatened by the liberal capitalist model. The issues that most concern reformists like Kujanpää, Forsman and Myllyaho include economic, social and political marginalization, racism, xenophobia, discrimination against women and the exploitation of children.

Kujanpää is fond of quoting, not without sarcasm (scathingly in *Birth of a Salesman*), then president Tarja Halonen's second inauguration speech from 2006:

> Yet we also have our problems. Income differentials are again growing, and new poverty has emerged in Finland. The pay for a full-time job is not enough to

support a family. Women still earn about 80% of what men earn on average. There are problems with the system of welfare services, and employees have difficulty coping at work. Social inequality takes many forms.

The reformists, in their myriad plays, testify to the veracity of this statement. But it is the following from the same speech that fuels their ironic ire:

> Although the welfare society is a generally accepted objective, it is an objective that is not attained in the lives of most people. We have regional and social inequality, and this clashes with the Finns' sense of what is right. Things do not need to be like this. The welfare of citizens and the international competitiveness of our country are not mutually exclusive; they are mutually complementary and mutually supportive [Halonen].

The incongruity between the problems and the solutions offered by the government, as the progressive playwrights see it, is absurd. To be fair, the pragmatism of a country's political agenda is debatable on several levels, but in the case of contemporary Finnish theatre, one truth is indisputable: straight political theatre, as a vehicle to promote leftist social causes, is dead, ineffectual. The radicalism animating the late 1960s and 1970s has been effectively stifled by the "success" of liberalism, and theatre, politically impotent, is unable to promote the intellectual discourse necessary to sustain a political movement. Contemporary audiences quickly tire of the manifestos and the haranguing of soapbox dramas.

Myllyaho is also quick to acknowledge cycles in history, and he views recent developments in theatre in a dialectical context. He points out that the influential experimentation originating in Berlin stems from Brecht and his rejection of naturalistic theatre. The experimentation popular in the 1960s in turn led to a revival of psychological drama that in its turn led to the experimentation in vogue today. "You must know history to change it," he says, matter-of-factly, reinforcing his own status as a contemporary practitioner with a respect for tradition, a trait that separates the merely trendy from the actual trendsetters.

And even though many directors and playwrights are concentrating more and more on form, theatre in Finland remains a potent vehicle by which to critique the status quo, to examine in graphic, immediate images and language the social realities confronting the post-modern, post-political world of cynical self-indulgence that Myllyaho addresses, for instance, in his play *Chaos* (*Kaaos*).

Designed to complement his previous piece, *Panic*, which dealt with three men coming to terms with the collapse of their once secure lives, *Chaos* involves three professional women — Sofia, a teacher; Emmi, a journalist; Julia, a therapist — dealing with their various personal crises. A series of minimal scenes moves the women through memory as they review their last six months. The characters speak to the audience, a convenient device that allows each character to argue her point of view but that also seems too convenient and contrived to maintain adequate dramatic tension. The most dramatic moments are recollected in monologues, and the action is contained in conversations and arguments among the three women. Structurally, the piece might have been more effective as a short story.

But the structure is clever. The women play all the roles, allowing the actors to improvise, especially when playing the male roles in a teasing style of drag. One highlight is how Myllyaho handles Julia's lover, a man being treated for a split personality disorder. The other two actors each play one side of the man's psyche, the "fearful man" and the "fiery man," for appropriate comic effect.

This strategy, according to Irene Aho, who directed *Chaos* at the 2009 Tampere Theatre Festival, was worked out in the last few days of rehearsal before the premiere.

"That's how Mika works," explains Aho. "He continues to write and revise right up to opening night."

In the end, the anti-heroic women are admirable in their resistance, their struggle to maintain some semblance of dignity in a world that constantly threatens them with petty humiliations. They learn that it is not the drugs or alcohol, the violence or casual sex that can save them, but their camaraderie and mutual support and understanding.

If this sounds facile and too convenient, the play does not pretend to be anything more than it is: a stylized glimpse into the wackiness of contemporary professional women overwhelmed by localized hypocrisy and existential compromises that threaten to destroy their will and character. The production is slick — some might describe it as "boulevard" — i.e., like a soufflé, an airy pastry without a lot of substance.

While each illustrates her particular dilemma, collectively all of the women suffer from disillusionment. What they considered a relatively stable professional and personal life is suddenly threatened by unforeseen circumstances, although the complaints are all too familiar, if not mundane: loss of family members, marital difficulties, the normal issues involving home life and work. What is unusual, what drives the play, is the drastic response each woman employs in reaction to what are arguably ordinary problems. The over-reaction on the part of the women indicates a fundamental imbalance in their lives and in modern life generally.

Sofia, frustrated by events at her school, inexplicably lashes out at a man in a café, attacking him and drawing blood. Her anger simmers until she finally explodes, threatening to kill a woman who has parked illegally in a pedestrian area. Julia enters into an unethical sexual liaison with a married patient. Emmi, floundering in an insecure marriage, assaults a woman flirting with her husband on a cruise by knocking her head off a glass bar. Petty violence seems to permeate society. Emmi complains to Julia, "A man broke his hand banging it against a wall, a woman kicked her neighbor's dog to death."

Plagued by their private manifestations of this societal madness, the women rationalize their actions, and then seek medication, casual sex and alcohol. In a rather expedient epiphany, Julia realizes, "There are two worlds.... The world of harmony and the world of chaos." Balancing the two — between "love, order and goodness" and "weakness, fear, childhood"— seems to be the key to that elusive happiness the women seek. The resolution occurs after all the calamities have been reviewed and the women have reevaluated their reactions. Sofia is now the principal of her school, Emmi has quit her job to uphold journalist ethics, and Julia is setting up a private practice. All have rebounded nicely from their collective and individual excursions into angst, depression and self-doubt. They learn the simple lesson: "Hate gives birth to hate." The ending echoes Candide's advice, to tend one's own garden. Cleaning up the messiness at home will invariably contribute to cleaning up the messiness of the larger society.

The play also explores what happens when people fail to follow the old maxim: "Don't sweat the small stuff." It neatly illustrates the disconnection between what is truly important in life and what is trivial. Confusing the petty with the significant leads to misplaced values, unnecessary stress, and finally, as the title implies, chaos. This conflict in the human psyche between the destructiveness of desire and the orderliness of logic is an old story, but Myllyaho adds a new twist to the ancient tale by citing Naomi Klein's 2007 study *The Shock Doctrine: The Rise of Disaster Capitalism.* Klein argues that global corporations exploit disasters, whether natural like tsunamis and hurricanes or man-made like the war in Iraq or terrorist attacks, to further their economic hegemony. The problem with Myllyaho's application is that he never explores the implications of Klein's thesis; he merely hints that globalization has something to do with the anxiety felt throughout the local communities where the women live and work. When Julia suggests that the psychic tension in the general public is a result of "these kinds of shock situations where people make snap decisions," Sofia blames "outsourcing" for her problems at work.

Flirting with Klein does not advance the human story Myllyaho wants to tell. A more reliable explanation of the women's dilemma might be found in Sartre's notion of people being condemned to freedom. Responsibility causes anxiety. In the end, the women suffer from their inability to make good choices.

In *Satan Comes to Moscow*, Tatu Mönttinen as Master fantasizes about his love, Margarita, played by Elena Spirina. Esa Leskinen uses video projections to break down the inner and outer lives of the characters. The technique intentionally conflates the world perceived by the audience on stage with the mental images of the characters. Implicit in the performance is a critique of surveillance and the political impulse to control and pacify citizens with image clusters. The result is a portrait of a politicized society where life is played out in front of a video screens and individuals are isolated from actual experience (photograph by Tanja Ahola).

With all its emphasis on the problems of social cohesion, the interest at The Group in experimentation and new forms of theatrical language is strong. So it is not surprising that Leskinen, as part of 2007–2008 program at The Group Theatre, chose *Satan Comes to Moscow* (*Saatana saapuu Moskovaan*), a stage version of *Master and Margarita*, Michail Bulgakov's macabre, surreal, kaleidoscopic *tour de force* of life during the Soviet crackdown on dissidents in the 1930's. Given how the Finns lately, if tentatively, have begun to appropriate the new prevailing style of visual, metaphorical and physical theatre popular with Baltic and Russian directors like Eimuntas Nekrošius and Vladimir Ageev (a style slow to catch-on with mainstream Nordic directors), this play is a perfect excuse for indulging in a bit of postmodern extravaganza.

Directors who decide to stage *Master and Margarita* must themselves be a touch demented. Of course, Bulgakov's novel has been staged often since its posthumous publication in 1967, by university troupes, amateur ensembles and professional — even prestigious — companies. But as Polina Barskova noted in her review of Vladimir Bortko's 2005 television film version, "Numerous theatre directors [have] attempted adaptations of the novel, all to various degrees of failure." Or as D.J.R. Bruckner wrote in a review of Jean-Claude van Itallie's 1993 stage adaptation, "Some of the book's most delicious fantasies simply cannot be enacted." So it might seem counter-intuitive for Leskinen to attempt to stage Bulgakov's phantasmagoric tome in a fairly mainstream house where the audience is sophisticated but still intrinsically conservative. The result, however, proved Leskinen's instinct was right.

The plot, if it can be simplified, begins when Woland (Satan) moves to Moscow at the height of Stalin's brutal purge. His entourage includes a seductive witch, a salacious cat, a magician, and a motley gang of mischievous misfits determined to wreak mayhem around Moscow, countering the nega-

Tatu Mönttinen as Master in *Satan Comes to Moscow*. When Soviet apparatchiks seek asylum from Stalin in the psychiatric hospital where political prisoners are held, they meet a novelist who calls himself Master. Driven mad by the rejection of his masterpiece — an unpublished book on the life of Pontius Pilate — he forsakes his writing and his love — Margarita — and frees himself from life in a world of madness (photograph by Tanja Ahola).

Elena Spirina as Margarita with an unidentified victim in *Satan Comes to Moscow*. For Esa Leskinen, the core of theatre is the image. He uses a visual, metaphorical and physical theatre to illustrates the contemporary anxiety regarding a newly aggressive Russia under Putin (photograph by Tanja Ahola).

tive energy of the Stalinists with a positive counterforce of their own. Their shenanigans terrify the Soviet apparatchiks to the point that even they seek asylum in the psychiatric hospital where political prisoners are held. One of the inmates is a novelist who calls himself Master, driven mad by the rejection of his masterpiece, an unpublished book on the life of Pontius Pilate. He has forsaken both his writing and his love — Margarita — and has withdrawn from life into a world of madness in the hospital. Margarita, determined to revive Master's lust for life (and for her), makes a Faustian deal with Satan and agrees to become a witch. She learns to fly, greets celebrated impresarios of historical evil, and presides over Satan's grand ball. In the end, she is granted her wish to have Master released, and they leave Moscow with Satan to live in peace but without salvation.

    Leskinen's performance sticks fairly close to the plot of the novel, as far as any stage production can, given the reductive nature of any adaptation, but especially considering the narrative permutations, pastiche, stories-within-stories, shifts in points of view, etc., that make this novel particularly rich and dense. Leskinen does conflate the character of The Poet from the novel with Master/Jesus in the play, and though he maintains the story in Master's novel of the life of Pontius Pilate and the Roman occupation of Jerusalem, it serves more as a subplot than the parallel historical narrative implied in Bulgakov's version.

Part of the strength of Leskinen's production stems from his decision to temper psychological realism with shades of vaudeville. The characters rarely pretend to be three-dimensional — the exception being in some of the painfully tender scenes between Master and Margarita — but for the most part the characters are cartoons. Leskinen insists that this approach is in harmony with the spirit of the book, which itself is absurd and hilarious. By plying the comic in the obscene, Leskinen risks treating torture as entertainment. At the same time, this tactic might be the only way to deal with the human tragedy of trying to make sense of a senseless situation, where the raw brutality of power-politics trumps quaint notions of humanity.

One of the strategies Leskinen employs not only to reinforce the vaudevillian aspect of his production, but also to challenge the boundaries of theatrical space and the limits of stage presentation, is his use of tremendous banks of television monitors on either side of the stage. Not only does this approach underscore several themes running through the performance but it also illustrates his exposure to the new production values stemming from Berlin, Lithuania and some of the more experimental Russia directors like Ageev. The audience experiences the external action while simultaneously witnessing fantasies projected on the monitors. This breakdown of inner and outer lives intentionally confuses the world perceived by the audience on stage with the mental images of the characters, challenging which version represents a "real" life experience. This effect also allows action begun onstage to continue offstage, so that "offstage" is no longer an operative concept. A character exiting a door onstage into an apartment or onto the street appears on the monitor in real time, so that the action is extended beyond the confines of the immediate *mise en scène*.

Often the video and stage images intersect. When an editor in Moscow is decapitated, the crime is depicted on the video in what appears to be claymation, but then the "actual" head rolls out onto the stage. Other times the images qualify and comment on the action, as when desires repressed in the stage action are projected onto the monitors. Other times, the images enhance the action, especially effective in showing Margarita's joy and fascination when she learns to fly. On stage, the magician runs across the stage holding a doll dangling from strings, but on the monitor the audience can see an actual woman flying across the countryside.

At times, the images acquire more meaning and reality than life. For instance, Pilate embraces a television image of Jesus, and later, in a scene from Jerusalem, he lugs the television with the image of Jesus around the stage much as Jesus hauled his cross to Calvary. His engagement with the image seems more significant than his interaction with the actual man. Pilate's behavior mirrors the dehumanizing effects of video, illustrating how it is easier to deal with an image than an actual human. This ploy by Leskinen underscores the alienating effect of electronic renderings, how they sanitize the reality of war atrocities and natural disasters; the simulation is abstract, safe and therefore entertaining.

In a terribly comic scene, one that Leskinen invented outside Bulgakov's story but which is based on an actual event in Bulgakov's life, the monitors show Master receiving a phone call in his apartment. No matter how often he hangs up — even ripping the cord from the plug — the phone continues to ring. When he finally answers, a voice says, "This is Stalin calling." Stalin actually did call Bulgakov when the writer had asked permission to work in Paris. Stalin told him that even though he thought it was a bad idea, of course Bulgakov could go. Bulgakov understood the implication and decided to stay, explaining that perhaps a Russian writer should, after all, work in the Soviet Union.

Although the scene provides an effective bit of comic relief— a typical bit of Finnish black humor, especially for older members of the audience more immediately familiar with the historical Soviet penchant for the political cult of personality — it illustrates a serious, contemporary anxiety regarding a newly aggressive Russia under Putin as well as the resurrection of that pernicious cult. Leskinen jokes that the scene is reminiscent of what he calls a "Finnish decision," a cold war term used in West Germany indicating, as in Bulgakov's case, "a decision being made" which is really a *fait accompli*, no decision at all. Bulgakov "decides" not to go to Paris when, in fact, he had no real choice. During the Soviet period, Leskinen quips, "You couldn't cough in Helsinki without Moscow asking, 'What was that?'"

Leskinen insists that, despite the odd invented scene, he wanted to maintain the historical integrity of the original text while integrating contemporary elements. One of the historical bits he emphasizes is the magic show. Near the end of the first act, Woland stages a magic show intended to ridicule the *nouveau riche* Muscovites. Featuring a real magician, along with preposterous (and impressive) special effects (including disappearing acts, a body dancing after being sawn in half, amazing card tricks and Vegas-style flamboyance), the magic show seems like a set piece out of sync with the main narrative. Leskinen acknowledges that some critics found it distracting, but he defends his decision to stage what is essentially a separate performance — a real magic show — because, he says, "the novel blends so many styles" and he wanted this performance to stay true to what he considers the essence of the book.

Another historical element to which Leskinen said he tried to remain faithful was the presentation of Woland as a Blakean/Nietzschean positive force in a corrupt world of weak-willed spirits that have become victims of their disordered desires. His Satan is a Robin Hood figure, a prankster mocking the materialistic greed of the Soviet Party elites; he celebrates the creative spiritual forces he recognizes in Margarita, Master and Pilate, whose decision to allow the execution of Jesus changes the world. For Leskinen, casting Woland as an existential champion complements Bulgakov's vision and explains why Master and Margarita are granted peace without salvation. Because of their passion, their faithfulness to their earthly, sensual existence, Woland decides they do not deserve salvation: devoted to their corporeal freedom, to be condemned to the conventional notion of eternal paradisiacal existence, devoid of strife and passion, would be a truly evil punishment.

Notwithstanding Leskinen's fidelity to the mad world of Bulgakov's novel, he uses the performance to highlight contemporary issues. The most visible, literally, is his use of the imposing TV monitors stacked in banks on either side of the stage, along with film clips strategically cut into the action. Leskinen claims that the production demanded the use of projectors and televisions, but he also says the approach allowed him the opportunity to explore the impact of video streams on everyday life. Especially effective were the opening sequences, in which images of exotic dancers, punctuated by ragtime music and stylized reels of silent film, are desexualized by repetition, inter-cut with images of Stalin and religious fanatics. The result is a mesmerizing exercise in the pornography of propaganda.

Other sequences reinforce the pernicious aspect of surveillance and the political impulse to control the populace by pacifying them with image clusters and monitoring their lives. The sense of electronic intrusion is point blank throughout the production, as is the conflation of life as lived and life as projected, again feeding into the myth-making machine of mass media. Aligned with the idea of a coercive, politicized society is the sense of alienation, both in the Brechtean sense and also as a mode of modern existence, in which so much of life is played out onanistically in front of a video screen, destroying community standards and creating individuals isolated from actual experience.

For Leskinen, "the core of theatre is the image." Not the cold, distant gray of a television or computer screen but the dynamic presence of live performance. Like many of the new directors working in the Baltic and Nordic arena, he dismisses psychological realism as a decadent form no longer viable as a vehicle for exploring the contemporary situation. When it comes to the theatre experience, he says, "understanding is not everything. Truth should be experienced." And though in this production he utilizes technological solutions, he thinks new forms are possible without relying on gadgetry. "New theatre," he says, "is an ethical question. Directors must have the courage to fail."

KOM Theatre began as an independent group within the conservative Swedish Theatre in Helsinki; its lifeblood was a revolt against the general repertory policies of conventional theatres. But, according to Denis and Elsa Carroll, KOM was also inspired by a leftist political agenda. Its name signals the radical duality in the initial project, KOM being a conflation of the Swedish verb "come" and the first syllable of the Finnish word for "communist," the upper case reinforcing the imperative form. It adopted Swedish as its performance language and its "leftist convictions were muted" (Carroll, "KOM-teatteri" 377). When this arrangement did not work out, ostensibly for "'financial' reasons" (378) but clearly because of its identification with the Communist Party and socialist causes, KOM emerged in 1971 as an independent progressive theatre. Since 1984, KOM has occupied its current premises in a quiet, posh section of Kapteeninkatu, with its offices and a chic restaurant/bar adjacent to the main stage house, seating capacity 292.

Although its identification with the Communists and leftist activism has been diminished (if it can even be called vestigial), it retains its commitment to developing new writing, especially work that stresses social consciousness. According to Pekka Milonoff, one of the original visionaries behind the KOM concept and an old-school, if slightly reformed leftist whose radicalism has been tempered more by political realities than age or cynicism: "'The idea is to create conditions in which writers are able to develop their ideas in conjunction with theatre workers and in which new contacts will be made, through which the works will reach the stage'" (qtd. in Kurki 36). This emphasis on plays that deal with contemporary communal issues explains why, according to Producer Marika Agarth, KOM prefers social realism to experimental plays that focus on new visuals. She admits that KOM is "less political" now than it was originally, but she stresses that the company still believes in theatre's "power to communicate messages about world events."

Didactics aside, KOM has produced some of the most important writers in recent years, including Marjo Niemi, Ari-Pekka Lahti, Tuomo Aitta, and Reko Lundán, one of the most promising playwrights of his generation, who died in 2006 at the age of 37. Agarth attributes the success of its protégés to the KOM writers-in-residence program (literally a "text hatchery") begun in 2000. Writers are encouraged to submit scripts in an open submission format, and if a piece is accepted, KOM provides the structural assistance to polish the work, offering professional actors and directors, performance space and publicity, plus the prestige of being affiliated with one of the most acclaimed theatres in the country.

A major problem in bringing new work to the public is finding small performance areas suitable for material that by its nature does not require a full stage and is more suitable for intimate black-box productions. To resolve this predicament, KOM must rent out small venues around the city, which adds to the expense of development and underscores a dilemma not unique to KOM, as many of the major theatre companies interested in promoting new writing confront the same problem: finding appropriate space where fledgling playwrights can stage their work. "There are fewer dramaturges than before, and the demands of profitability do not encourage risk-taking" (36).

Another facet of KOM's commitment to finding new writing is to keep its venue indigenous. Contrary to the commitment of theatres like Q and Koko to internationalization, KOM favors new work that addresses themes relevant to Finland today. Its audience expects familiarity and prefers plays that offer insight into the Finnish community and that explore Finnish issues. Milonoff explains, "'New plays address themes and matters which concern writers and audiences here and now. There develops an image of humanity which is contemporary, recognisable'" (36).

Accentuating this commitment to using theatre to reinvigorate interest in Finnish culture, Agarth suggests that theatrical performances should not try to compete for young audiences with new-fangled media gimmickry, but instead should offer young people an alternative, truly different experience that only theatre can provide. MTV, video games and Internet access do not create social connections, and it is this communal function of theatre that Agarth hopes KOM can maintain. Complementing the social awareness and educational aspects of theatre, KOM's productions tend to avoid mixed-media performances and metaphorical theatre, and Agarth is unapologetic about KOM's preference for psychological realism. "Realism is pretty standard," she says, which at KOM means traditional staging and reluctance, in Brechtian terms, to "break the frame."

However, now and again KOM produces work which by any definition challenges naturalistic theatre. For instance, Pekka Milonoff's adaptation of Juha Itkonen's novel *Towards* (*Kohti*), which opened on KOM's main stage in 2008, dispenses with KOM's trademark psychological realism and presents a pastiche of styles and modes that demonstrate what happens when mixed media is used with mixed results.

One of the young directors associated with KOM, Johanna Freundlich, explains that Milonoff's natural inclination is to eschew experimental theatre. He usually avoids tactics like addressing the audience, overly stylized acting, metaphorical interludes and overt physicality. But in *Towards*, he uncharacteristically challenges the nature of the so-called "fourth wall." His motive, Freundlich suggests, has less to do with aesthetics than with intention.

"Young people don't care about politics," she says. "The problem, then, is how to make politics interesting." Because the roots of Finnish theatre are planted firmly in the tradition of a popular, "people's theatre," audiences have a natural aversion to a theatre of engagement. They are equally suspicious of metaphor and stylized acting, of infusing drama with video, dance and "alienation" techniques. But because of the contemporary situation, with Russia reasserting itself and creating tension around the Baltics (though it is often not "polite" to discuss it), young people are becoming more attuned to the political situation. The difficulty is to find new forms that will engage the young without simply preaching from the pulpit or trying to stimulate them with snazzy electronic effects.

With *Towards*, Milonoff seems torn between his desire for an old-style radicalized performance and the need to bring new expression to old themes. The minimal set consists of an upstage office area separated from the rest of the set by a Plexiglas partition behind which several members of the cast watch as the audience files in. At stage left is a band with a piano; downstage right a mattress, a bass guitar and an amp represent an apartment. During the play, various scenes are projected on the back wall, as the action is intermittently interrupted by actors reading from texts, breaking character, commenting on the action and performing songs.

The plot centers on a mother, a father, and their two children, a daughter and a son, all coping with death, abandonment, loneliness and personal allegiances. When the play opens, the mother has died of cancer but is represented on stage by her ghost. Distraught at her mother's death, the left-leaning daughter has run off to Thailand to join a tsunami relief program. The father, the lead guitarist in the stage band, and the right-leaning brother set off to find the daughter, whom they discover living with her peace activist boyfriend, also the bassist in the band. The family history is played out in flashbacks, involving, among other soap-opera elements, the son's pregnant girlfriend and the father's pregnant lover.

The action, punctuated by songs and narrative sequences, presents a family drama cast through a Marxist economic-deterministic lens. It portrays a contemporary Finnish household struggling to find meaning, values and fidelity in a balkanized world destabilized by post-modern philosophies, desensitized by liberal capitalism, and fractured by post–Kantian historicism. Conveniently in the end, the brother and sister reconcile their differences, harmonized by their common humanistic and familial bonds that transcend their political differences. Milonoff's adaptation of *Towards* (co-written for the stage by the author) is evidence of an established director's attempt to provide a new form for traditional material relevant to social issues confronting contemporary Finns, but the theme of the play tends to underscore the fact that its appeal has more to do with its story than its visual presentation.

More in line with the traditional psychological realism preferred by both the audience and the principals allied with KOM, and a vivid testimony to the success of its writers-in-resident program is *Ähtäriin* written by Iira Halttunen, a then-14-year-old dramatist from Tampere. The play explores the lives of an eleven-year-old girl and her teenage brother, their relationship with two friends, a transvestite and a nerdy geek, and their dysfunctional family. The action is set in a small town in contemporary rural Finland in 1994, when the rock band Nirvana was at the pinnacle of its popularity in the grunge music scene.

The play begins on a green grassy space slanted upwards in the back and thrust out over the audience downstage. A young girl sits among a swing set, a boom-box and fashion magazines, enjoying a summer day, the toys of adolescence highlighting the fragile illusion of innocence ripe to be shattered. A set of bunk beds stage right delineate the private space the brother and sister share, emphasizing their isolation from the world and values of their drunken, selfish and abusive parents.

The title is a variation of the name of the town; in Finnish it implies "to Ähtäri," meaning something like "come spend some time with us here." The girl narrates her story to the audience, but this device never seems intrusive or "epic"; her explication, at times delivered through a portable megaphone/recorder — her diary — functions to provide context for the scenes played out by other members of the cast in a fairly straightforward psychological-realistic fashion. But in a twist on the cliché of a *bildungsroman* detailing the rites of passage for typical teens — experimenting with smoking, drinking, living vicariously through music and media — the brother, ambiguous about his sexual identity, has a crush on his sister's best friend, who is really a boy. His misadventure turns out to be virtuous, however, as he realizes that he loves the person, not the "identity."

As in a proper allegory, each character stands for a symbolic value. The sister and her nerdy friend provide a normative value in the play, representing level-headed pragmatism and an optimistic stoicism that sustain them through their various crises. The brother represents the passionate extremes of emotional yearning. The transvestite object of the brother's desire illustrates an ethical rejection of categorical reality. The brother's volatility is a result of his frustration, and to assuage his disillusionment he becomes obsessed with Nirvana, investing his existential self in their music and living under the sway of the band's persona. When he learns about Kurt Cobain's suicide, his world collapses. After he crashes a car that kills his lover, he and his sister come to understand that running away from their problems — by literally lamming from town — will not bring them the peace and self-fulfillment they desire, so they decide to stay in Ähtäriin. Their reality-check complete, they awaken, as it were, from their fairy tale and accept the fact that, in the end, changing their lives is their responsibility.

Different in concept and execution, the plays by Milonoff and Halttunen nevertheless typify themes in contemporary Finnish theatre and represent the best traditions of KOM. Both plays offer an unvarnished look at the new Finnish family: educated, affluent, comfortable in the fraying but still viable social security safety net, yet prey to traditional maladies like alcoholism, adultery, divorce, absent parents and existential angst. The plays also expose more recent disorders like professional mobility, the stress of ambition, lax social mores and the dubious virtue of what is defined as success, plus the more institutional crises involved in national, sexual and ethnic identities — all factors threatening family cohesion and creating dissatisfaction with the nature of a "progressive" Finnish culture.

Taxing the strength of the family forces some, like the young woman in *Towards* and the brother in *Ähtäriin*, to seek meaning and self-realization outside of themselves and their familial, private spheres. At the same time, given the new paradigm by which the family units seem to have abandoned any familiar sense of moral guidance, the plays reaffirm traditional values of self-reliance, fraternity and altruism, no matter how weakened or damaged the traditional model becomes. Milonoff concurs: "'New plays address themes and matters which concern writers and audiences here and now. There develops an image of humanity which is contemporary, recognisable'" (36).

Q Theatre was founded in 1990 by freelance actors who graduated from the Finnish Theatre Academy. Since 1991 it has had its own venue located in a former cinema house in the heart of Helsinki. Subsidized by the state and by the City of Helsinki, the aim of the group is to make independent and original theatre and to develop new types of rehearsal methods. Almost all of the members work on a freelance basis. Q now hosts a 200-seat main stage, and a 50-seat small stage (called "Half-Moon" — the letter "Q" in Finnish sounds like "moon" in English), providing space for established plays, experimental work and outdoor spectacles. Though it is now a state-sponsored theatre, it is one of the most experimental and innovative contemporary independent ensembles in Finland. As the original initiator of the Baltic Circle, started in 1996 to create a forum to promote cultural dialogue among artists and theatres from Finland, East Europe, the Baltics and Scandinavia, Q remains the coordinator of the festival and a major agent in the creative development of new works from Finnish writers and directors as well as artists from abroad.

While dissimilar in styles, the plays selected by Q all tend to explore the uncertainties of an often unfamiliar, globalized world destabilized by forces beyond local control. Most importantly, they illustrate the diversity contemporary Finnish theatre is capable of. Q supports a newly emerging aesthetic in Finnish theatre and willingness on the part of directors to experiment and take risks, complemented by an audience hungry for innovative dramatic forms.

Heikki Kujanpää's *Birth of a Salesman* (*Kauppamatkustajan syntymä*) is a good example of the kind of drama promoted by Q Theatre: experimental, but with a strong focus on social issues. Kujanpää places an asterisk on the "success" of the liberal capitalism adopted by the Finnish government after the collapse of the Soviet economy. Recalibrated according to a Western model, the new economy jeopardized the social safeguards many Finns had come to rely on to help those less able to adapt to the new system. Kujanpää, critically acclaimed for his writing, directing and acting, is equally respected for being one of the founding members of Q Theatre.

Birth of a Salesman opened at Q in 2007. It illustrates some of the difficult social issues affecting marginalized citizens during the transition period of the early 1990s, after the collapse of the Soviet economy caused a recession in Finland, troubles which then resurfaced during the Finnish recovery of the late 1990s. Kujanpää's play follows a new tradition in which Finnish playwrights use theatre to explore the deleterious effects of economic determinism and the weakened social network inherent in the capitalist model. Exploring this theme, *Birth of a Salesman* resembles other plays like *Border Crossing, Mobile Horror, Panic* and *Can You Hear the Howling?*

The story begins in 2000, then shifts back and forth in time from the 1980s and 1990s to the present, portraying the desperate and dysfunctional relationships among Holger, a traveling salesman — actually a tinker selling rugs and novelties — living on his wits and trying to provide for his two children, Matti, a boy who thinks he is Holger's true son, and Henkka, who thinks she is adopted. One of the ironies operating throughout the play, which provides the dramatic dénouement at the end, is the fact that Henkka is Holger's actual daughter and Matti is his adopted son. Holger had decided early on that his influence and power within the family could be played to his advantage if his children remained ignorant about the truth of their situation, and as the children grow older, he operates from this position until Matti and Henkka (scandalously) become lovers.

The plot sounds like a soap opera but plays more dramatically on stage, in part because of Kujanpää's non-linear narrative and the shifting power relations among the trio. The action opens with Henkka — in a mansion she has acquired with the wealth she earned as a shrewd, amoral executive of her

own firm — interviewing candidates being considered as her new CEO. The interviewees are presented as still photographs projected from television monitors hung high above the set on either side of the stage. The impression created by the monitors and the slideshow portraits of the candidates is of a cold corporate world devoid of real human contact, where anonymous two-dimensional figures vie for power.

The interview is interrupted by the arrival of Matti, who has not been as successful as Henkka but has nevertheless managed to amass a sum of money that he hopes to use to buy the mansion back from Henkka for their father. Holger's father once owned the mansion, and now that Holger is fatally ill he wants to reclaim it as a place of wonderful childhood memories as well as a place to come to die. Angry with her father for having squandered their earlier fortune on his drinking and profligacy, and for not having properly provided for them as children, Henkka refuses. The scene then shifts to the early 1980s, when, as children, Henkka and Matti follow their father from village to village as he sells his wares. A series of scenes depicts their economic rise through several business ventures, their decline, and finally their dissolution as Holger devolves into drunkenness, violence and debauchery. The narrative continues to shift through time to illustrate Henkka's success, Matti's fall — following the model of his father — until finally it returns to the opening scene and Holger's arrival at the mansion where Henkka refuses to forgive her father but Matti embraces him. Holger dies in his stepson's arms.

Kujanpää acknowledges that the title *Birth of a Salesman* echoes Arthur Miller's *Death of a Salesman*, though he claims his play should not necessarily be interpreted as related to Miller's work. His idea, as the title implies, was to start with the result and then explore the process that led to it. Henkka is a woman considered successful by modern standards. Her name is usually a man's name — a nickname for Henry — reinforcing the masculinity of Kujanpää's heroine, a necessary quality if she is to compete in the masculine business world of contemporary Finland. She is wealthy, professional, powerful, independent, influential and ... soulless. For Kujanpää, she is a product of the times, a creature of a social crisis that privileges materialistic values —"game

Opposite, top: Annu Valonen (left) and Elina Knihtilä play American-style entrepreneurs as mud-wrestlers in Heikki Kujanpää's *Birth of a Salesman.* Kujanpää's play exemplifies a trend in Finnish theatre of highlighting the deleterious effects of economic determinism and the weakened social network inherent in the liberal capitalist model (photograph by Patrik Pesonius). **Bottom:** Asko Sahlman and Elina Knihtilä in *Birth of a Salesman,* a scathing indictment of the laissez-faire marketing philosophy threatening social welfare policies in contemporary corporate Finland. The quest for materialistic success depletes the spirit, leading to madness, illness and death (photograph by Patrik Pesonius).

show mentality," as Kujanpää puts it — over genuine humanistic concern for the welfare of the community. (Kujanpää also references the Darwinian capitalism exemplified by Donald Trump's *The Apprentice*, a television show popular in Finland at the time.) He purposely designed the time line of Holger's rise up the economic ladder to parallel the Finnish economic arc from the depression in 1992 to the recovery in 2000. For Kujanpää, Henkka represents the pernicious downside of Finnish consumerist logic, that fierce desire for corporate success that disregards spiritual values.

To further illustrate this theme, Kujanpää creates a subplot interwoven into the main story that deals with one of what the successful "winners" in the capitalists game call the "losers" — the bums excluded from the new Finnish economic policies. Street people, according to Kujanpää, are a recent phenomenon in Finland, a by-product of the liberal capitalism adopted by Finland after the demise of the Soviet market. Kujanpää's bum was once a successful businessman — a rival of Holger, competing with him for clients — but he, too, became a victim of his own success, wasting his life on meaningless extravagance, trashing his friends along with his health. Unable to accept responsibility for his predicament, he blames the yuppies, the successful professionals and social climbers indifferent to the plight of the less fortunate.

He decides to take revenge by attacking a television station, hoping to kill the news anchor in a nihilistic expression of rage. But before he can carry out his plan, he suffers a sort of spiritual revelation. He awakes one morning wearing a halo, depicted on stage as an actual circle of white light crowning his head. Preferring his disdain for the system, in an act of Miltonic defiance he resists his "conversion," enlisting his friend to pry off the halo (at one point trying to blast it off him by hooking it to jumper cables). Exasperated, he decides the only way to destroy the halo — this universal symbol of benevolence — is to kill God. Employing the help of his ex-girlfriend, who visits him in a vision as an angel (having killed herself because he rejected her in a moment of crisis), he arranges to meet God in order to assassinate him. As delusional as Don Quixote, he accomplishes his mission — except the man he thinks is God turns out to be a businessman in a gentleman's club playing cards. Shot while fleeing the police, the bum experiences a genuine epiphany, coming to realize before he dies that people are not abstractions, not ideas, and that everyone suffers equally.

The bum's lesson, or vision, expressing the universality of suffering, the need for compassion, and the human desire for a loving community, is lost on Henkka. She is left in the end with nothing but her anger and self-serving wealth, position and power. Matti, on the other hand, has experienced the fragility of the human condition. Recognizing in himself the same potential for failure, he accepts Holger for what he is, what he has been, just as he must accept himself. In a convincing final scene, Kujanpää hints at resurrection. After the two deaths, presented simultaneously on stage in spaces representing a confluence of worlds — Henkka's mansion and the alleyway of the bum — Holger arises with the help of his son to limp off stage. The bum, in the arms of his faithful Sancho, wobbles into eternity, both having learned the uselessness of rage and envy and the value of unconditional love and friendship.

The theme within the action is not as saccharine as it sounds, as Kujanpää uses a deft touch of comedy — especially in the scenes with the bum — to undercut the tendency for sentimentality the script might otherwise imply. The play is full of spectacle, with scenes of mud-wrestling, vaudeville acts, drunken lunacy, and one remarkable scene in which Holger "flies" across the stage in a helicopter — actually a wheelchair with a Plexiglas shield and assorted gizmos enhanced by sound effects and strobes. Despite its heavy-handed didacticism the play never bogs down in tedious sermonizing. (Kujanpää admits he has difficulty resisting the Lutheran impulse to deliver from the pulpit.)

A good example of Kujanpää's ability to undercut his own seriousness occurs in a scene wherein Matti reads a document with all the sincerity of an earnest schoolboy giving an oral report on civic duty. The text is a proclamation from the "new" government elected in 1995, whose platform pledged to care for the needy and to insure the viability of the social safety net that the Finns had incorporated into their social philosophy for years even as they introduced liberal capitalism and "reforms" into the economic system. The document, however, is encased in a dildo, so as Matti reads the high-minded political rhetoric, the audience can only laugh, both at the implication of the citizens getting screwed and at the Orwellian nonsense couched in government propaganda — especially given the fact that the family is desperate and truly in need of the vaunted social services that are clearly being portrayed as empty political promises.

Kujanpää's mischievous approach to the production — utilizing non-linear narrative, mixing naturalistic dramatic styles with metaphorical scenes, irony and slapstick — does not distract from his straightforward investigation into the social issues that emerged after the recession of the early 1990s and the anomie created by the resultant bottom-line marketing philosophy of the boom years that followed at the end of the decade.

For Kujanpää, "Finnish culture is so young" (qtd. in Alftan), and because of this, playwrights, from his perspective, have an essential duty to explore and, to some extent, explain the social changes that occurred after World War II. Instead of buying into the official jingoistic ideal, he hopes the Finns will

Elena Leeve and Tommi Korpela, both from Q-theatre, in Heikki Kujanpää's *Falling Angels*. The play underscores the fragility of agency, as the authority of experience is challenged by memory, and the convenient diametrical distinctions — outer and inner lives, private and public selves, personal and artistic personas — collapse. In the film version of the play, Leeve and Korpela won the best actor/actress prizes (in Finland called "Jussi" instead of "Oscar") (photograph by Patrik Pesonius).

began to comprehend the present by viewing it through the past. For him, understanding historical contexts is a moral imperative for living ethically in the present. "It is a question of what has happened to Finland," he says, "what has happened in the post-war Finland."

To expedite his sense of moral historicism, in 2005 Kujanpää, along with Sami Parkkinen and Heikki Huttu-Hiltunen, created *Falling Angels* (*Putoavia enkeleitä*), based on the tumultuous relationship of Lauri Viita and Aila Meriluoto, two of Finland's most accomplished and well-known post–World War II poets. For Anglo-American readers the story, later made into a film, echoes that of Sylvia Plath and Ted Hughes, the American and British poets, respectively, whose volatile marriage, roughly during the same era, was equally creative and destructive. In structure, the play resembles Marsha Norman's 1979 play *Getting Out*, in which a younger version of the lead character ghosts her older self, critiquing herself and acting out flashbacks to illustrate present circumstances.

The complex narrative of *Falling Angels* unfolds like a mystery novel, a palimpsest slowly revealing through a series of interviews, recollections, imagined scenes and eyewitness accounts, the Cubist personalities of the two poets. Throughout the play, questions of identity underscore the fragility of agency, the authority of experience is challenged by memory, and the convenient diametrical distinctions — outer and inner lives, private and public selves, personal and artistic personas — collapse.

The action opens in 1973. Meriluoto visits Helena, the daughter she had with Viita, to inform her that she has just signed a contract to write a memoir of her marriage to the poet, covering the time she met him in the late 1940s until they divorced in 1956. Meriluoto seems uncomfortable with her commitment to the project, as if prying into their relationship and trying to capture their past lives in prose constituted a form of betrayal, underscoring the impossibility of simplifying the intensity of their time together. The story then unfolds in a series of overlapping sequences that shift back and forth through time, largely based on Meriluoto's 1974 book *Lauri Viita*. Various witnesses recall and relive events through taped testimony, biographical notes and dramatic reconstructions. The action centers on Viita's last creative years, when his life was shadowed by schizophrenia. After struggling to love his madness, to cope with his abuse, and finally, to sacrifice her career and independence in a desperate attempt to save Viita from himself, Meriluoto recognizes the limits of her indulgence and accepts the irreconcilable tragedy of the situation.

The premise of the play reflects the dilemma faced by Meriluoto: the moral ambiguity of exploiting the suffering of another for artistic purpose. The conflict for Meriluoto is explicit throughout the text. She hesitates even to consider the book project, and then falters in her early attempts, resisting the accounts of Viita's other acquaintances, personal and professional. She accuses others of exploitation, of misrepresenting her relationship with Viita, of claiming a "truth" that she knew was essentially and necessarily conditional. Even after Viita stabs himself and threatens physical harm to others — including the infant Helena — Meriluoto urges the doctors to release him from the institution and to stop prescribing medication that tames him. When the choice is between madness and creativity or docility and sterility, she chooses the wild, irrepressible genius of poetry. Her decision begs the question: Is she acting in the best interests of Viita or sacrificing his welfare for art?

The same issue might be raised regarding Kujanpää's decision to stage the work about which Meriluoto had so many ethical qualms and reservations. The story, in the end, could be reduced to a portrait of any relationship rent not by the actual elements of tragedy — in which the protagonist

knowingly and willfully chooses self-destruction over alternative, safer, compromising options — but by circumstances beyond the protagonist's control.
(To struggle against illness is admirable, but not the stuff of tragedy.) Likewise, Meriluoto's self-abnegation, and her subjugation of her will to his, can
be interpreted as pathetic, pathological and sycophantic, her love bordering
on idolatry. For the audience, witnessing this familial dénouement threatens
to devolve into voyeurism.

But Kujanpää's deft handling of the material keeps the play from slipping into mere prurient indulgence. Most immediately impressive is how he
integrates the poetry, clearly a by-product of the symbiotic tension inherent
in the couples' relationship, into the text. A more significant aspect, and one
that elevates the significance of the play beyond its particulars, is the meta-
theatrical structure not only illustrating Meriluoto's personal ontological
dilemma but also challenging the very efficacy of any artistic attempt to represent reality. The characters constantly allude to the impossibility to recreate the truth of experience though memory. Helena accuses her mother several
times of committing the very infraction Meriluoto objects to in others. At
one point she says, "How many times did you define me and my life in that
one accounting?" (Kujanpää 3). Later she reiterates the charge: "You're afraid.
Afraid to finish this book. Because you have started remembering things"
(112). Another character asks Helena, "So which of you is the real author?"
(16), and then warns her, "Your mother may not be the first one to trust" (14).

The play is as much about the creative process as it is about the people
doing the creating. This struggle between those that represent and those that
are being represented leads finally to a scene in which Helena and her mother
argue about the accuracy of the immediately preceding scene that the audience has just viewed as fact. Everything being related becomes conditional as
the shifting perspective of each character's subjective experience qualifies
another's.

As important as the aesthetic question of how memory shapes reality,
and how art, imperfectly and problematically, attempts to recreate this process,
is Kujanpää's interest in how art — especially theatre — can reinvigorate Finnish
culture. *Falling Angels* reminds the audience that there was a time when art
mattered, when aesthetics were married to theme. Kujanpää complains that
theatre in Finland occupies a sort of dramaturgical DMZ where the concerns
of artists seem bifurcated between plays that focus on aesthetic experimentation and those that hope to raise social conscience, with Kujanpää (a principal on Q's board of directors) solidly in the latter camp. Q Theatre's
productions, however, are certainly not restricted to plays dealing with civic
amelioration.

One case in point is Q's production of *The Tin Drum* (*Peltirumpu*),

Outi Kavén as Oskar in Fiikka Forsman's adaptation of *The Tin Drum* by Gün-ter Grass. Forsman sees an analogy between Oskar's dilemma and the situation faced by Western democracies as they confront inequities inherent in market-driven economies (photograph by Patrik Pesonius).

based on the 1959 novel by Günter Grass. Adapted by Seppo Parkkinen and directed by Fiikka Forsman, the play is both an aesthetic extravaganza and an exercise in containment. One immediately apparent virtue is that Fors-man manages to control the sprawling narrative of Grass's novel without spoil-ing the expanse of the original text. The minimal set features a solitary polished circular "tin drum" center-stage with its mirror image hanging on the wall behind, framed by silhouettes of Roman-style arches backlit in stucco relief. Within this minimalist field, the action unfolds through a series of vivid scenes rendered with an economy that never diminishes the intensity of the action. Romantic trysts in seedy hotels, Nazi party marches, the chaos and anarchy of street combat — orchestrated by the diminutive Oskar, flailing on his drum or breaking glass with his piercing scream — are all the more powerful pre-sented in lucid flashbacks and tightly structured vignettes without sensational special effects or the clutter of unnecessarily detailed *mise en scènes*.

The story derives from the fictional autobiography of Oskar Matzerath, who decides after he is given a drum for his third birthday not to grow any older. Set in Danzig (now Gdansk, Poland) during World War II, Oskar's account of his exploits becomes an allegory for the supposed lack of German conscience and accountability for the rise of Nazism and the criminal atroc-ities committed by the army in the name of the German people. Like Oskar, the collective will of the Germans during the war seems to have been suspended, in arrested development, and Oskar's preoccupation with his drum suggests the petty personal preoccupations — pursued to the point of madness — by which ordinary people survived the extraordinary events perpetrated by the Nazi regime.

The narrative takes the form of a memoir Oskar writes while incarcerated in a sanatorium. He recalls the significant episodes of his life that parallel events in Germany before the war, during the holocaust, concluding with post-war Europe into the 1950s.

Oskar is an obstreperous child, who not only drums away incessantly on his toy whenever he witnesses what he perceives as the crass hypocrisy of the adults around him — adultery, duplicity, exploitation and stupidity — but who also learns to scream at such a high pitch that he can shatter glass, and he does not hesitate to use his destructive powers as a weapon to punish those who threaten his desire. Oskar's moral outrage stems from the fact that his reductive ethical expectations are too simplistic; he cannot reconcile the complexity of human behavior with his moral compunctions.

Outi Kavén as Oskar in *The Tin Drum*. Fiikka Forsman insists that necessity, not the more edgy gender-identity politics, dictated the casting of a woman to play the male lead. She admits that mixing all the ages of Oskar while mixing his gender was a bonus (photograph by Patrik Pesonius).

Oskar's education begins early. As a child, he witnesses his mother's affair with her lover Jan, a Polish citizen executed for defending a Polish post office, and her subsequent descent into madness and death; his father Alfred's embrace of the Nazi Party, his marriage to Maria, a young woman Oskar claims is his lover; and the birth of a son, Kurt, to Alfred and Maria, although Oskar insists the child is his. During the war, he entertains German troops at the front line, but when his new lover is killed by Allied troops, he returns to Danzig where he becomes the leader of a criminal gang. When the Soviet army captures the city, Alfred goes into seizures while swallowing his Nazi Party pin and is killed by the invading soldiers. Remarkably, at his father's funeral, Oskar throws his beloved drum into the grave and begins to age again, although he remains stunted.

After the war, Oskar, Maria and Kurt move to West Germany, where Kurt, now a savvy entrepreneur, establishes a profitable black market business with Maria. Ill at ease about his son's profiteering, Oskar leaves his family to become a grotesque nude model and also to work engraving tombstones. He falls in love with a nun, becomes a drummer in a jazz ensemble — which leads to a successful solo career — until finally, in his account, he is falsely accused of murdering the nun with whom he was infatuated and is convicted of the murder. Sentenced to a sanatorium, he writes the account of his life.

Mixing myth, magical realism and historical fact, the novel is difficult to classify. More than an allegory, Oskar's unreliable narrative account of Germany during the Nazi years may ring more true than straight historical reporting. The surreality of that era defies easy explanations, and the aftermath, framed by silence, denial, overwhelming guilt, broken taboos, distortions, over-generalizations, intricate collusions and hypocrisy, may well best be portrayed in the notes of a madman full of sound and fury.

But given the strict historical context of Grass's novel, the question becomes: Why this story, now? Does Forsman see parallels between contemporary Finland and Germany in the first half of the twentieth century? Or is she merely interested in bringing that story and those characters to the stage? That the play, for all its technical and dramaturgical virtues, was not selected after its premiere for presentation at the influential 2008 Tampere Theatre Festival, for which it was eligible, illustrates that the questions of appropriateness are not idle ones.

According to Forsman, the impulse to stage the novel was personal. "*The Tin Drum* has been following me since I first saw the film at the age of eleven," she says. Haunted by the story, Forsman suggests that the production was like an exorcism: "After reading the book in my late teens, this devilish version of Peter Pan began to preoccupy me." As for her minimalist approach, she admits that stripping the novel to its basic elements was the "only possible way to bring the multiple strands of the narrative and the characters to stage." Necessity, instead of the more edgy politics of gender-role reversals, also dictated a curious bit of casting: a woman, Outi Kavén, plays the lead. "After Outi's name popped up for the role," Forsman says, "it wasn't a question of her size"— she is diminutive —"but the sheer joy of mixing all the ages of Oskar while mixing his gender too."

Although Forsman's approach is grounded in psychological realism — her characters are less stylized than in metaphorical theatre — Oskar plays to the audience. In this role he is more of a functional device than an actual person. His humanity is undercut by his role as Oskar, the director, signaling events and qualifying the reality as it is presented. Forsman concurs, to a point.

"My aim at this moment is to develop my theatrical expression towards magical realism," she says, admitting to a new tendency in her work toward stylized acting. "But I also try to help my actors to see their characters as internally complex, just as I see the people around me in general. In the case of Oskar, the role developed from making the subject somebody who is actually a bystander, someone looking at the situations from the outside." After all, she points out, "the whole story takes place in his head." Forsman saw no other way to depict the action and stay faithful to the unreliable narrative aspect of the novel than to have Oskar conduct the performance as if conducting a tragic human circus.

Technical and aesthetic issues aside, Forsman considers the play a relevant piece of social theatre mirroring uncomfortable contemporary truths. For her, the over-arching theme of *The Tin Drum* is Oskar's "daring to grow up and assume the responsibility of an adult. This question about responsibility is so clear in the novel because of the historical time that gives the background to Oskar's story." She sees an analogy between Oskar's dilemma and the situation faced by Western democracies as they confront inequities inherent in market-driven economies. "We cannot simply live our everyday lives and close our eyes from the injustices of our time, like poverty, inequality and global warming."

Forsman, like Kujanpää (and others associated with Q Theatre generally), is optimistic about the continuing relevance of theatre in Finland and its ability to maintain its relevance with younger audiences. Because the base of the Finnish theatre is still rooted in the working class, and an amateur theatre tradition, Forsman is quick to point out that "the social point of view never really leaves the stage here. At this moment, in a world of new liberalistic globalization, many of the young writers and directors are trying to give a voice to those less fortunate, the poor, children, unemployed, single mothers." She is convinced that theatre, as a particularly immediate medium, is well positioned to connect themes with audiences through an aesthetic experience. "Theatre," she says, "is one of the last places in our world where real human beings can give something human and emotional to other people. It is one of the last possibilities for live connection of ideas between human beings."

The idea of a "live connection," as opposed to the plastic arts like video, cinema, virtual media and even formal art, also animates Antti Hietala, the artistic director of Q. Hietala recognizes a connection between the unique performance value of live theatre and its relevance as a viable medium in Finnish culture. Although he admits that competing with popular media like television, video and cinema for audiences is difficult, the challenge is also what keeps theatre vibrant. The problem, he says without apology or nuance, is that the general theatre-going audience in Finland is lazy. They tend not to travel and resist investing their time in watching foreign work.

"People worry that Finns might lose some kind of cultural purity if they cooperate with foreigners," he says. "We might lose our originality." Such sentiment, however, is "never said aloud but seems to be the nature of their thinking." Instead of worrying about losing some undefined "identity," Hietala suggests that audiences become receptive to outside influences and move away from what he calls the "coded language of local cultural signifiers."

This desire for Finnish theatre audiences to open up to outside influences explains Q Theatre's interest in creating and sponsoring Baltic Circle. Hietala acknowledges that Finnish theatre traditionally consisted mainly of musical and lyrical performances that, while still popular today, are not taken seriously. He also acknowledges a tradition of activist theatres associated with social and political movements that tend to stress message over aesthetics. He agrees with critics like the Carrolls that "Finnish theatre historians and commentators [...] have connected the emergent Finnish theatre of the late nineteenth century with the new importance of spoken and written Finnish, with nationalist (i.e., anti–Swedish and anti–Russian) aspirations, and with the working man through the labor, youth and temperance movements" (Carroll, "Contemporary" 41).

Critics identify "two major lines within the indigenous Finnish theatre, i.e., that which involves the performance of indigenous plays and theatre pieces. One is the mainstream sociorealistic line, the other a more surreal and metaphysical one which has at certain periods — recently the late 1950's and late 1970's — become prominent" (41). The homegrown nature of Finnish theatre, "engendered in the problems and ideals of ordinary people and the concomitant form of naturalism" (42), aroused misgivings about the more experimental styles by both the audiences comfortable with naturalism and the radicals that preferred a theatre of engagement: both were suspicious of aestheticism and withdrawal.

In the late 1990s, however, the initial impulse of the principals at Q Theatre, including Hietala, was to promote new Finnish work that, for the time, could be considered experimental. Intrigued by the work coming out of the Baltics, especially Lithuania and the way the Lithuanian directors were appropriating and transforming the styles from Berlin — incorporating video, visual symbolism, non-textual approaches to stage language — they envisioned new artistic directions for Finnish playwrights and directors.

According to Jukka Hytti, then one of the principal producers of the Baltic Circle, during the first phase of the evolution of Baltic Theatre (1996–2000) the organizers recognized a need to explore Finland's unique position within the geo-cultural sphere of the Nordic region. With Finland situated inside a triangle formed by Russia, the Baltics and Scandinavia, but not necessarily connected to these neighboring countries, this group of enterprising writers and directors decided the best way to explore Finland's situation was to organize a series of workshops and co-productions that would unite theatres in the region. By importing plays from other cultures for production in Finland, the Baltic Circle introduced new work to the theatre-going public who otherwise would not have access to these productions. By exporting Finnish plays — or, at least, co-productions — they likewise introduced foreign theatre-goers to Finnish theatre. Most critics now recognize Baltic Circle as a well-established producer of collaborative performances, a venue for showcasing and exporting Finnish theatre, as well as a sponsor and coordinator of international theatre festivals.

But not everyone agrees that Baltic Circle is still the thriving, vital organ of innovation it once was. Erik Söderblom, one of the original members of Baltic Circle as well as a founding member of Q Theatre, says that at the time of its inception the rationale for creating Baltic Circle was clear. The Finns were simply not curious about foreign theatre and had become complacent, satisfied with their amateur theatres and the "radical" theatres recycling the political theatres of the 1970s. For those interested in outside influences, no clear channels were open to the outside. Complicating their isolation was the difficulty of traveling freely in the former Soviet Bloc.

"Until the 1990s," he explains, "the Soviet empire was like a refrigerator with all these 'frozen styles' stored there," inaccessible to the greater part of the Western world.

After the Iron Curtain lifted, Söderblom and others began to travel throughout the new territory, networking, observing performances and organizing co-productions that culminated with a definitive festival in 2000, when Helsinki was selected as the cultural capital of Europe. The city hosted performances from former Soviet bloc countries that were exotic, unusual and exciting for the general theatre-going public, as well as for those in the business. Now, however, Söderblom feels the Baltic Circle organization reflects a theatre in crisis, a victim of its own success. In his view, the performances have become predictable and uninspiring, hardly new or unique.

"All of Europe drained the talent," he says. Eastern and central Europe are now facing another crisis of relevancy much like the one they faced after liberation: "There are no themes," he says. "Some interesting productions, especially from some of the Lithuanians and [Latvian Alvis] Hermanis, but mostly that theatre is now empty."

Theatre Siberia (Teatteri Siperia) is truly an outlaw organization. It has no fixed home, no artistic director, and an eclectically democratic ensemble in which, according to Antti Nikkala, one of the principles, it is hard to reach a "consensus." They adhere to a process that keeps the troupe dynamic and unwilling to compromise. Nikkala, like many of his peers, found himself in Helsinki after graduating from the Theatre Academy and looking for a chance to perform. A native of Tampere, he soon realized that, though the majority of "free theatres"—that is, non-institutional theatres—are in Helsinki, the competition was intense and distracting, so since, in his words, "Tampere is a theatre city," he decided to return and try to establish himself in his hometown.

The name Siberia refers to the historical factory area of Tampere located along the dark waters of the canal joining the two main lakes and bisecting the town. Workers called the main factory Siberia, now a major shopping district. But for Nikkala, the name also referred to a virgin area where people go to start their lives over anew, as he felt he and his theatre comrades were doing when they decided to branch out on their own. Only half-jokingly, he also notes that all of the founding members of Theatre Siberia worked steady jobs at Tampere City Theatre, so when they left their jobs it was like moving to Siberia.

Because of the tight-knit ensemble design of their theatre, the members of Siberia tend not to solicit outside work, preferring to develop their own performances through collaboration within the group.

"In City Theatre the audiences were middle-aged, and the productions catered to that audience," Nikkala says. "We are a generational theatre."

Theatre Siberia was formed specifically to deal with the concerns of young people, which Nikkala says the more established theatres simply cannot address because young people are not their primary audience. This conundrum creates a paradox: because theatre audiences tend to be older, the theatres must gear their productions to their preferences, but the more the theatres work to accommodate the established audiences, the more they isolate younger generations. As a result, young people tend to turn away from theatre as a source of entertainment.

Nikkala is convinced that theatre will recover the attention of young people only if it offers themes that have a direct relevance to their lives. He suggests that his generation was born into a period many Finns describe as the "therapy generation" and that "young people in Finland are not doing very well." He and his peers are the third generation after World War II, and the war still haunts Finnish youth. Their grandfathers are considered heroes, but for Nikkala's generation there are no important battles to fight. The welfare state guarantees they will not have to struggle for the basic necessities of life, and while this safety net assures them a healthy life, it also eliminates challenges, creating social anomie and threatening the sense of shared community values.

Young people tend to reject the middle-class dream that animated their parents, suspicious of the idea of sacrificing personal goals for the chimera of a house, family, car and a few weeks of vacation a year. Instead of working to establish themselves in a community, these young people, nurtured by the state and raised in relative security, cultivate drug dependency, aimlessness, and in extreme cases a cult of mutilation. (Recently in parts of Scandinavia teenagers were amputating body parts simply for the thrill.)

Indicative of Siberia's attempts to explore these themes is its performance *All the Love That Belongs to You* (*Kaikki se rakkaus mikä sinulle kuuluu*), a carnival-style production based on the stories of six young people acting out their experiences growing up in contemporary Finland. The title ironically refers to a popular marriage therapy book, implying pathetic attempts by parents to study their situation, hoping to find answers to the challenges of their relationships in a how-to manual.

At times heavy on dialogue, and often relying on selective use of psychological realism during some of the encounters, the production is decidedly more Meyerhold than Stanislavsky. The characters are stylized, even during the realistic scenes, but often they are puppet-like and representative. During the opening scene, several of the players are propped in a closet, like dolls stored in a toy box, which becomes a repository for the characters as they emerge in different roles. The conflicts ambitiously run the gamut between generations, parents, the sexes. The action mocks popular entertainment, including karaoke bars, game shows, glitzy newscasts and political commentary. The characters explore the trendy banalities of dating, parents trying to revive their relationships, children looking for meaning in theirs, all of them suffering the awkwardness of needing significance to justify their otherwise mundane lives.

Although the play never pretends to be anything more than a study of teenage angst and dysfunctional parenting, it manages to avoid the schlock of a network-style after-school special. It maintains integrity more by its dramatic presentation than by the acting. The themes are presented through a series of clever, poetically physical vignettes, heavy on representational visuals (though the inevitable inter-cut video scenes are unnecessary, clumsy, and do not advance the story).

For Nikkala, the key to the play is the gift, what the parents want to leave to their children, an idea reinforced visually by the myriad boxes the characters utilize throughout the production. He explains that the gift is never the right one because the parents tend to think they must leave their children something specific, an inheritance or artifact, or else an ideal by which to live. Instead of focusing on materialism, or being productive, or establishing careers, good jobs, a family, the best gift the parents can pass on to their children is the opportunity to pursue a passion, and the ability to choose for themselves.

Siberia's ironic treatment of *All the Love That Belongs to You* fits Nikkala's interest in the direction he thinks theatre should take. He wants to move away from the authority of the text, allowing for improvisation and surprise during performances. He also stresses collaborative performances that diminish not only the text but also the role of the director during the conceptualization process. Contrasting his approach with the popularity (and dominance in European theatre) of the Lithuanian productions, he perversely describes the work of a luminary like Nekrošius as "melodramatic," suggesting that Lithuanian productions are "too grand" and the metaphors "too heavy." He insists that he is "more urban," finding metaphors in mundane items, "like appliances."

Of the established theatres in the metropolitan Helsinki area, Koko Theatre is refreshingly quirky. During the 2007 Baltic Circle theatre conference, for instance, the bar area, which feels more like a cozy living room than a café, doubled as a meeting place for a heady mix of artists, aficionados and academics from the Baltics, Finland, Scandinavia — a truly international gathering. At one moment a Norwegian troupe was discussing its performance of the night before while interpretive dancers improvised on tabletops, and the next minute a comedian came through the window from the street, unannounced, and began his routine.

This is the scene artistic director Anna Veijalainen cultivates. Her fascination with transnational hybrid ensembles is a natural extension of her affinity for hybrid performances. Trained at the Theatre Academy as a dancer and choreographer, she named her theatre Koko intentionally to refer to "the making of 'complete' works by bringing several art forms under the same roof" (Maukola 20). The Finnish word "koko" connotes completeness, wholeness and entirety. True to its name, Koko Theatre incorporates various forms and genres into what Veijalainen calls "crossover" theatre. Mixing styles to create more visual rather than narrative performances, she is quick to express her antagonism toward mainstream Finnish theatre. Her dissatisfaction is especially directed at classical formulaic performances that cater to rather than challenge popular expectations.

"At one end of the repertoire is drama," she says. "At the other is contemporary dance. At the meeting point of the two exists hybrid theatre, the fusion of different forms of artistic expression."

Ideally, these different genres of dance, music, acting and visual arts merge, creating what she calls a "theatre of inclusiveness."

After the 1960s, excluding a fairly rich period in the 1980s, the major theatres in Finland until 1990 offered a steady diet of generic, typically Scandinavian plays: realistic, text-based narrative family dramas, musicals, farces and comedies. Veijalainen attributes the predominance of this style of theatre to two familiar factors: the natural insularity of the Finnish people and a system of funding in which the most money goes to the most traditional theatres.

According to Veijalainen, the situation changed after 1997, in no small part because of the influence of the Baltic Circle organization, where Veijalainen has served on the selection panel. The Baltic Circle's emphasis — indeed, insistence — on opening up Finnish audiences to foreign styles of theatre exposed Veijalainen to more experimental production values.

(Her inclination toward internationalization parallels that of other smaller theatres in Finland actively working off the trend begun by Baltic Circle in the late 1990s. Examples are plentiful, including notably the Swedish-language theatre group Viirus, which staged several performances with Lithuanian Cezaris Grauzinis, the group's director from 2005 to 2008. Other foreign directors like Latvian Alvis Hermanis have also begun to collaborate with various Finnish theatres to create international performances.)

Convinced that smaller, "profiled" or specialized theatre companies were the wave of the future, Veijalainen decided to risk box office numbers and dedicated Koko theatre to the pursuit of new forms of expression, challenging the nature of "mainstream" performances and promoting international productions. In a phrase, she has not looked back, and her theatre is now one of the most innovative and respected in the city.

Faithful to its original philosophy, Koko remains an authentic "outlaw" theatre and receives no support from the theatre law funds, relying instead on fifty percent of its budget from annual discretionary state and city grants, and the other half from ticket sales, rental of space to outside theatre groups, and bar sales. Although concerned and often frustrated by the financing difficulties inherent in operating outside the theatre law, Veijalainen is militantly proud to be an outlaw. For her, independence allows Koko "self-governance," which translates into "the freedom to (re)define art and the ways of making it." Outlaw theatres typically eschew "results-driven bottom-line thinking," and the status of Koko as a true outlaw means, in Veijalainen's view, "total artistic expression and freedom." She sounds as if she is bragging when she claims her theatre "doesn't make a profit" (Maukola 22), and she is convinced that what she lacks in funding is offset by opportunities unavailable to theatres operating within the auspices of the law. "The freedom of being an independent theatre means that we don't need to worry about spectator figures — we can carry on taking risks, which is a good thing from an artistic point of view" (22).

By 2006, Koko produced 50 premieres and listed 50 members, including actors, dancers, musicians, directors and choreographers, although much of its workforce is not paid. Koko manages to stage 130 performances a year, including visiting troupes and in-house productions. The theatre usually premieres a new play, then runs it 20 times before changing, keeping its schedule manageable but fresh. Koko encourages development of new plays, including workshops and readings, while also producing foreign and independent performances. Configured like an Italian box stage, the performance area operates more like a black box with bleacher seating for 91.

The evolution of Veijalainen's interest from pure conceptual performance to more "traditional" dramatic work is apparent when comparing her *Dragonfly* (*Odonata*), an early production from 2001, to *Romeo and Julia* (*Romeo ja Julia*) by Estonian playwright Andrus Kivierähk, staged in 2006.

Even though dragonflies actually live longer than 24 hours (contrary to urban myth), Veijalainen exercises a bit of poetic license to present her balladic dance metaphor, paralleling the life trajectory of her *Odonata genus*— from its emergence from a larva to fruition as a viably defined creature — with a young woman's emergence into self-realization. Oddly, and accurately in terms of the production piece, the term *Odonata genus* refers to a dragonfly nymph, the "teenage form of the dragonfly, before it transforms into an adult" ("Dragonfly nymph"), and this is the basis for Veijalainen's extended metaphorical treatment of a young woman's coming of age. Combining atonal, jazz-infused music, voice accompaniment, expressionistic lighting and poetic tableaux with modern dance choreography, Veijalainen creates an existential hue to the young woman's progress through the various stages of adolescence into adulthood.

After a first tentative foray outside of her larva-like womb, the dancer reemerges to play in several circles of white light pooling on the dark stage floor, testing the possibilities of motion and the mechanics of movement, as each circle provides varying emotional contexts for her to explore. She continues to experiment with the limits of her potential, tentatively becoming aware of her body and expressing the fascination of freedom. In one especially effective and startling scene, two children and an adult violently thrash a doll about their playroom while the dancer mimics the doll's actions with a human response. Finally, the dancer acquires enough confidence to move beyond the awkward questioning of her body's rhythms to a more fluid awakening of sexuality and eventual maturation.

If *Dragonfly* illustrates Veijalainen's founding philosophy, in which her "background in dance [allows] her a freer attitude towards theatre ... so that she consciously leaves some loose ends" (Maukola 22), *Romeo and Julia* shows that she is not averse to staging more straightforward dramas, though she still manages to integrate physicality, music and metaphor into the narrative to create the sort of hybrid theatre that has become her trademark. Her choice of Kivierähk's adaptation also illustrates another aspect of Koko's evolution: the internationalization of her production schedule, in line with her desire to expose Finnish audiences to the possibilities of new kinds of performances. Kivierähk is well established in Estonia, most noted for his 2000 novel *The Barn Keeper* (*Rehepapp*) and witty plays satirizing the stereotypical Estonian national character. His take on *Romeo and Juliet*, as absurd as it is irreverent, reinforces his reputation as a scathing critic of contemporary Estonian society. But the charm and power of his work rest in his ability, while capturing the local color of Estonian issues, to illuminate universal questions about the human predicament, and this, even more than the outrageous events in his ribald narrative, warrants inclusion in the current Koko canon.

The performance will not be recognizable to anyone familiar with Shakespeare's original. First, in Kivierähk's version, the action takes place in the countryside of present-day Estonia, where most of the inhabitants have moved to the city, leaving behind a restless crew of simple-minded farm boys who satisfy their desire by having sex with animals. As in the original, Romeo falls in love with Julia, but in this rendering Juliet is a wild deer living in the forest, and when Romeo's family objects to the relationship, they turn her into a vat of meat jelly, into which Romeo dives, a suicide. Second, the production, directed by Mikko Kaukolampi and choreographed by Veijalainen, is a bare stage performance piece, heavy on imagery, ensemble folk music and ritualistic dance. The tragic elements of the story are often reduced to travesty, but the sexual interaction between Romeo and his cervine lover are convincingly tender and keep the piece trembling toward pathos.

In context, the play critiques and satirizes the modern phenomenon of urbanization in Estonia based on the recent change from an agrarian to a marketing economy. High-tech industry, tourism and banking concentrated commerce in Tallinn, and this shift in trade and industry corresponds to a shift in philosophy and lifestyle. Inflationary pressures and job competition create a competitive attitude that runs contrary to the traditional (and stereotypical) image of communal folk living in harmony with nature. Kivierähk's tale pits the voices or reason and education against the more instinctual impulses of Romeo and his love of nature. Veijalainen's choreography underscores the contrast between the innocent rural spirit and the corrupting influence of the city's business logic (a common Romantic conceit) by juxtaposing the poetic, sensual duets performed by Romeo and his beloved deer with the flinty, comical blustering of the family and the stooges supporting them.

This dislocation and spiritual crisis is not lost on the Finns. They share with Estonia a population still dealing with the cultural shock of the new post–Soviet economy, in which the rural lifestyle of traditional farmers has been disrupted by the transience and fluidity of urbanization.

Koko's progression from an experimental, performance art venue to an institution interested in presenting more diverse, ambitious and international theatrical productions (while remaining decidedly outside the mainstream), is perhaps best evidenced by its 2007 production of *Chicken* (*Kana*). Written by the Russian writer Nikolai Koljada, staged by a Russian-Finnish director, Viktor Drevitski, and featuring Finnish and Estonian actors, the performance embodies the sort of international ensemble Veijalainen considers indicative and ameliorative, representing both the new reality of the Euro-zone countries and a vehicle of inclusiveness that unites instead of separates the various national identities that compose the region.

The play is set in a small Siberian town during the years of *perestroika*, circa 1989. Two couples, one married and one recently divorced, are rehearsing Chekhov's *Uncle Vanya*. Into this quarrelsome quagmire — the couples' primary occupation, at the expense of their thespian talent, is sniping and mean-spirited score settling — comes a beautiful and talented young actress who sparks intense reactions from all four actors: the men want to sleep with her, and the women are predictably jealous. Each of the players projects his or her insecurities, desires and expectations onto the newcomer. She, exasperated with their amateur affectations and professional pettiness, announces that she is going to kill herself by throwing herself into the Volga River.

In her absence the couples continue to bicker, selfishly unfazed by her melodramatic gesture, but when the actress returns, having decided that performing in the play is, after all, more rewarding than martyrdom, she becomes the catalyst that forces the couples' to reevaluate their relationships and come to terms with the lives they have, not the ones they dream of. Their mutual reconciliation expresses a stoic security that allows them to apply themselves to their art and successfully stage Chekhov's play. Throughout the text, Koljada weaves lines from works by classic Russian writers, interspersing them in the dialogue and having the characters repeat them until the allusions become a leitmotif that shapes the action while simultaneously creating inside jokes that both comment on the action and produce provocative inter-textual ironies.

Having progressed from staging performances without texts, focusing on metaphor and physical theatre, to creating dramatic pieces spiced with an eclectic mix of dance and musical accompaniment, to presenting standards like Sarah Kane's *Blasted* and playful hybrids like *Chicken*, Veijalainen does not shy away from political theatre. In 2007 she adopted five monologues for stage taken from *Putin's Russia*, the 2004 exposé by Anna Politkovskaya, the Russian journalist murdered in 2006. Because relations with Russia are still a sensitive topic, Veijalainen notes that the response from the critics was typical. They dismissed her performance and said her theatre should deal with Finland's problems, not Russia's.

"But Russia's problems are Finnish issues," she says.

The shadow of Finland's relationship with Russia during the cold war, in her view, still lingers. She singles out Putin's use of "natural gas as a weapon." Echoing sentiment in neighboring Estonia, Veijalainen believes economic terrorism — manifest in the exploitation of natural resources — along with profit-driven economies — embodied by the outsourcing of industry — define the dominant political issues of the future.

4

The Cult of Primitivism: Old Themes, New Forms

A playwright and director active in Helsinki during the 1980s, Jouko Turkka was one of the most controversial teachers at the Theatre Academy. Turkka's directing style has been described as "sadistic" and some critics "likened the method to brainwashing, or to those of religious cults" (Jouko Turkka). Commentators recall an infamous incident "when a group of his students held a performance by invitation at which they cut themselves to bleed, smeared each other with excrement, and performed a crucifixion."

The Finns speak of a "Russian soul" in Finnish people, which means they harbor volatile emotions — what one acquaintance identified as an "inner excessiveness"— behind an outwardly sedate surface. This mentality also applies to the Finnish acting style. The simplest action can suddenly reveal an intense reality, a burst of emotional self-exposure. Turkka was one of the best at exploiting this tendency in Finnish actors. Using (some say abusing) extreme psychophysical training exercises, he provoked actors to tap into authentic personal expressions. He believed in an essentialist truth of human nature, discoverable in the primitive unconscious.

Critics like Helavuori refer to a post–Turkka tradition. "He emphasized subjectivity," she says, "and challenged theatre professionals to be fully engaged. For him, theatre is comprehensive, holistic, a way of life."

Admire him or despise him, Turkka's tenure at the academy was a turning point in Finnish theatre. The strong radical social movements of the 1960s and 1970s were over. The conventional modes popular in the rural areas like northern Finland, which is intransigently right-wing and where the popular theatre consists of non-political situation plays, family dramas and musicals, were as redundant as the naturalistic Scandinavian style of theatre on which they were based. The major political players were aging and tired and settled into private life. With the putative Cold War ending, and the capitalist model accepted by the working majority, the leftist movement was mostly ignored and its aesthetic passion at a dead end. The new-wave audiences ignored politics, preferring the comfortable trappings of middle-class affluence and electronic media that reflected Finland's new prosperity. Simply put: Brecht was out, Stanislavski exhausted, political theatre finished, and popular theatre decadent.

This disillusionment with political activism in theatre at the time mirrors the dissatisfaction with the aesthetics of the period. For Antti Hietala, the artistic director of Q Theatre, who studied with Turkka, Turkka's new approach was a form of rehabilitation. He revolutionized technique and reassessed the possibilities of performances in both form and content. According to Hietala, it was common practice before 1988 for actors "to sit around smoking and drinking coffee, discussing the play, analyzing the characters' motives." Turkka changed the rehearsal process, forcing actors, in Hietala's words, "to learn to swim by being thrown into the water." Turkka's approach was structural and phenomenological, utilizing physicality, coordinating mind with body. Instead of casting actors who would come to work to act and then leave the theatre to resume their ordinary lives, Turkka insisted that the actors think of their job existentially, as a way of being. For his actors, theatre was a way of thinking, each member of the cast training to always be ready to take a role, carrying the rehearsal process into their lives, further erasing the difference between acting and becoming.

Politically, Turkka's ideas were no less rebellious (and, to many, traitorous). According to Hietala, Turkka was an avowed leftist, but by the late 1980s he was convinced that the leftists' ideas "ran out of fuel." Hietala insists that "he was not so much against the aesthetics of the left, as far as technique, but he recognized that there had to be new themes, new thinking, a new direction." Turkka rejected both political theatre based on didacticism and long-winded proselytizing from the stage, as well as the stale Brechtean concepts of alienation and self-reference. Leftist critics and colleagues, objecting to his aggressive directing style — demanding physicality, imposing strict discipline (even slapping his actors) — accused him of being a Fascist. Likewise, the conservative city theatres, objecting to his methods, regarded him as an anarchist, and he had trouble keeping a job. But his actors defended him, sometimes going on strike to support him.

The play by Turkka that inspired Hietala's aesthetics was his adaptation of Hannu Salama's 1972 novel *Where There's a Watcher, There's a Doer* (*Siinä Näkijä Missä Tekijä*), performed at the Helsinki City Theatre in 1976. Salama was already notorious for his 1964 novel *Midsummer Dances* (*Juhannustanssit*); its sexuality was too frank for the time of publication and Salama was accused of blasphemy, although he was never convicted. *Where There's a Watcher* cre-

Jani Volanen as Franz Biberkopf in Antti Hietala's *Berlin Alexanderplatz.* Hietala incorporates techniques learned from studying with the notorious director Jouko Turkka. While training actors, Turkka exploited what the Finns call the "Russian soul," referring to volatile emotions repressed beneath an outwardly sedate surface (photograph by Patrik Pesonius).

ates an unflattering portrait of the Finnish Communists during World War II, depicting them not as heroes of an idealistic movement but as saboteurs and traitors. Some critics claim the novel hastened the demise of the Communist party in Finland.

The Soviet sympathizers despised the novel, and were equally incensed that Turkka would want to stage the text. But of more consequence than Salama's realistic and revisionist version of Communist activism during the war years was Turkka's directing. He utilized simultaneous action, stressing physicality and non-realistic metaphorical scenes that contradicted the expectations of the audience and reinvigorated the stylized acting reminiscent of the experimental spirit of the 1970s, but without the leftist polemics.

Applying Turkka's style to his own work, Hietala says that his definitive play was his 1998 adaptation of Alfred Döblin's *Berlin Alexanderplatz* (1929). The expressionistic novel tells the story of Franz Biberkopf, an ex-convict trying to rehabilitate himself, and whose moral disintegration mirrors the frenetic amorality of the mad urban chaos of Weimar Berlin. (Predictably, the novel ends with a typically modernist sea-change resurrection with Biberkopf reconstituted through his suffering as a redeemed man-of-the-times.) But aside from the modernist themes, the novel's montage narrative and the idea

Where the action is: The Shipyard bar and theatre in Tampere, Finland's "second city" (courtesy Shipyard).

of its being set in Berlin provided the fascination and challenge for Hietala. The set was an empty stage with crossing streets in a parallel grid, the audience sat in a bleacher space within the four blocks, as if occupying Alexanderplatz, while all the props were on wheels — the restaurant booths, the band stage — everything choreographed in motion, including simultaneous scenes (a style Turkka explored in *Where There's a Watcher*), capturing the turbulence of Berlin before World War II but, in Hietala's words, "aesthetically beautiful."

Tampere is the so-called "second city" of Finnish theatre. A lot of the action, both socially and professionally, buzzes around The Shipyard Theatre (Teatteri telakka). Once a warehouse for storing farm implements, then deserted for years, the building was restored in 1996 by an enterprising group of theatre renegades who wanted to stage productions outside the purview of institutional theatres. According to Hanno Eskola, one of the founding members, the initial impulse was to create a space for several disparate groups operating with no fixed base.

"It's difficult to get an audience," he says, "when they can't locate you."

Eskola, who grew up in Tampere and as a child hauled sacks of oranges around the original building — back when "oranges were fairly exotic," he says — planned to refurbish the site, creating a performance space on the spacious top third floor. But while Eskola was setting the scene for his play *A Coin in the Hat of Love* (*Lantti rakkauden hattuun*), which required the use of a sawn-in-half Volvo Amazon, the fire marshal stopped the production, insisting the performance had to be on the ground floor because it was the only space that had two doors for exits. The space on the first floor was too small, so Eskola abandoned the performance and, for the time being, the proposed restoration.

Eskola and his compatriots decided that a better idea would be to open a bar instead. The point, Eskola explains, was to create an alternative performance space, as well as a meeting place for actors and artists, and a bar seemed to be the perfect venue.

"We were actors, writers and directors," he says, "having fun selling beer."

Though they managed some formal performances, including cabaret, improvisation and some experimental one-acts, running the bar was the real performance, a profitable bit of street theatre. The actors in the shows worked for free, focusing their energy in the bar. And their dedication paid off. After just one year in business, the principals were able to buy the building and bring it up to standards so that they could support a true theatre space on the third floor, as originally planned, a gallery, business offices and a community room on the second floor; and the bar, restaurant and beer garden on the ground floor.

The Shipyard was always mainly about the bar, Eskola insists, and though the theatre has evolved into a powerhouse in the alternative theatre scene, the main attraction remains the bar, a stimulating and unpretentious gathering place for artists, writers, actors and directors from around the region.

With respect not just for preservationists but for artistic integrity, those responsible for the restoration took pains to maintain the character of the original building. They were even given old timber from some dilapidated barns in the countryside so they could retain the acoustics. Combining business loans with some support from the state, but mainly financed by income generated by the restaurant and bar, the structure was finally transformed into a nexus of artistic energy.

As romantic as the venture sounds, by the time he and the others conceived of The Shipyard, Eskola was already a veteran of the alternative theatre scene in Finland. After graduating from the Theatre Academy in Helsinki, Eskola joined with Antti Hietala and others to form the original Q Theatre. At that time Q was just beginning to make a name for itself, and the critics were paying attention. Q—alongside The Group, KOM and the Swedish-speaking theatre Viirus—was proving a viable model for small companies throughout the country looking for more autonomy than the institutional theatres could allow and yet also wanting to establish a base of operations, as it were, a location, a place with which to be identified. Many of these early independent theatres were "outlaws," but as Eskola is quick to point out, Q (and many of the others, like The Group and KOM) joined the system so quickly that their status was never really "outlaw" in the true sense of the concept.

"People used to think only the 'free' groups produced radical theatre," says Eskola, "but now they all do avant-garde, even the municipal theatres." To illustrate his point, he cites The National Theatre's production of Kristian Smeds' *The Unknown Soldier*. Even so, he notes that Finnish playwrights, no matter how controversial the subject, still for the most part rely on a Lutheran, text-based model, heavy on dialogue and suspect of metaphor, physicality and overly stylized acting. He traces this preference for text-based theatre to the relative youth of Finnish literature, pointing out that since the mid-nineteenth century, when Finnish literature came into its own, art was expected to address issues associated with the emerging Finnish nation. The early chauvinistic approach to art as a propagandistic and inspirational vehicle never lost its influence. Audiences well into the twentieth century expected art, theatre particularly, to explore social issues, to be politically relevant, its theme more important than its form.

As Eskola points out, again referring to the relatively brief history of formal Finnish literature and the fact that since its inception it has been associated with the emergence of a national identity, "there is no tradition of aesthetical theatre in Finland." Formalist and experimental theatre simply never caught the mainstream public's imagination. Theatre was always expected to carry some form of social commentary. Any deviation from this pulpit-style exercise in communal amelioration seemed extravagant, self-indulgent and irrelevant. Simply put, the mainstream audiences feel more secure with imports, especially plays written in what Eskola calls the "American British style ... all talk and analysis" than with homegrown theatre that deviates from the psychological-realistic model and delves into mixed media, metaphor and more poetic performances.

The phenomenon Eskola identifies—the Finnish preference for socially relevant plays performed in a fairly straightforward manner—is strikingly evident in Juha Jokela's *The Fundamentalist* (*Fundamentalisti*). The play, which foregrounds the social issue at the core of the drama over the theatrical possibilities of its delivery, presents an argument between a secularist—a lapsed clergyman—and a literalist believer—the fundamentalist of the title—but

Dick Holmström and Maria Udd in Juha Jokela's *The Fundamentalist*. The play depicts an argument between a secularist — a lapsed clergyman — and a literalist believer — the fundamentalist of the title. The story unfolds in a discursive *pas de deux* about sexual guilt and the impetus of desire. The effect is that of an old-fashioned a sermon illustrated by dramatic interludes (photograph by Petri Kovalainen).

offers little new in an old debate. The performance seems more like a lecture illustrated by dramatic interludes that advance the story strictly through dialogue. The play was widely celebrated, immensely popular, and was selected to represent Finland in the 2008 Nordic Drama competition. The form achieves nothing surprising beyond the impact of a dramatized lecture. The social theme is timely — discussing how fundamentalist tendencies can be used to counter a perceived secular hedonism — but it is also trite. The appeal of the play is based less on aesthetics than a hunger for theatre to renew its social relevance. The play is the antithesis of metaphorical or physical theatre. Ironically, given its subject, it is painfully Lutheran. Significantly, in his opening line, Markus, the narrator, asks the audience if they have all "managed to find a pew."

Markus opens the play by explaining that as a twenty-two-year-old youth minister he was involved in a "dysfunctional and sexless" marriage. One night during a Confirmation retreat he found himself alone with Heidi, an eighteen-year-old parish helper, and he was suddenly "given permission to roam across this young, attractive woman's back," to relieve, he says, her tense muscles. Caught up in the sexuality of the "physiotherapy," Markus massaged her buttocks and then slipped his hand further down her pants. Heidi sat up, stunned, rushed from the room and vanished from his life.

This back-story leads to the present situation twenty years later. Markus is now a popular writer known for his book *Purging the Cathedral*, a reformist tract promoting a more balanced, historical and reasoned approach to the scriptures. His comfortable and self-assured secularism is shattered by the sudden appearance of Heidi, now thirty-eight and married to a fundamentalist preacher, the head of a born-again alliance called The Church of the Living Word. Predictably, Heidi has come to "save" Markus. He counters her passionate appeals with logic and exegeses. As the dialogue progresses Heidi eventually succumbs to his point of view, denounces her belief and becomes his lover.

His sophistry is summarized in a Hegelian sleight-of-hand: "The nature of truth exists in the simultaneous presence of opposites," he tells her. To Heidi, this means, "Jesus both died on the cross and didn't die." When he professes his love for her (more carnal than platonic), she is primed to abandon one doctrine for another, swapping, in her mind, the divine for the devil. Markus refuses to accept her "conversion," telling her that she is merely running from "one addiction to the next." Heidi, angry at what she perceives as his betrayal, suffers a nervous breakdown and tries to commit suicide.

Confined to a mental hospital, she is finally well enough to have visitors. Markus learns that her desire for the certainty of the fundamentalist church and her need to live a strict life of adherence to incontrovertible truths stemmed from a traumatic event in her youth, that night at the Confirmation retreat, when she felt "like a sweet little girl on the arm of a wise and warm-hearted bear" until "the bear's paw does something it shouldn't do to little girls." Cloying, even for a woman who was eighteen at the time, Heidi's confession is overly convenient, and any sympathy for her evaporates with her sappiness. To the end, she blames Markus for her slide into a life of desperation, addiction and mental illness. Trust for her, she whines, leads to pain. This clinical romanticizing of disillusionment becomes a catchall to explain her inability to control her actions and make existential sense of her life.

Throughout the play, Markus addresses the audience directly, explaining the situation and setting the context for each of the several dramatic scenes with Heidi that alternate between his lecture and the acting-out of each illustrative episode. The American archetype is Thornton Wilder's *Our Town*. But in Jokela's play, with only two characters in a discursive *pas de deux* about sexual guilt and the impetus of desire, the play comes off as little more than an old-fashioned sermon.

For his part, Eskola prefers physical theatre and insists that if Finnish theatre hopes to progress, writers and directors — and in the end audiences — must embrace a more ambitious, self-conscious theatre. A director and professor of acting at University of Tampere, Eskola stresses movement and what he calls "formalism — although it's a 'bad word' in Finland." He admits his technique puts him in a minority in Finland, but he considers himself a traditionalist, in the "tradition," he says, without a trace of irony, "of Meyerhold" and stylized theatre.

Instead of the concentrated search for emotion or spending hours analyzing texts, Eskola begins with the physical aspects of the performance. Students selected for his acting classes, he says, could just as easily have been auditioning for dance. When he begins work on a piece, he gets the blocking down fast, then the language. To him, the emotions are obvious. What he seeks is a "form" to contain and express the essence of the situation. He calls the technique "sonar-mobile": sound-movement, in which the actors fuse language and action with emotion, an exercise in trans-linguistic expression.

"Most Finnish actors still tend to go for meaning in the words," he complains. "I want abstract sound and action that creates meaning."

Part of his training routine involves having his students perform a play in a foreign language that they haven't mastered. No Finnish. No English. This distancing from any immediate word connotations tends to disrupt familiarity and ready-made verbal phrasing so that the lines are fresh and surprising. He also feels that this program restores a sense of what he describes as "seventeenth century discipline" to the training, suggesting that during the Renaissance actors could sing and dance and display a variety of skills that gave them a deep reservoir of experience to draw from during a performance.

That is one reason Eskola does not direct at The Shipyard, and acts there only when he thinks the play is right for him.

"These are not my kind of actors," he says. "Plus, at the university I don't have to operate within the formulaic structure of rehearsing for two months then, bang, going on stage."

The second reason, he says, only half-joking, is that "these are my friends, and, you know, the Telakka has always been about the bar."

Given Eskola's appreciation for non-verbal form and his disdain for plays based on dialogue, his move from Helsinki back to Tampere seems fittingly ironic and absurd. Echoing the urban myth about how critics killed the English Romantic poet Johns Keats, Eskola mischievously tells the story of his short-lived affiliation with Q and his self-imposed exile from Helsinki. He had written a play, performed at Q, the title of which Eskola translates with some difficulty as *Between Dead People* (*Vaina jat keskenään*). It was an absurd, farcical piece relying heavily on physical theatre and sight gags. To increase the dissonance, he directed his actors to speak very quickly, running their words together in nearly nonsensical patterns.

The leading critic of the day, Jukka Kajava, having lavished praise on Eskola's previous plays, trashed the performance. Paradoxically, given that Eskola's premise was to focus on physicality and minimize the importance of language in the play, Kajava's central complaint was — and Eskola gleefully quotes him verbatim — "you can't talk that much in a play." This criticism was especially odd to Eskola, since his piece was a direct attack on the typical Finnish style of the times: a text-based model heavy on dialogue. Eskola, flabbergasted, felt the critic had willfully misconstrued the play and decided that, instead of trying to work in a city where the foremost critic was exercising a personal vendetta against him, he moved home to Tampere and never looked back.

While writers and directors at Q, KOM and The Group seem determined to keep theatre socially engaged, not so much as an editorial exercise or a rehabilitative vehicle but certainly as a window opening into a communal world of ordinary people facing both practical and existential issues of love, loss, fidelity, grief, security, anxiety and, basically, the situation of a people struggling for meaning in their lives, Eskola remains staked out soundly in the art-for-art's-sake camp. But even he recognizes a disconcerting shift in perspective between the days of politically engaged theatre and the commercially driven nihilism plaguing the current generation.

To dispense with socially driven art, whether couched in the polemics of propaganda or the more subtle forms of psychological realism — that is, to pursue an art of aesthetics, requires a benevolent reassessment of sensibility. But these days Eskola identifies a movement in the new young Finnish professional classes that he labels "abstract politics," a subversive form of marketing cynicism aligned with no particular ideology but capable of adopting whatever philosophical position is required to satisfy the matter at hand.

The result is a generation unanchored from any guiding principles, operating like chameleons, affiliated only with the politics of exigency.

"They aren't interested in concrete projects," he says, "just fictional statements."

The current literary elite, those in their fifties and sixties, cut their teeth in the years when politics were taken seriously, when people were associated with specific movements — mainly among Socialists among the Finnish intelligentsia. Now, according to Eskola, "This new generation is pleased to slip radical statements into Coke commercials." Theirs is a politics of posturing. They are committed to nothing but the bottom-line.

Eskola's sentiment might seem odd, since he is based in Tampere: home of the Workers Theatre, built on the site where Lenin and Stalin first met and which houses the only Lenin Museum in the world; stronghold of Soviet sympathizers even into the late 1980s; where the concept of art as a tool to promote social awareness began in Finland.

But Eskola's aestheticism is a product of his cosmopolitan past. Although he was born in Tampere, he has traveled extensively. Steeped in Meyerhold, whose opposition to social realism is well documented, and whose technique focused on using energy and gestures to reveal emotions, Eskola was equally influenced by Pina Bausch, the famed German choreographer whose work evokes a subjective, surreal engineering of motion into poetry.

"For me," Eskola says, "acting is hidden dance."

Indicative of the passion and allegiance The Shipyard inspires in the local theatre literati, theatre manager Marja Laitala describes how she began as a waitress on the ground floor, acted in several performances in the third-floor loft, left for a year, and then returned to take over the day-to-day business in a second-floor office.

"I am both philosophically and concretely a part of the concept," she says. She emphasizes that each floor represents a very different and separate aspect of the conglomerate. She also stresses that understanding the synthesis, how each floor is symbiotically associated with the others, is essential for a proper appreciation of the operating vision, or mission, of the theatre.

The performance space occupies a sixty-five-seat black box of brick and wood. It is intimate but professionally equipped with enough technical gadgetry to assure first-class sound and visual effects when needed. The seventeen members of the association include artists from all areas of theatre: actors, writers, directors, stage designers and musicians. But the small coterie that actually decides which plays are accepted for production consists of only five individuals, four actors and one costume designer. This creative oligarchy chooses to stage only two or three new productions, and they typically stay booked for three years in advance. They prefer plays that are still being developed so that the collaborative process can shape the play to meet the standards of the artistic committee and the expectations of their audience.

Although the artistic directors are especially interested in promoting young local Finnish playwrights, all productions are not homegrown. The Shipyard's production of Alfred Jarry's *Ubu Roi*, for instance, featured a French text, a Spanish director, and Finnish actors. The performance language was English.

Sirkku Peltola, also based in Tampere, is a good representative of what Eskola defines as the "brutal" Finnish acting tradition, exactly the opposite of the more documentary style of *The Fundamentalist*. Peltola is one of the most widely produced playwrights in Finland. Her play *The Finnhorse (Suomen*

(Left to right) Lasse Poser, Antti Mankonen, Piia Soikkeli and Antti Haikkala in The Shipyard's production of *Ubu Roi* illustrates Finland's international collaboration. The performance featured a French text, a Spanish director, and Finnish actors. The performance language was English (photograph by Kimmo Hokkanen).

hevonen) and its companion piece *I Ain't Taking Mama in My One-Room Place* (*Yksiöön en Äitee ota*) describe the lives of the underclass with a tenderness and affection that places her squarely within the camp of writers that both romanticize and ironically exploit characters like Uuno Turhapuro in the classic comical tradition. While Peltola's work describes "bizarre families and misfits" (Introduction to *The Finnhorse* 6), her plays also address "the problems of the countryside, where the simple, rural life-style is doomed to extinction by the demands of an increasingly bureaucratic EU" (6).

The devastating effects of European Union regulations on traditional farmers do form the basis for *The Finnhorse*, but it is Peltola's understanding and astute treatment of those who populate her landscapes that make her plays so successful. On the surface, with her focus on the noble poverty of the underclass and her ear for the poetry in rural dialogue, she seems to borrow heavily from the American playwright Sam Shepard. But that influence in no way detracts from the originality of her vision. At the center of the play is the Finnish work horse, a staple of rural Finnish life, but for Peltola the horse represents all that is unique and wonderful about the character of the

Maria Aro in Sirkku Peltola's *Finnhorse*. The play explores the lives of the under-class and the devastating effects of European Union regulations on traditional farmers. In this context, the play is an allegory representing the demise of the rustic Finnish character and the destruction of the rural Finnish way of life, but Peltola's critique never strips the characters of their individualism (photograph by Ari Ijäs).

Finnish farmer: "[...] even-tempered. Headstrong yet meek. [...] Content with its lean pasture [...] earnest and long-suffering" (Peltola 14). In this context, the action becomes allegorical, representing the sacrifice of the rustic Finnish character and the destruction of the rural Finnish way of life.

The central cast consists of a divorced couple, Aili and Larri — passion-less non-achievers — their slacker son Jay, his sister Jenni, her friend Kristi-ina, Larri's new girlfriend Meri and Aili's mother Gram. The plot centers on Jay's plan to sell his grandmother's horse Rowan to buy a Harley-Davidson motorcycle. He is convinced that the horse can be sold profitably to a com-pany that will haul the beast and sell it to a restaurant in Sicily, where he has heard the citizens are "as mad for horsemeat as for wild mushrooms" (13). What follows is a comedy of errors.

Jay and his father arrange for a Latvian driver to transport the horse to their restaurant buyers while hiding news of the sale from Gram, who thinks her beloved horse has simply died and hopes that it will be given a decent burial. She laments that horses are eaten in some countries but notes that "in this country we have a deeper relationship with our horses" (26). Events escalate when Meri drops by. She confesses that her innocent flirtation during a chance encounter on the highway with the Latvian truck driver caused him to wreck the rig, killing all the horses. Fearing Gram will find out the truth about Rowan, Larri rushes out with a meat grinder to make sausages of the horsemeat.

While the family, none the wiser, nonchalantly munches on meatballs made from Rowan's carcass, Kristiina visits Jenni and tells the family how her step-brother tried to kill himself because he failed to file a form notifying the EU authorities in Brussels of the removal of livestock. About that time Jay rides up on a Harley, purchased with the funds from the unfulfilled sale of the horses. When the horse buyers demand their money back, since they never received the horses for which they had paid Jay and Larri, Jay refuses to sell the motorcycle and initiates another scheme to pay off them off.

A month later, the hardships continue. Aili has stolen Gram's coffin money and given it to Larri to pay off, unbeknownst to her, the debt for the dead horses that Jay used to buy his Harley. Then Aili receives a note from the Ministry of Agriculture explaining that Larri's subsidies will be cut off and his last three years of subsidies will be reclaimed. Gram discovers she has been robbed and demands to be buried beside Rowan, Jenni has become pregnant from an affair with a "bog-standard ball scratching" (118) bass player from a local band, Jay's motorcycle is stolen, Larri confesses that the meatballs they are eating have been made from Rowan's remains, and Gram dies. The final indignity: a valuable painting by Ilya Repin of Leo Tolstoy, which they discover in their possession, is carved up by Jenni and Kristiina for their "community center EU-homepage project" (150).

The genius of Peltola's style is that she manages to present her gallery of grotesque, gothic characters with a touching humanity. Her critique never strips the characters of their individualism even as they double as representatives illustrating Peltola's social and political concerns. Gram clearly operates as an ideal, the only sensible member of the family who respects traditional mores and self-reliance. Her love of Rowan and her disdain for Woolworth's and television distinguish her from Jay, Jenni and Kristiina, who have been seduced by the "new" Europe: a homogenized zone of predictable fads and crass behavior. Meri is ineffective and humorless, Larri impulsive and impotent, Aili broken and bitter.

For Peltola, it seems the corrupt geopolitical bureaucracies of the EU replicate in the communities that subscribe to them, ruining both the Finnish national character as well as the ethical makeup of the culture. Gram's death is the death of historical Finland.

Perhaps the most radical of the dramaturges operating within this primitive style, and perhaps representing the most authentic Finnish theatre in the current theatre catalog, is writer, actor and director Leea Klemola. With no pretense for subtlety, her play *Kokkola* and its companion piece *Into Colder Climates* (*Kohti kylmempää*) — parts of a proposed trilogy — defy a logical synopsis, but the surreal caricatures who populate her plays seem to feel right at home in their kaleidoscopic reality, their stoic acceptance of their bizarre existence rendering Klemola's work even more hallucinatory.

The charm — if that's the word — of Klemola's plays will not be found in subtle acting but in the themes. She deals with people who are lifesavers, survivors who hold other people together. No matter how absurd the situation, there is a centrifugal drive to maintain order in the middle of chaos, and this attempt to control both the natural and manmade calamities creates a dark humor popular with Finnish audiences.

The title, *Kokkola*, refers to Klemola's hometown. A hamlet on the west coast of Finland, "on the same latitude as Greenland's capital, Nuuk, [...] this Artic connection — people living in cold dark places dreaming of faraway lives and looking for intimacy and ways to express their emotions — was the starting point of the play" (Kurki).

Kokkola is a calamitous slapstick production, punk cabaret, the parts of which are greater than the whole. The intense scenes often seem isolated, like stand-alone comedy skits knitted together by a thin narrative thread that frays long before the end of the performance. While the plot resists a neat synopsis, the action revolves around the central character of Marja-Terttu Zeppelin, a role originated by Heikki Kinnunen, one of the most famous comic actors in Finland. Marja-Terttu, a sixty-year-old drunk who frequently loses control of her bladder and bowels, is determined to travel from Kokkola to Greenland. Caught up in the petty ignominies of small-town life, she equates coldness with purity and believes that she can achieve a kind of transcendence by moving to ever-colder climates (the literal title of the second play in the series). Subplots involve Piano, owner of Individual Servicing Company, his girlfriend Minna, Marja-Terttu's daughter Maura, and other assorted oddballs involved in various homosexual, heterosexual and incestuous relationships. The central conflict focuses on Marja-Terttu's attempts to resolve her unnatural affection for her brother Saku, who in one scene is accused of "beating up his own sister out of love."

As these characters lurch from one mini-crisis to the next, each resolution opens into another comedic situation that replicates the process, until the play collapses from exhaustion more than from any logical conclusion, cause and effect, or conventional sense of a narrative arc. Marja-Terttu sums up her motivation by explaining: "When it gets cold, all energy is bent on maintaining the vitals. It's not so lonely when you're in the company of your own body." Her faith in withdrawal, like that of an anchorite recoiling from the madness of the world, culminates in her self-imposed exile on a frozen piece of sea. In the final scene, the motley gaggle of characters gathers to witness a miracle: Marja-Terttu transformed into a seal. While the others argue the plausibility of this phenomenon, she emerges from her disguise. Undeterred by this charade, the clan climbs into the bus with Piano at the wheel and heads off for Greenland.

The core crisis in the sequel, *Into Colder Climates*, centers on the existential dilemma implied by global warming, which, in Marja-Terttu's cosmology, threatens not only the ecological balance of the planet but also the moral potential of mankind. One of the prime contributions to the warming, however, is the fact that Marja-Terttu has fallen in love — she is literally in heat — and her passion is melting glaciers. Although a new cast of misfits populates the landscape of *Into Colder Climates*, the situations are no less absurd than the action driving *Kokkola*. The Needendal family, believed to be the last remnants of the original Neanderthal race, join a trio of personified dogs (named, in an orthodox bit of inter-textual frivolity, after characters from *Kokkola*), a crazed Greenlander priest, a few leftovers from the last expedition, and a motley collection of other incongruous characters, all striving

Leea Klemola's *Into Colder Climates* defies a logical synopsis, as the surreal caricatures populating the play endure a kaleidoscopic reality. Her characters are survivors who hold other people together, no matter how absurd the situation. Their attempt to maintain order in the middle of chaos and control both natural and manmade calamities creates a dark humor popular with Finnish audiences (photograph by Harri Hinkka).

Into Colder Climates: Heikki Kinnunen, left, one of the most famous comic actors in Finland, originated Marja-Terttu Zeppelin, the central character in Klemola's trilogy. With Klaus Klemola (photograph by Harri Hinkka).

for satisfaction, significance, meaning and a sense of order in the sexual and geographic chaos they encounter during the ensuing absurdity.

Marja-Terttu is now in Greenland operating a kiosk she has named Polar Grill. One by one the others gather, some literally dropping in from a helicopter. Through a series of ridiculous scenes, mainly composed of scatological humor, sight gags, bestiality and politically incorrect jokes intended to insult an impressive array of stereotypes, Marja-Terttu decides it would be best if she were launched to the moon. "There," she says, "it's absolutely cold." After hallucinating that she does indeed visit the moon, she returns to reality long enough to organize the characters into yet another improbable venture designed to cure Marja-Terttu of her sudden emotional warming: a trek toward the coldest regions on the planet.

Antti Nikkala from Theatre Siberia describes Klemola's work as quintessentially Finnish. Echoing comments from the Finland-Swedish community, as well as directors like Mikko Viherjuuri and Hanno Eskola, Nikkala suggests that Finnish acting is "fierce," but he sees this as a virtue. He recalls working with a French theatre group in an exercise where they were asked by the director to create a myth. It only took a minute, he says, until the Finns were naked and fighting. "There was nothing subtle about it," he says, approvingly.

Dan Henriksson, artistic director of the Swedish-speaking Finnish theatre Klockrike Theatre, traces the brutal humor and savage acting techniques employed in Klemola's plays to a tradition of stock characters in Finnish literature and the influence of the controversial acting professor Jouko Turkka during his tenure at the Helsinki Theatre Academy. The archetype of the "noble" peasant, best represented by Ilmari Kianto in his 1924 novel *Jooseppi from Ryysyranta* (*Ryysyrannan Jooseppi*), allowed the Finns to mock themselves in his shiftless, lazy bootlegging antihero, while at the same time romanticizing his simplicity and survival instincts.

Later, this type morphed into a craze surrounding the success of Uuno Turhapuro, the hapless character at the center of a series of wildly successful films in Finland spanning several decades from the 1970s to 2004. Uuno is a Finnish loser with bad teeth and tattered clothes whose marriage to the wealthy daughter of a mining executive allows him to pursue his favorite pastimes: lying around, eating hotdogs, and seducing women.

Klemola's work can be seen as the logical continuation of this tradition, combining the graphically coarse character of a Finnish redneck with Turkka's brutal, in-your-face style of actor's training to create her own brand of raw comedy.

Revisiting classic novels and bringing them to stage has been a staple of theatre for years; there's nothing new in the process. But whereas the trend in the past — especially during the Neo-Classical period — was to maintain a fairly strict fidelity to the text, the new generation of directors continuing in this tradition tends to exercise a liberty with the original text that locates them in a wholly different mode.

This new generation of directors views the text as a possibility, disregarding the novelist's characterization, imagery, sequence of events and internal logic. Many of the more radical directors are reluctant even to consider performing material that is explicitly written for the stage. They eschew "scripts" loaded with stage directions, *mise en scène* and specified behavior and opt instead for scripts that ignore conventional theatrical considerations. (Martin Crimp's *Attempts on Her Life* is a good example. No voices are identified as character or gender, no scenes are set, no action predetermined.)

Many of these new Finnish directors also avoid what might be called stage-specific plays, works written to be performed as theatre pieces. The *cri d'coeur* is "nobody knows how to stage a novel." One complaint about Forsman's production of *The Tin Drum*, as well as similarly timid approaches to radically altering the narrative of a novel, is that she didn't stray far enough from the text; each of the most vivid scenes in Grass's original — the ones that drive the story forward — she adheres to faithfully. In Leskinen's case, production necessities, as much as his own desire to rethink Bulgakov's original text, led him to radicalize the performance.

Not necessarily the most notorious but perhaps the most striking and memorable example of this trend in Finland of radically reshaping novels for stage may have been Kristian Smed's staging of Väinö Linna's 1954 novel *The Unknown Soldier* (*Tuntematon sotilas*), which opened at the Finnish National Theatre in 2007. This best-selling and most-revered novel in Finnish literary history has been appropriated by various artists to question the idealization of war and the promulgation of patriotic propaganda that glorifies heroism while mitigating or denying the horror of actual combat. And given its status, it is ripe for exploitation, any treatment or deviation from its original purpose certain to cause a cultural ruckus and social infamy. After all, "[t]he main theme of the work is the national spirit, and masculinity, heroism and defeat" (Ruuskanen 8) — that is, Finnish mythological identity.

Linna's novel provides a sympathetic view of the ordinary soldier suffering extreme privations while risking his life for the sake of others, at times to promote the careers of incompetent politicians whose feckless diplomacy often results in unnecessary wars. (Finland's ability to avert conflict with the Soviets through an alliance with Germany in 1938 is debatable and problematic.) The story, an unsentimental, realistic depiction of war, follows a machine gun platoon fighting Soviet forces in the Karelia region of Finland during World War II. The genius of the novel lies in how Linna manages to personalize his characters while simultaneously creating representative types drawn from various social strata and geographical regions to represent an accurate cross-section of Finnish society: Sergeant Lahtinen, the Communist sympathizer; Sergeant Hietanen, the apathetic fatalist; Lieutenant Kariluoto, the privileged idealist; Lieutenant Koskela, the tough pragmatist; Sergeant Lehto, a working-class sadist; Private Rahikainen, a scammer and raffish lady's man; Sergeant Rokka, the cocky and self-assured no-nonsense realist. The list of characters is long and impressive, illustrative of the diverse social types thrown together, despite the petty quarrels highlighting their individuality, by the common fatal necessity of war.

While the characters elicit sympathy and complexity, the action and motives of the men are never glamorized, and Linna seems to go out of his way to debunk the notion of war being an opportunity for male bonding and selfless glory, producing heroic sacrifice for noble causes greater than self-survival. The men are human, terrified, ridiculous, disrespectful and businesslike. Most of all, they represent that archetypal Finnish quality *sisu*, "a stubborn, unwavering strength of purpose and integrity in the face of suffering and external pressure" (Carroll, "Contemporary" 36). While the grunts slogging it out through the violence exhibit the expected vicissitudes of war — cowardice, heroism, naiveté, bravery, cruelty and indifference — the lieutenants commanding the men, regardless of their ideology, are loyal and dedicated, without pretensions or delusions of grandeur. They understand their role as actors in an absurd drama that will play out despite their intentions. Linna saves his scorn for the officers and politicians whom he depicts as pompous propagandists and cynical opportunists. He also mocks the notion of patriotism embodied in hollow imagery and empty slogans, intentionally resisting any epic context or romantic idealism and focusing instead on the gritty brutality of war.

At its heart is the years-long conflict between Finland and the Soviets, which reached its climax in World War II. But the effects simmered throughout the Cold War, continuing even beyond the collapse of the Soviet Union in the late 1980s. The West was lulled into a complacency accentuated by, in some Western countries (particularly the United States under the Bush administration), a foolish triumphalism that allowed Vladimir Putin the opportunity once again to create an aggressive Russia eager to test the weakness of its immediate neighbors (including the Baltics, especially Estonia). Reinforcing the sentiment expressed by Esa Leskinen in his decision to stage *Satan Comes to Moscow*, Smeds points out, "'The previous war was so long ago that the current generation have labeled it bad. Our time is very tense, and relations with Russia are still traumatic'" (8).

Smeds' version more closely resembles a typical West End/Broadway musical than the subversive *piece de resistance* its avid admirers (especially the popular press) make it out to be. To his credit Smeds focuses on Linna's disdain for the political classes whose whimsical ambitions send men into the dehumanizing experience of war. But too often, the attempts at contempt seem juvenile, as when a huge portrait of Mannerheim, the leader of Finland during the Continuance War, morphs through computer image manipulation first into a distorted Francis Bacon–esque miscreant, then into Donald Duck. In another scene, a live effigy of a pompously decorated politician is dragged from the audience and abused, his wife accosted, both historical icons humiliated, any pretense of respect stripped away in a slapstick "caricature" assassination. In a facile effort to connect past events to Finland's current situation, portraits of the party's ruling cabinet at the time of the original production are likewise abused, the disillusioned soldiers shooting at them and shouting, "Finland is dead!"

The most serious problems with the production do not concern the politics of Smeds' adaptation. As Paavo Arhinmäki, a member of Parliament and first vice chairperson of The Left Alliance, points out:

The original book is anti-war. In fact it described well how the warlords and simple sons of the tenant farmers are against each other in the army. Later on the message of the book has been sought to be seen as very patriotic, and of course there are patriotic elements in the content, but the book is definitely not fanatically patriotic. [...] The total insanity of war became very clear to the audience. [...] People need to be reminded about the madness of war and the class division of our society [Arhinmäki].

The problems have to do with the staging, which relies heavily on special effects and, surprisingly for such a grimy naturalistic story of heroism in the face of gory futility, cabaret. The performance is literally wet and mushy where it needs to be gritty and dry. It opens with the soldiers training in a pool. Later, in a famous scene from the novel in which the troops brew home-made beer, they dunk and spill and spew the beverage across the stage until, after several drunken and drenched sing-alongs, they douse each other with buckets of beer.

Smeds is most effective when he is faithful to the text, creating an impression of deprivation and convincingly portraying the life of the troops living, fighting and dying in the frozen swamps of the Karelian peninsula. They are wet, cold, exhilarated, exasperated and exhausted, some like teenagers pumped up for a soccer match, others romanticizing the conflict, and still others fatalistic about the impending violence and death awaiting them in the icy lice-infested forest.

Interspersed between the splashing on stage, the soldiers embed themselves with the audience, mingling in the seats, reconnoitering the aisles and sniping from the cheap seats. All of this gallivanting, clowning inter-cut with the serious business of warfare, is video linked to a huge projection screen over the stage. While this element is effective at times, it is also distracting. In one episode totally invented outside of the text, the video shows an angry drunken soldier on leave in Helsinki wielding a sledgehammer and demolishing a Lada (the ubiquitous emblem of the Soviet era). The sequence is a mildly humorous clip filmed with all the panache of a happening, a bit of surreptitious street theatre that smacks of the puerile antics of the popular American television spoof series *Candid Camera*.

The video works best when it provides a platform depicting the action from a simultaneous but alternative perspective that adds to the intensity and interpretation of the action instead of, as is too often the case, competing for the viewer's attention. Inevitably viewers tend to watch the big screen, so that the acting on stage seems like a drama being staged for the camera, which, of course, it is, but cutting back and forth from action on the stage to the video disrupts the continuity of the stage action, weakening instead of strengthening the projected intensity.

Two scenes, however, illustrate the efficacy and potential for dramatic enhancement this mixed-media approach offers the director. In one, the soldiers play with a Russian *matryoshka* doll, discovering one ever-smaller doll within the other until each soldier begins to lick and suck his individual toy. The action, shot close-up by the video cameraman and exaggerated into an overtly sexual act, underscores the longing and loneliness of the soldiers while stressing their camaraderie and boyishness as they act out their homoerotic bond. The tight video intensifies the sexuality and grotesqueness of their play with the dolls, an effect that otherwise would have been difficult to achieve, the action possibly indecipherable to the distant audience. The other scene depicts one of the soldiers in agony after being wounded, shouting desperately for help from his comrades, some of whom have deserted him while others are pinned down by Soviet machine gun fire. The solder, eerily lit in a distressingly close shot, manages finally to find his rifle, swallow the barrel and shoot himself to death. The effect on the audience is palpable, and the use of the video projected on the huge screen offers the viewers little distance from the immediacy and violence of the act.

When Smeds leaves the video in his toy box, his focus appropriately returns to a startling fresh theatrical language through which to viscerally tell the story. At one point, the soldiers attack the metal liners of washing machines with sledgehammers, capturing the violence, noise and senseless destruction of war and rendering much of the video work, by contrast, unnecessary. It seems as if Smeds, who obviously is not interested in a strict re-telling of Linna's novel, did not trust his own stagecraft and felt the need to reinforce the narrative with his clever cinematic devices. His strategy creates three plays in one: a raucous musical, a video show, and a meta-linguistic metaphorical performance. This is fine if each element is integrated, but in this performance the various elements compete or interfere with each other, disrupting instead of advancing the narrative flow.

Disrupting narrative is, granted, a legitimate postmodern technique when used to question the viability of logical connections (the bugbear of David Hume's demolition of cause and effect), but when the effect is merely annoying, clearly the application needs to be reconsidered.

Smeds' *The Unknown Soldier* did cause a calculated effect: it reinvigorated interest in theatre in a country where many critics feel the theatre has become static and, to some, irrelevant to the contemporary lives of its citizens. Suddenly, here was a play that people were not only talking but also arguing about. Politicians were less amused than outraged, even those who had not seen it.

"At the time of the premiere there was a big fuss about the play in the Finnish media. The adaptation of Smeds was said to be too modern, too politically incorrect and not patriotic enough. For example Prime Minister Matti Vanhanen and Foreign Minister Ilkka Kanerva were able to judge the play beforehand without even seeing it for themselves" (Arhinmäki).

Newspaper critics fawned, agreeing that Smeds' production was the play of the decade. A Russian magazine, *Kommersant*, gushed after its premiere that it was the most important theatre event of the month. Many of Smeds' colleagues, wary of being accused of sour grapes (the play sent Smeds' reputation into overdrive), usually parried suggestions that the performance was overrated by suggesting it could only properly be understood in a Finnish context. It was, after all, designed to be iconoclastic. It dealt irreverently (no matter how accurately in its essence) with the sacred text of Finnish literature, it attacked the politicians of contemporary Finland, and it was staged at The National Theatre, the revered hall — cathedral, in some minds — of all that is patriotically synonymous with Finnish culture.

One of the most important aspect of the "Finnish context" alluded to by Smeds' apologists is the director's re-examination of the mythical Finnish character. Finns are described in their own literature as angry, stubborn, shy, dysfunctional, resentful, and more interested in sports than politics. And in the face of the new Finland, where individualism is replacing community values, and the welfare system is threatened by privatization, the common man feels impotent and increasingly irrelevant. Ostensibly depicting a war considered by many to have been avoidable, even unnecessary, that was particularly nasty, brutal and ultimately futile (the Finns suffered a humiliating defeat, reduced to selling their wedding rings to pay reparation to the Soviets), Smeds holds a mirror up to Linna's engagement with the phenomenon of war to reflect the current state of Finnish culture and its pressing social issues. The idea is to shock complacent citizens into reassessing their government and inspire them, if not to direct action, at least to recognize their current situation.

Drawing parallels to the exploitation of the masses during the run up to the disastrous Continuation War, and the manipulation of people today through deceitful marketing and appeals to patriotism, propagandistic advertising strategies and empty promises of affluence through globalization, sacrifice and hard work, Smeds creates an anti-war and anti-authoritarian performance. By his clever manipulation of poetic images, he tries to restore both social and artistic integrity to theatre.

Whether his attempt was successful is a matter of sensibility. Clearly, with appropriate qualification (not available from the Finnish chattering classes) his adaptation of Linna's classic was a radical media success and a source of national pride in the new Finnish aesthetics.

Mika Myllyaho's version of *The Unknown Soldier* is purposely a more traditional treatment than Smeds'. Performed as part of Helsinki's summer theatre program, the production resembles regional historical theatre once popular in tourist areas, where historical organizations team with university theatre groups to produce crowd pleasers like *The Lost Colony* and *Unto These Hills*. As in those parochial productions, the audiences patronizing the summer festival in Helsinki are invariably mainstream and expect a rather straightforward play without much deviation from Linna's original text.

Myllyaho's approach is not without its clever aesthetic surprises. The location itself, on the fortress island of Suomenlinna, allows him to exploit the contemporary mode of site-specific theatre. The setting of the play is not a semblance but a space where the action might actually occur. The space reinforces the theme, not metaphorically but ecologically, integrating place with action.

The audience gathers outside the massive stone walls of the fort until a soldier appears in uniform above the main gates and declares that the performance is beginning. Entering through the brick arches, the audience must navigate through a narrow channel — at one point having to stoop single file to squeeze through a portal gateway into the performance area. The impact of being part of a defensive team under siege is immediate.

The split bleacher seats surround a dirt center space, a low barracks structure squats behind it, and to the rear a wooden platform overhangs the barracks. As the audience files in, the soldiers are playing a sloppy tavern-style folk-blues, a lighthearted ditty that serves as a wistful prelude to the seriousness of the task ahead. The effect reinforces the barracks mentality already established by the site-specific location. The soldiers' goofing around expresses both the naivety of young untested recruits who will soon have any romantic notions of combat shattered by the actual violence of war and a haunting nihilism, a macabre dance of death, an existential abandonment of identity in the face of certain annihilation. Myllyaho uses a light hand here, not overplaying the fatalism but effectively contrasting the soldiers' initial innocence with the reality of what will come. Their horseplay resembles that of a team in a locker room before an important match, the laughter masking fear, the boisterousness a sign of nerves, the sentimentality a defense mechanism designed to deflect the audacity of their duty.

As Myllyaho says, "They are teenagers. They are so young. When I walk the streets and see these kids — eighteen, nineteen — I think: they are fighting these wars. It's incredible."

One of the elements most faithful to Linna's text is Myllyaho's juxtaposition of comic relief and sheer terror, of the silly schoolboy antics with the heroism and fatal sacrifice of men in violent conflict suffering and dying in miserable conditions for a cause lost before they began. The battle action is economically played across the meager space of dirt, allowing Myllyaho to contain the sprawl of the novel but also to underscore the small area of land — in the human scheme of things — the men are dying for. They attack across the dirt and then turn around and fight their way back again.

Especially effective is Myllyaho's use of freeze-frame, during which the soldiers suddenly stop in action — as if caught in a photograph — while one of the soldiers addresses the audience and comments on the action. In one sequence, a soldier hand delivers a bullet from the barrel of a rifle to the back of a Russian prisoner slowly across the stage while discoursing on killing. Myllyaho admits he intentionally employed this Brechtian device to allow the players to explain, from their individual perspectives, the nature of their characters and the action to the audience. The use of these cinematic and "epic" effects (Brecht's term for exposing the illusion of verisimilitude in theatrical performances) can appear sophomoric and interrupt the flow of action, and Myllyaho takes a few chances in his application of the technique, but more often than not the strategy effectively isolates and highlights significant scenes.

Less effective is his deviation from the text to flesh out the stories of a few of the women who in the novel are peripheral characters. Their involvement is fine when they are used as foils to reflect the desperation of the soldiers and their desire to retain some sense of normalcy in the absurdity of their situation, but to dwell on the lives of the women seems imposed and gratuitous, not intrinsic, and this subplot adds nothing to the overall impact of Linna's original theme. Myllyaho is more successful when he sticks to the stuff that matters: the tragic comedy of men in no-win situations, fighting with no clear understanding of what they are fighting for or why; their contempt for their fastidious officers, who are obsessed with rules and formulas while the men under their command kill and die; the petty and fatal loyalties and betrayals by which the men measure the worth of their existence.

Given the nature of the text, the audience's reverence for it and the purpose of the venue, Myllyaho manages to capture the essence of the novel without compromising his aesthetic integrity. Minor anachronisms could seem gimmicky and unnecessarily intrusive, but Myllyaho seamlessly blends these devices into the narrative to provide both verisimilitude and contemporary context. When the soldiers have taken a village — one of their early small victories in their struggle against the Soviets — they admire a Finnish tank which they pathetically assume will increase their chances of winning (Soviet tanks outnumbered Finnish thirty to one). The tank is a battery-operated remote controlled toy. The point, of course, is to highlight the soldiers' naivety. They thought they were in for a quick success with superior forces. Likewise, the pop songs played as pathetically as a cheap USO show to alleviate the stress of combat only intensify it, contrasting the soldiers' outward nonchalance with their actual apprehension. In the novel, Soviet tanks plague the men, so the use of the toy is an appropriate expression, psychologically and emblematically, of their desire to reduce this threat to something manageable and harmless. Meanwhile, the songs serve as leitmotifs and reminders of the surreal experience of war.

Myllyaho's adaptation works best when he resists pretending that it is anything other than a crowd-pleasing visualization of the most popular novel in Finnish history. His production is patriotic without being patronizing, a traditional treatment that seems fresh, expressing the fragility of life and the arbitrariness of death at the center of Linna's novel. Myllyaho debunks the romance of war and nationalism with the grim reality of combat. His sympathies, like Linna's, are clearly with the soldiers as they try to make the best of a bad situation. He combines faithfulness to the text with adroit visual stimulation to lift the performance out of the mundane, creating an authentic theatrical experience.

Both Myllyaho and Smeds depict war as nasty, freaky and chaotic, an adrenaline rush that leaves the combatants feeling both exhilarated and guilty. They also exemplify the trouble with much of Finnish theatre: as directors search for innovative techniques in their impulsive need for something "new," they discover clichés. The self-referential tricks employed by Myllyaho too often have no metaphorical or thematic context within the action, and so the use of these strategies seems designed only to satisfy the whim of the director. In Smeds' production, he abandons all pretense of "story-telling," an effective device if employed as part of a coherent scheme, but his ubiquitous use of video and his facile insults directed at government officials diminish the other more powerful aspects of his production. Like many young directors just coming to power in Finland, both Myllyaho and Smeds feel obliged to sample strategies from Castorf and the more radical Lithuanian directors, and especially in the case of Smeds this fealty to these earlier innovative dramaturges now seems more derivative than authentically fresh or original.

One of the best indications of Finland's new sense of internationalization is evident in Martina Marti's *7/1 Sons* (*7/1 veljestä*), which had its premiere at Q theatre and was later produced on the small stage of the Tampere Workers Theatre during the 2008 Tampere International Theatre Festival. Marti is a French-speaking Swiss who learned Finnish "out of necessity" when she moved to Finland after taking her degree at Canterbury, England. Her script — a one-man performance — derives from one of the most classical of Finnish texts, *The Seven Brothers* (*Seitsemän vlajestä*) by Aleksis Kivi, published in 1870, the first novel written in the Finnish language.

Even more interesting — and perhaps bizarre — is that Marti had the courage (or gall) to take on, as a foreigner and a woman, another of the sacred texts in the canon of Finnish literature, which also happens to be the essential study of Finnish masculinity embodied in a myth of the untamed wilderness spirit that is finally civilized in an emasculation ritual of domesticity, achieved through education, civic duty and marriage. Parallels can be found in tales about settling the American West, in which a savage inhospitable nature had to be cleared, cultivated and made safe for settlement and commerce. But Marti brings a stylistic and thematic feminine touch to what is traditionally a rite of passage for male Finnish directors who must come to terms with the definitive Ur text of what it means to be a male in Finland.

Kivi tells the story of seven brothers who live in a Finnish country village, circa 1860. The father is a failed farmer and a drunk who is killed by a bear while hunting. The mother tries to raise the boys, but they grow up rough and uncouth. When the mother dies, the boys, now ranging in age from eighteen to twenty-five, are left with some land but without the discipline, knowledge or inclination to manage it. Illiterate, they are also deemed social misfits because during this period the church stressed literacy as a civilizing tool (and a way to salvation, as a parishioner was expected to be able to read the scriptures). The boys resist the influences of the church and school and prefer to continue living as anti-authoritarian ruffians, more interested in drinking and fighting than literacy. They manage in one of their drunken evenings to burn down their sauna. To complicate their familial relationships, they all fall in love with the same woman, a village wench named Venla. In its reformist zeal the church refused to marry anyone who could not read, so the boys, frustrated and outcast, decide to withdraw from society and move further into the woods.

They lease their home and roam like nomads through the forest. At one point, they try to settle down, but they stay so drunk they burn down their new home and have to return to their original house and beg the renters to let them live there. One day, foraging like nomads, they shoot a bear on a wealthy landowner's property (revenge for their father's death) and are attacked by the man's herd of bulls. The boys take shelter on a rock, but after several days they are starving and decide they must shoot all the bulls or die. They massacre the landowner's herd and when they reach safety they confess to the man what they have done, offering him the meat from the bulls as reparation, but the man refuses their payment and demands cash. The boys return to their original homestead, and this time they grow enough grain to pay off their debt.

During these epic travails, one of the brothers has a religious vision: the devil says he is his friend and invites him to the moon with him. On the moon, the brother finds a tower made of boot leather, and from this vantage he witnesses the destruction of the world. He glides back to earth on a piece of leather on which is written a warning in red, that the brothers will be destroyed. Heeding this omen, the brothers decide to return to civilization and work to urbanize the wilderness. They ask forgiveness from all the people they abused in their past and work to atone for their sins. The youngest learns to read and becomes a scholar. All but the one who had the vision find wives — the eldest marries Venla — and they settle down to lead productive lives.

The original story has been performed in a variety of styles throughout Finland's modern history, but the tendency these days, evident in an adaptation by another male director, Mikko Roiha, confronting his gender-performance demons, is to situate the brothers in contemporary Finland. Reshaping Kivi's nineteenth century text into an unblinking critique of the country's disillusioned youth — jobless, bored, idle, resentful, with no ideological allegiance — Roiha casts the boys as an inner-city gang who must develop a social conscience. They attack rival gangs and the elderly with equal glee and abandon, retreat into a head-banging band, drink and fight, their raucous escapades punctuated by superstitious visions and fear of divine punishment.

Staged during the 2008 Tampere Festival at the Tampere Workers Theatre, the opening scenes are played on the extreme downstage area on a narrow space between a huge curved black backdrop and the edge of the stage. The opening action — the father's death, the mother's despair, the priest's frustrations, the impatience of the townsfolk — play out in the gray claustrophobic enclave at the foot of the stage. The wooden backdrop rises only to allow the dead to enter and to remind the boys of their lost youth and innocence as they pound on the implacable divider. When the backdrop is finally raised completely, a magical stage reveals wild images and scenes from the novel, expanding the story to illustrate the learning curve the boys must experience on their trip from savagery to civilized behavior.

School and textbooks become both defensive and offensive weapons that the boys trash in rebellion. A drunken couple addicted to television occupies their former home. Their sauna is a deep pit that literally explodes from their clash of egos. Violent visions of divine wrath constantly threaten them.

While the success of Roiha's poetically relocating the play from the nineteenth century to the twenty-first is in part based on the audience's familiarity with the original, allowing him to rethink and de-familiarize the images without alienating the audience from the narrative, he sticks fairly closely to the original text.

Marti, in her version, deviates almost completely from the original, a process that relies even more on the audience being familiar with Kivi's novel. She combines, in a sort of gestalt theatrical device, traits of all seven broth-

Top: Mikko Roiha's adaptation of *The Seven Brothers* by Aleksis Kivi reshapes the original nineteenth century text into an unblinking critique of Finland's disillusioned youth—jobless, bored, idle, resentful, with no ideological allegiance. Here, their sauna is a deep pit exploding in a clash of egos. *Bottom:* In *The Seven Brothers*, director Mikko Roiha maps the learning curve the brothers make from savagery to civilized behavior. In their journey from being an inner-city gang to becoming integrated citizens with a fully developed social conscience, violent visions of divine wrath constantly threaten them (both photographs by Jyrki Tervo).

ers into one, represented by Juhani, the eldest (thus the title *7/1*— seven brothers in one). Adapted by Anna Viitala, and incorporating improvisation from the young Finnish actor Jussi Nikkilä, the idea remains faithful to Kivi's intent — even the rap songs are taken directly from his text.

Metaphorically, Marti decided that the key to understanding the story was to focus on the notion of retreat. Just as the brothers retreated from their home to the wilderness to reform their lives, Marti depicts a more contemporary form of retreat, having Juhani withdraw to a small apartment and live as an urban recluse.

Explaining why, for her debut performance in Finland, she chose to adapt one of the most significant novels in Finnish literary history, Marti claims that it was a natural choice. To learn something about the essence of her adopted country, she felt a classic text like *The Seven Brothers* would be the best source for exploring the character of the Finnish people. After all, she wondered, why was this text so important to Finns? What was it about the novel that made it so culturally significant? And like Roiha, while exploring historical aspects of the story, she wanted to make a connection between the Finland of Kivi's novel and the contemporary Finland in which she was living. As a practical matter, Marti knew that the Finnish audience could recite the text by heart, so there was no need for her to re-tell it and she could instead experiment with the familiar aspects of the story, manipulating them to fit her vision of the action.

In a larger context, she reads the novel as an allegory, delineating the process of becoming human, tracing the path from primitive existence to a civilized state. This process can also be cast in Freudian terms, as the brothers must learn to control the impulsive behavior sparked by their collective id and develop a sense of super-ego through which they sublimate their desires and create, instead of anarchy, productive social projects. Focusing on one of the brothers but incorporating all seven of the characters into one allows her to concentrate the essence of Kivi's theme.

Beyond these abstractions, there is still the very literal story of the brothers and their adventures that Marti wanted to transpose. The action opens with Nikkilä, as the actor in the play, speaking directly to the audience, narrating the well-known vision of the brother's trip to the moon with the devil. He also introduces himself and the play, but soon tires of telling the story because he assumes the audience already knows it. He reads from the novel, skipping huge passages, until he gets to the part where the brothers leave their village for the wilderness and decides to begin his presentation of the story there, in the moment of withdrawal.

While sticking to Kivi's text, Marti transforms key episodes from the novel the way James Joyce, for instance, translates scenes from *The Odyssey* into images in modern Dublin. Juhani's kitchen table, for instance, acts as the rock of refuge that in the novel saved the brothers from the bulls, while in Marti's depiction the bulls are merely people from the city that terrify Juhani in a fit of agoraphobia. To connect the interests of contemporary Finnish youth with the travails of Kivi's character, Marti has Juhani rap parts of the narrative through a microphone, just like any other teenager entertaining himself with contemporary electronic media.

To prevent the audience from slipping too far into the familiar story, and in order to keep them attuned to new aspects of the text, she disrupts the expected narrative events with improvisation. Juhani listens silently to Venla, the country girl from the novel, the object of desire for all the brothers, softly singing next door. Her voice reminds Juhani of the beautiful but destructive attraction of desire, drawing him, like a moth to a flame, toward temptation from the world outside. At Christmas, in despair, he tries to hang himself with his microphone cord, but then he hears Venla singing through the walls, and he remembers a story of a beautiful maiden saved by a prince. He decides to leave his apartment, convinced that one day he will achieve a middle-class version of happiness: a wife and a child, a house in suburbia, a cliché that Marti acknowledges but explains by suggesting that his vision is one of hope, a future without destruction.

Revisiting classics and adapting them to contemporary situations, while not a new phenomenon, has reemerged as a sub-genre in Finland as in other European countries — especially "young" ones like the Baltic States — that utilize a relatively small reservoir of traditional literary texts both to celebrate the rich nationalistic themes inherent in their literary histories and to question and critique those very nationalistic tendencies — to explore the idea of "national characters" and map their evolution in the rapidly changing "New Europe." This revisionism tends to relocate historical works — like Shakespeare's — within a relevant contemporary social context that keeps those works vital, significant and alive as the various cultures are assimilated into the greater geo-political entity of the European Union. But while Shakespeare has become global property, Finnish works like *The Unknown Soldier* and *The Seven Brothers* maintain historical and social references that keep them culturally specific, a colonization Shakespeare's plays continue to resist.

The same holds for Ilmari Kianto's *The Red Line* (*Punainen viiva*), a work published in 1908 that evokes nationalistic sentiments in its audience before they even take a seat. And while some directors are interested in staging a retelling of the text, others will exploit the audience's expectations to probe those very assumptions.

One such deconstructionist director is Juha Luukkonen. His adaptation of *The Red Line* is re-titled *An Ideological Karaoke Night in the Non-Ideolog-*

ical Finland (*Aatteellinen karaokeilta aatteettomassa Suomessa*). Luukkonen situates Kianto's realistic classic in a landscape of garish, neon-lit internet cafes and karaoke clubs. A cabin in the forest is a boxing ring. The couple's starving children are plastic baby dolls. Creatures of the forest, most prancing through song and dance routines in reindeer suits, threaten the sanctity of home. The infamous bear of the novel makes eerie emotionless speeches to the audience, removing its mask to reveal only the implacable face of nature.

The original text was published before the rise of Socialism and the Finnish Civil War, which pitted the Reds against the Whites; still, the novel is remarkably prescient and in retrospect can be interpreted as an allegory. The bear from the east warns that he will kill if he is awakened, and the identification of socialism as a means of political reform is explicit. In the end the social democrats do win, but their victory seems futile and irrelevant when the bear kills the common man. The evocation of the color red is associated with the bear, with the east, and with the awakened threat that leads to death. In Finnish history, given the nation's struggle to remain free from at first Russian and then Soviet dominance, the story is hauntingly accurate and the national poetic themes even more acute in hindsight.

However poetically Luukkonen transforms the original, the story is rendered with a clarity that matches the naturalism of the novel. Topi and Riika live a life of not-so-quiet desperation as they try to cope with the deprivations of the Finnish wilderness. They argue and dream and despair but can do nothing to mitigate their hardship. The unctuous, officious local vicar offers only platitudes and piety, offering to bury the couple's children at a discount because they are so small he can use one coffin.

Meanwhile, rumors of a new political movement — social democracy — are circulating among the villages, and soon the Agitator arrives preaching the gospel of reform. The citizens debate the pros and cons of the new policies, pitting the church and reactionaries against the working poor and the radical politicians representing them. Torn between the doctrines of the social reformers and the traditions of the church, they hold the election. (The first formal election in Finland took place in 1907.) The illiterate voters are instructed to draw a red line on the ballot. The socialists win the election, but the awakened bear kills Topi, slitting his throat and leaving a red line of blood on the ground.

In Luukkonen's direction, the melodramatic elements of the story are subverted by cynicism and absurdity. Arguments are settled in the boxing ring. The Agitator uses media appeal and music to convey his message. Unusually for a Finnish play, the operating tenor of the performance smacks of *commedia dell'arte*. The scenes are crowded with caricatures and clowns. The acting is overly stylized, so that any sense of realistic psychological identifica-

Heikki Pirhonen (left) and Sanna Kemppainen in Juha Luukkonen's adaptation of Ilmari Kianto's *The Red Line* staged at Lappeenranta City Theatre. Luukkonen exploits the audience's expectations to probe romantic sentiments of Finnish nationalism. In Luukkonen's direction, the melodramatic elements of the story are subverted by cynicism, absurdity and metaphorical imagery. Unusual for a Finnish play, the operating tenor of the performance smacks of *commedia dell' arte*. The scenes are crowded with caricatures and clowns (photograph by Ari Nakari).

tion with the characters is flattened. And to intensify Kianto's central theme — the dominance of nature over the petty ideals of mankind — Luukkonen inserts his own political observations into the text of the play, attacking organized religion with Nietzschean zeal and peppering the audience with leftist ideological commentary. More controversially, he includes provocative quotations from Pentti Linkola, a radical Finnish environmentalist and misanthrope best known for his apocalyptic proclamations promoting genocide and eugenics to control population. But political inanities, Church hypocrisy and the imaginative inadequacies of the middle-class are easy targets, and Luukkonen's production is weakest when he indulges his prejudices against these convenient red herrings.

Invective is the least effective means of theatrical polemics; it too easily becomes the very rhetorical drivel against which the speaker rails, even when

Anne Niilola in *The Red Line*. In Juha Luukkonen's version, the infamous bear of the novel makes eerie emotionless speeches to the audience, removing its mask to reveal only the implacable face of nature (photograph by Ari Nakari).

In *The Red Line*, Juha Luukkonen situates Ilmari Kianto's realistic classic in a landscape of garish neon, internet cafes and karaoke clubs. Both domestic and political quarrels are settled by simulating professional wrestling matches. The acting is overly stylized, so that any sense of realistic psychological identification with the characters is flattened (photograph by Ari Nakari).

the critique is couched in the mouthpiece of a charmingly outlandish manikin with a microphone. Luukkonen's best strategy is irony, as when he transforms the schlock of a karaoke bar into a reverential chapel of solace for the disaffected. In his view, Finland has become a nation of isolated souls suffering from extreme loneliness and lacking any sense of communality, victims of a new world driven by empty technology and capitalistic ethics. At least in public karaoke bars, people can create a comfortable self-image, not unlike religious identifications in the past, and can recover a sense of place in the community. The neighborhood bar — the church that houses the altar of karaoke — has become the new nexus of localism. The participants bond through mutual recreation, creating idealized selves that are as transcendent as any religious identification — and in the balkanized world of the post–Soviet era more fun and more relevant. The religion of escapism and disengagement is as viable a response to anomie as political or social activism.

But to old-school contrarians like Mikko Viherjuuri, resident director at Tampere Theatre, these "experiments" in style associated with Luukkonen's productions, in the end, offer nothing new. "Attack on form is old," he says. "Imagination can blow up any form, but you get nowhere if you don't work through the actor to reach the audience."

Viherjuuri believes that the current crop of metaphorical and physical theatre is nothing more than a rehash of the political avant-garde popular during the 1970s, and even those productions merely represent the refried formalism of Meyerhold, Brecht, Kantor and others. His position implies that any successful production depends on the actor's capacity to emotionally engage the audience; no matter how intellectual the performance, the audience must connect the action to their own human experiences.

As for the success of a play being attributed to a strong director, and the current cachet afforded the Lithuanians, Viherjuuri is incredulous. For him, the actor's craft is the most effective and necessary element in the making of a successful production. Contrary to contemporary trends, he diminishes the role of the director.

"Directors should not be clever," he says. "They should be wise."

For Viherjuuri, the point of theatre is to get the audience to believe the experience, and this process does not rely on the director's signature. No matter how radical the form, "the play needs good actors."

He admits that the process is different if the point is to stage a "happening," which usually lacks a narrative, often involves improvisation and audience participation, and tends to flow spontaneously, creating surprise without the framework of a plot. Viherjuuri concedes that there is, indeed, a difference between performance and "reality," though he is not much interested in trendy explorations of the phenomenological distinctions between the two.

"Theatre by its nature is the most naturalistic form of art," he explains. "And illusion is the key. The director must get the show from the stage to the audience, and the only way to do that is through the actor."

The trick is not to create illusion, as in self-conscious theatre designed to expose itself, but to erase the illusion, so that the actual performance occurs in the imagination of the viewer.

"Theatre is pretending," he says. "But the minute the audience thinks the actor is pretending, the actor loses contact and it's over."

Viherjuuri suggests that the predominance of strong directors and self-conscious productions is not as important in Finland as it is, for instance, in Germany, where theatre is more political and the *auteur* tradition is stronger. Finnish dramaturges are by tradition and inclination text-based, preferring to work through the script with the writer and actors, privileging the play and discounting the artistic "vision" of the director.

While resisting the fad of promoting the director as *auteur*, Viherjuuri likewise does not believe good directors need to be trained as actors. In his view, directors can bring experiences to a production from diverse areas of experience; in the end, the director's job is to facilitate the acting. If the purpose of the production is to address the form of the performance, actors become secondary tools in the manipulation of theatrical elements, and though this tactic might generate an intellectual response, the result is usually cold, cerebral and merely interesting. Viherjuuri prefers life-enriching theatre from which the audience, immersed in the illusion, emerges as if from a dream. For him, only skillful acting, not a director's clever schemes, produces this transposition.

As a model for good acting, Viherjuuri looks to the actors trained in the United States, where he has worked extensively. He cites the influence of the Moscow Theatre, which is much more pronounced in the U.S. than in Finland.

"In the States," he says, "actors use their own personalities — as if they fear physicality — creating a more subtle style — lightly believable. Finnish acting — and directing — is more heavy-handed."

In his opinion, Finnish actors and directors need to move toward more subtlety, but "light acting is difficult for Finns," he says, and he hopes that the academies will soon begin to train actors "not as engineers but as violin players."

5

Performing in the Duck Pond: Finland-Swedish Theatre

Finland's Swedish minority is not considered a minority in the sense that they are excluded from any constitutional guarantees. They are fully integrated citizens, vital to the social fabric of the country, though they account for only six percent of the population (approximately 300,000 people). They maintain a completely separate educational system, separate theatres, radio and television stations, and proportionally more members in their own writers' association than their counterparts, the Finns. Constitutionally, "state authorities support Swedish cultural life 'on an equal basis'" (Ahlfors 4).

Yet, as assimilated as they are, their status, given this cultural divide, leads to some awkward tautological phrases, such as when then President of the Finnish Theatre Centre Raija-Sinikka Rantala, in a 1998 edition of *Finnish Theatre* dedicated to the country's Swedish-speaking theatres, distinguishes Swedish-speaking Finns from "Finnish Finns" (2). Still, the thriving Swedish-speaking community does provide, in the view of Rantala, "an impressive resource in the Finnish scheme of things" (2).

Like that of its Hanseatic neighbors in the nineteenth century, Finland's early formal theatre can be traced to the influence of Germany's touring companies. (The opening performance in 1827 at Finland's first city theatre was in German.) But Finland's natural political, cultural and historical affinities were with Sweden. (Swedish was the official language of Finland until 1863.) And while most commentators define the roots of traditional Finland-Swedish theatre as "Scandinavian," based in Stanislavski and psychological realism, there are some major differences between Swedish theatre proper and that of the Finland-Swedes.

The established companies still productive within the contemporary network of Finland-Swedish theatre are the Swedish Theatre in Helsinki (Svenska Teatern), Turku Swedish Theatre (Åbo Svenska Teater), and Wasa Theatre

(Wasa Teater) in the northern region of Ostrobothnia. The Swedish Theatre dates back to the nineteenth century. It is an imposing building situated along Mannerheim Boulevard and adjacent to the Esplanade, a fashionable section in the center of Helsinki just above the old harbor and market square. The building houses four proscenium stages and employs over 80 staff and actors. The theatre boasts an average of 12 premieres a year with an average annual audience attendance over 100,000. The Turku Swedish Theatre occupies Finland's oldest theatre building. It usually manages six premieres a year with an average of over 200 performances and an annual attendance of over 25,000. Located in a mainly Finnish-speaking part of the country, the Turku Swedish Theatre serves the Swedish-speaking community by its extensive touring theatre program. Wasa Theatre is the only professional Swedish-language theatre in Ostrobothnia, in the north of Finland. Its main stage seats 270, and its studio 80. Like its counterpart in Turku, Wasa maintains an active touring program that serves the region's schools and educational establishments.

The complaints about the major theatres like the Swedish, Turku and Wasa sound familiar. Even though all three of these huge and historically important houses offer smaller stages and programs designed to encourage and develop new and often experimental work, they exist primarily to satisfy an audience that continues to demand the standard fare for large production companies: musicals, classics and popular imports heavy on psychological realism, all featuring well-known stars of the repertory theatre. A professor from the academy responding to a query about Turku Theatre replied, wryly, that Turku rented its first floor to McDonald's, and rejoined, "That says it all." The publicity literature available from all three of these major theatres stresses popular entertainment in the form of musicals like *Evita* and *The Sound of Music*, comedies like *The 39 Steps*, stand-up, improvisation, and specially commissioned Finland-Swedish plays. All three are also involved in children's theatre, including educational programs.

Like their Finnish-language counterparts, the smaller, more independent theatres — some outlaws, others government sponsored but operating at the fringe — allow writers, actors and directors more freedom to pursue independent collaborative performances without necessarily having to worry about catering to the bourgeois expectations of an audience that does not come to theatre to have their views challenged. Of course, the problem with financing through the grants process keeps the wolf perpetually at the door. Ideally, the remedy for funding problems would be to attract a more sophisticated audience of young viewers whose expectations of theatre are more in line with those currently at the cutting edge of theatrical performances, but most cultural directors agree that this is not happening and that, in fact, drawing an audience from the thirty to fifty year old demographic has proven extremely difficult. Of the smaller houses, Klockrike Theatre (Klockriketeatern) and Viirus have established themselves as two of the most innovative, producing original, progressive performances. Other important independent companies include the several theatres loosely aligned with Universe (Universum), the Sirius Theatre (Sirius Teatern), Mars Theatre (Teater Mars) and Venus (Teatteri Venus).

To understand the contemporary situation of Finland-Swedish theatre, it is instructive to view the developments as part of a continuum that parallels movements throughout most of modern Western Europe.

In its simplest form, the recent history of progressive Finland-Swedish theatre can be reduced to three phases. Theatre in the 1960s, as in most Western countries, began to focus on social and political themes, stressing a message and call to action. The late 1970s and 1980s were the era of postmodernism, when the emphasis was on questioning the nature of performance and the notion of theatre itself. The new theatres support the emergence of radical feminist voices, an awareness of physicality and metaphor, and the importation of new styles from the international community, especially from what was until the 1990s considered Eastern Europe.

In Finland-Swedish theatre, personalities like Martin Kurtén and later Dick Idman are associated with the early stages, having come of age in the sixties. Kurtén was also a product of the traditional Swedish training system with a heavy emphasis on the Stanislavski model, a process he carried into the Swedish Institute and which Idman continued during his tenure at the Academy. Idman continues to play a major role in all aspects of theatre, in both the Finnish and Finland-Swede communities, famously declaring that he wanted to separate art from culture—meaning that sipping Chardonnay and pontificating about modern art was not synonymous with the rigorous task of producing authentic emblems of the human experience. The writer and director Joakim Groth and his brother Marcus, an actor, cut their teeth during the postmodern period, integrating Gestalt psychology into a system of actor-training that produced an acutely naturalistic approach, as opposed to the pretentious, emotional style in vogue in popular theatres at the time. The brothers have maintained their independent spirit with their work at Mars Theatre, which gives them the freedom to experiment outside their bread-and-butter work with the more established theatres.

Many of the new personalities are graduates of the Theatre Academy, trained in the international style stressed by Erik Söderblom. A short list includes Paula Rehn-Sirén from Pure Theatre (Rena Teatern), Jakob Öhrman, Elmer Bäck and Rasmus Slätis from New Ramp Theatre (Nya Rampen), Kim Gustafsson from The Finland-Swedish Theatre (Finlandssvenska Teatern), Martin Bahne from Mestola Theatre (Teater Mestola), Pekka Strang from

The Little Theatre (Lilla Teatern), Sonja Ahlfors and Joanna Wingren of Blaue Frau, and Maria Lundström from Theatre 90^0 (Teater 90^0).

The new generation includes a plethora of new talent, much of it dispersed throughout the network of small, independent theatre companies. Most, like Pure Theatre, New Ramp and the groups collected within Universe symbiotically attach to an established theatre but remain free to experiment aesthetically, choosing a host that suits their purposes for different productions and helps with financing.

A common trait the Finland-Swedes share with the Finnish theatre — identified by both camps as a potential malady — is inherent in any small cultural clique: insularity. The Finns — especially neophytes trying to break into the establishment — complain that all of the major players have been to school together, have often dated or married one another and work together almost like a close-knit family suspicious of outsiders. In the case of the Finland-Swedes, this insularity has led playwright Bengt Ahlfors to point out, "Our audience base is small, our world is a closed one, there is a danger of inbreeding. In literature, there is talk of a 'confined space.' Most people know most other people" (4).

That was in 1998. By 2009, the situation had not changed. The major players of the 1990s are still in positions of influence; if anything, many of the younger Finland-Swedes working within the theatre market feel marginalized even within their own community, in part because more new actors are graduating from the Drama Academy than can be absorbed by the current job market, but also because the biting issue of cultural identity seems to play with more vigor outside of theatre — in the political arena, for instance, and the press — and is not shared by the larger general population; it festers among the Finland-Swedes, and paradoxically further insulates them as an identifiable minority.

Even with the sentimental and cultural connections between Sweden and the Finland-Swedish population, Ahlfors acknowledges differences between the two populations. First, the common language of the Finland-Swedes is historically different from Swedish and was deemed unacceptable by the establishment of the time as a language suitable for cultural performances. This schism between the Swedish cultural elite and the Finland-Swedes led in the nineteenth century to the creation of autonomous venues like the Swedish Indigenous Theatre in Turku and the Popular Theatre (Folkteater) in Helsinki, both of which promoted the artistic expression of life as lived by the Finnish-Swedish natives. When the Swedish National Theatre of Finland was established in 1915, "the Swedish actors went home to Sweden" and the indigenous line won a narrow victory" (8), although, among Swedish nationals, "prejudices against the Finland-Swedish way of doing things were still strong in the 1950s" (8).

Though the different priorities of style caused a decisive split between the high-minded Swedish practitioners and the Finland-Swedes, who preferred, in the tradition of Finland, more popular forms of common entertainment, there remained a continuity of style shared by the Swedes and the Finland-Swedes that continues into the contemporary theatre, a style that distinguishes Finland-Swedish productions from those of the Finnish-speaking theatres. Whereas the Finns experienced a major rebellion in the 1960s — using radical experiments with form to separate the more aesthetic, urbane and international style championed by the progressive artistic community from the "sweaty guy" amateurism that until then was the mainstay of traditional Finnish theatre — the Finland-Swedes retained a sophisticated nuance that favored more refined performances. In general, they continue to employ a lighter touch, more suitable in analytical plays stressing psychology and subtle irony.

Critics from both camps — the Finland-Swedes and the Finns — agree that the Finns lack the light touch and irony of true Scandinavian theatre (especially the Swedish variety) and tend to prefer a heavier, more melodramatic Finnish style. The operative cliché is that the Finnish actors tend to strip off their clothes and shout a lot. And while it is of course unfair to collectively describe Finns onstage as naked emoting hams, Finland-Swedish professionals do not hesitate to differentiate the Nordic style from the Scandinavian. Dick Idman, a former professor at the Theatre Academy, suggests that the Swedes "have a cultural heritage that comes more from the West (comedy, revue and farce) and we are less good at the blood, sweat and grime of which there is more in the Finnish tradition" (Jansson, "Finland-Swedish" 24). According to actress Mia Hafrén, "In the Finnish environment a lot more work went into the physical side of things, while we [Swedes] were more analytical and psychological" (24). Playwright and Finland-Swedish director Joakim Groth, discussing the Finnish production of one of his Swedish language plays, claims, "'In Finnish the play became heavier and sadder. [...] partly of course because Finland-Swedish comedy is lighter than the Finnish kind, more self-ironic'" (24). Adding a curious twist to the discussion of the difference between the styles, Erik Söderblom, former rector at the Theatre Academy, likens the Finnish theatre to rock music, suggesting that Finnish-speaking actors, like rock musicians, are not necessarily very skillful but produce interesting, if raw, performances.

Stereotypes, however, are not so easy to maintain. The usual complaints focus on those perennial bogeymen, class and nationalism. As Tomas Jansson points out, most of the clichés corresponding to Finland-Swedish theatre are "based on the notion that Finland-Swedes in general are upper-class [and] today there are no traces of that [...] background left" ("Finland-Swedish" 20).

Groth adds, "It's simply not the case that I would feel more comfortable in Sweden. [...] I have a context to work in here in Swedish Finland that makes me feel that what I do is important" (20).

These misperceptions may well have been debunked, or at least resolved years ago, but the complexity of living as a Swedish-speaking citizen of Finland continues to produce themes for dramatic exploration. Critics and artists agree that aesthetic concerns involving language, style and sensibility are the true markers that demarcate differences between the two populations and their approaches to theatre, but no matter how diplomats try to finesse this issue, using phrases like "different, not better" and "distinct, not superior to," the issue of identity within the Finland-Swedish minority is an essential fact of life underscoring their existential dilemma. Further, there remains a wisp of supremacy (not exactly arrogance) in the Finland-Swedes' sense of their acting tradition and current practice vis-à-vis Finnish performance values. Some dramaturges try to obviate the issue. Kristin Olsoni, a Finland-Swedish independent director, suggests that the difference in dramatic form between Finns and Finland-Swedes rests in the division "between people from the big theatre groups and people from the small theatre groups. Artistic form doesn't follow national boundaries" (22). Maybe so, but directors in, say, Lithuania would either scoff at this idea, or dismiss it as hopelessly naïve.

The sense among its community that Finland-Swedish theatre is special originates from its status as a hybrid form. It combines what Groth identifies as "the gravity of Finnish theatre" with the "lightness of Swedish theatre" (22). Living, as it were, between two cultures creates "a certain kind of lack of identity" (Jansson, "The Hunt" 26), and even though this existential condition continues to be explored thematically, the uniqueness of the Finland-Swedish theatre approach is more notable in dramatic technique than in the written content of specific thematically pointed work. The problem is similar to the theatre situation in a country, like again Lithuania, where directors dominate theatre productions. Because audiences are drawn to the presentation of the work — especially to how one director might reinterpret and stage her adaptation of a classic play — the emphasis on new writing is diminished. The directorial style reflects the contemporary operating ethos and ideology of the cultural situation more than the original scripts of young dramatists. The same is true of Finland-Swedish theatre: its uniqueness is based on its performance values more than any thematic textual content.

Still, Finland-Swedish identity theatre persists, not merely as a historical phenomenon but as a contemporary reality. As the Finland-Swedes were assimilated at the turn of the nineteenth century, and Sweden's geo-political influence waned, the Finland-Swedes continued to rely on classical Swedish texts without producing new work reflecting their actual life experience. This is changing, not only because Finland-Swedes continue to create identity-based texts that foreground the politics of national identity. Their status is not a choice, nor is it something that can be discarded as a snake sheds its skin. Identity politics do not necessarily predominate the concerns of Finland-Swedish writers. Many of the new breed tend to ignore their private cultural conundrums and focus instead on human events that connect cultures, that cross borders instead of defining or delineating them. But their minority status informs every willful decision in their lives. And this shift in focus from tribal issues to global themes — even within hybrids like the theatre of the Finland-Swedes — cannot mask their reality. What is new, and perhaps indicative of a new direction in Finland-Swedish theatre, is what might be defined as a turn to aesthetics. Cultural identity is no longer dependent on the text but is defined in its treatment. And even within this aesthetical approach, the Finland-Swedish theatre is actively experimenting with a more international style while not diminishing its unique situation.

As idealistic as this turn to aesthetics and a more international style sounds in theory, in practice, many of the leading theatre figures within the Finland-Swedish community remain skeptical. Actress and dramatist Paula Rehn-Sirén says flatly, "The identity issue will never be settled." As a child, she thought she should live in Sweden, but even there she would be considered an outsider. The reality of feeling like an outsider in Sweden or Finland, while speaking the language of one culture and having been born and raised in the other, creates in Rehn-Sirén's view a unique cultural conundrum, a community living between worlds in a "twilight" existence with only its peculiar language and cultural situation to unite it.

"Minority-language people produce good writers, especially poets," she says, "because the language is so important, the essence of cultural identity." This sense of cultural crisis also explains, in her view, why the Finnish-Swedes have such a strong audience allegiance to their theatres, motivated by a desire to keep the tradition inherent in the language alive and thriving.

In many ways Rehn-Sirén illustrates the typical situation for most Finland-Swedes pursuing a theatre career in Finland. She studied at the Swedish Institute of Acting at the Finnish Theatre Academy, the roots of which reach back to the Swedish Theatre of Helsinki, founded in 1908 mainly to promote Finland-Swedish as a serious language at a time when Swedish was the only language deemed acceptable for high culture. The training school evolved into the Helsinki Swedish Acting School, and then in 1979 into the Swedish Institute at the Theatre Academy. Recently, the institute began to stress bilingual cooperation. By 2009, for instance, one of the major professors of the Swedish students was Erik Söderblom, a Finn who survived training with the notorious Finnish director Jouko Turkka. But for the most part the two schools remain, if not culturally and ideologically, certainly artistically and technically segregated.

After matriculation, Rehn-Sirén joined the repertory at Turku Swedish Theatre (Åbo Svenska Teater), the oldest established theatre in Finland. She later moved to the Swedish Theatre in Helsinki (Svenska Teatern). Having spent three years working in repertory, she felt that she was not able to realize her potential and quit to begin freelancing. Whereas at the repertory theatres most of the actors work in three new plays a year, the roles are often uninspiring, and coupled with unpredictable personnel changes and personal conflicts, at the end of the day work in the repertory, at least for Rehn-Sirén, became stifling. She soon discovered that freelancing, though it offers the potential for more ambitious projects and challenging roles, has its drawbacks too, including an acute lack of financial security.

Undaunted when acting jobs became more sporadic and then sparse during the economic downturn after 2008, Rehn-Sirén began to focus on writing, producing her work through her own company, the Pure Theatre. She chose the name "Renan" because of its intentional ambiguity and multiple meanings in Swedish. It means pure and clean, but it can also connote chaos or disorder, as in a dinner party suddenly going awry, and it is also a play on her name, which incidentally is a homophone for the Swedish word for reindeer. Her love of word play is evident in her written work, which utilizes poetic elements of language, a minimalist dramatic form, and dialogue heavy on word games and free association.

Her first professionally produced play reflects her love of word play. *The Donkey Hot Show* (2000) phonetically recalls the English title of the classic Spanish novel from which she appropriated the two main characters, Quixote and Sancho Panza. In her contemporizing, the comical duo is involved in a television game show, tasked with performing good deeds in order to score points in the competition. The play, admittedly an exercise in juvenilia, was commissioned by the education department to tour throughout — significantly — Finnish-speaking high schools. The propagandistic function of the play in which one character speaks Finnish and the other Swedish, each at times mixing up the other's language in comical malapropisms, was to sensitize the Finnish students to the situation faced by the Swedish speaking communities as minorities. Ironically, the fact that the play was considered necessary underscores Rehn-Sirén's insistence that the identity crisis with the Swedish-speaking community is acute, persistent and perhaps irremediable.

Her next piece, designed for an adult audience but no less linguistically playful, was *Watercolored* (*Vattenfärgat*), which opened at Klockrike Theatre in 2008. The action is minimal. Two women — Rehn-Sirén and Nina Hukkinen (a well-known television personality) — sit on a bench on stage, fishing

and working out through a series of word games and free association our relationship with water and its importance in our lives. Directed by Mitja Sirén,
the play becomes a metaphorical discussion exploring how water has a will
of its own. Some critics read the play as an eco-political statement about con-
servation and preservation of perhaps our greatest natural resource, but Rehn-
Sirén insists, demurely, that the play for her was simply about "how water
colors our world."

Water figures in her next play too, *The Umbrella*, still in development
in 2009. Although Rehn-Sirén says the use of water is not a recurring motif
in her work, merely a coincidence, the image in this case becomes a convenient metaphor framing what she describes as a "poetical comedy [...] a love
story in three parts." In her minimalist style, the action is deceptively simple. A man has promised a woman that the next time it rains, he will visit
her. When it rains, they meet, and when the rain stops, he leaves her. Their
lives — and love life — become regulated by rain. The suggestive power of her
metaphor — feminine associations with water, nurturing, fertility rituals, and
the very notion of rain turning people inwards, toward each other — dovetails the mythical and practical connotations of rain into a powerfully light
treatise on the human habits of romance.

Not necessarily a strict essentialist, Rehn-Sirén does think women operate with a different theatrical language, whether directing or writing for stage.
She describes herself as producing "feministic theatre" but cautions against
reading too much into that characterization because the term "feminist" car-
ries too much political baggage to accurately depict the soulful method in her
work. And although she shares the concern of many women working within
the Finland-Swedish theatre (echoing complaints from the Finns too) regarding how women are underrepresented in the theatre-arts community, she has
noticed a recent upsurge in female voices emerging in contemporary theatre.
She cites with especial enthusiasm the work of Sonja Ahlfors and Joanna
Wingren, working under the aegis of Blaue Frau, and Maria Lundström from
Theatre 90°.

Another concern Rehn-Sirén passionately promotes is the development
of new plays by young dramatists writing in Finland-Swedish. She is vice
president of the Laboratory (Labbet), an organization begun by John Storgård
as part of the old, now defunct warehouse of the original Viirus Theatre before
establishing its independent status under the guidance of Anna Simberg. The
Laboratory offers courses in playwriting, actively tries to find producers for
plays, and maintains a bank of work by Swedish-speaking writers. The best
of these plays, she says, trend away from psychological realism and toward
experimental form, especially, she has noticed, toward surrealism.

The problem, she notes, is that most of the mainstream theatres are more interested in realistic drama, concerned about their audience's expectations and the proverbial bottom-line of their precarious profit margin, so experimental plays usually find outlets in the smaller, independent theatres. Timidity on the part of established theatres creates a vicious circle. They stifle creativity by rewarding new plays written in the old style while discouraging writing that challenges conventional forms. This tension between mainstream houses catering to audience expectations and young writers interested in a new theatre language is an ongoing problem. The two approaches will not be reconciled until the audiences demand more radical theatre, and for now, in both the Finland-Swedish and the Finnish theatre, this is not the case.

Although the Finland-Swedish theatre tends toward more conventional forms based on the Scandinavian model, radicalism is not stagnant. And one of the more resonant voices in the Finland-Swedish theatre community that best embodies both feminism and innovation belongs to Cris af Enehielm, an acting teacher in the Swedish Institute at the Theatre Academy. A freelance artist, director and choreographer who has been associated with the Academy for most of her professional life, af Enehielm joined the theatre department rather late in her career, and her appointment was controversial from the start. Some of her detractors felt that she was not qualified to teach acting, even though she was trained as an actor and graduated from the Theatre Academy. One reason may be that her primary passion and her early professional focus was dance, and she readily acknowledges the influence of dancers — especially, she says, the ones she met as a student trained in New York City — in her performances. Her stress on physicality, visual language, metaphor and hybrid performance values caused some of her students and colleagues in the field to suggest that her approach to formal acting was too eccentric.

Af Enehielm acknowledges that she is controversial, but in her view her provocative reputation is a result of the conservative values of her colleagues and of students that expect a more rigid training program. Academically trained actors, especially in the Swedish tradition, are notoriously regimented, very scheduled. The actors work on a strict timetable that resembles a business day; they work for a few hours, then take lunch, then work a bit more, then leave campus and pick up their work the next day, as if they were working in a nine-to-five job. Af Enehielm resists this regimentation, opting instead for a more intimate style of teaching; her students work not according to a set timetable but spontaneously, allowing the process to run a more natural course, the schedule dictated by the demands of the work at hand.

Af Enehielm also suggests that the more traditional teachers object to her relationship with the students. "I don't assume the position of pedagogue," she says. "I relate to the students as peers, because, you never know, I may be working with them in the near future in the professional world." She insists that her status says more about the conservative character of the Finland-Swedish theatre community than it does about her effectiveness as a professor.

Her methods are unconventional, at least by the established standards of the Swedish Institute. When she was a student, dance, art, acting and languages were interdisciplinary forms, not segregated as they are today. This balkanization of the departments cuts off vital crossover energy that af Enehielm prefers to utilize. She recalls, not so much nostalgically as with a sense of respect, the days when there was a less strict demarcation between Finns and Finland-Swedes, when theatre was a way of life, not just a profession. She recalls how she and her fellow students would study at school — mixing languages, theatrical forms, poetry, dance, happenings — and then after class they would continue the learning experience in other cross-cultural projects, some formal, others spontaneous. Once she and her colleagues graduated, they traveled around Europe, integrating styles and influences, creating a performance-based life, living and producing an ensemble mosaic that turned life into art.

Since the establishment of the formal program at the Academy, a bureaucracy of departments that discourages cross-disciplinary collaboration has diminished this eclectic approach. In response, af Enehielm combines forms — especially dance and physicality, movement and elements of surrealism — to create what she calls "strong pictures." Stressing the visual aspects of theatre — reflecting another facet of her career as an established painter — allows her to move away from text-based productions and toward more improvisational performances. This approach, too, proves controversial because it discounts the importance of language, and language is the key to cultural identity.

Cultural identity is at the core of the Finland-Swedish experience, the roots of which run deep in the acting program at the Academy. Af Enehielm is quick to criticize the resultant segregation at the Academy, preferring to work within a hybrid system that combines gestaltism with absurdism, dreamwork — i.e., exploring unconscious motives for action — with traditional techniques from Stanislavski, and Jungian deep psychology with Wilhelm Reich's theories of character. The result, to say the least, is unorthodox, but for those who support her, effective. As for the detractors, af Enehielm is stoical. "They think I'm crazy," she says, with no sense of irritation or even disagreement, only resignation.

From af Enehielm's perspective, the conservative nature of the traditional Finland-Swedish theatre is the consequence of two natural factors: geography and personality. Traveling from Finland to other countries besides

Russia and the Baltics is difficult. The country is surrounded by water except for the vast expanse of land connecting the northern perimeters of the Scandia aortic. She points out that people residing in what was once Western Europe below Scandinavia can easily move between countries, whereas Nordic Europeans cannot so easily traverse the landscape. Practically, the geographic reality makes it hard for theatre companies to mount productions outside their borders just because the physical logistics of touring with sets and technical support is daunting. This is true for both the Finns and the Finland-Swedes.

But perhaps an even more difficult drawback for the Finland-Swedish theatre community to overcome is what af Enehielm unhesitatingly defines as "laziness" combined with a lack of interest in exporting their theatre, a result of what she defines as "small vision." Marcus Groth, a former professor at the Academy who has taught both Finnish-speaking and Swedish-speaking students, concurs with af Enehielm. According to Groth, the Finland-Swedes "have less fire and passion" and need "help in projecting themselves" (Kaiku 38). Af Enehielm attributes this diffidence and self-imposed localization to a lack of confidence reinforced not just by their minority status within greater Finland but also by media that tend to treat the Finland-Swedes as invisible. She accuses the two main newspapers in Finland, for instance, of ignoring the cultural life of the Finland-Swedes. "They simply don't write about Swedish theatre," she says, not defensively but matter-of-factly. "Only about the Finns." This media blackout perpetuates a low self-image that is already endemic in the community simply as a result of its minority status.

Af Enehielm is quick to spread the blame for this predicament evenly between the two cultures. The Finland-Swedes have created a unique culture — what they refer to affectionately as the "duck pond" — with their own language and their own quirky existence — not Swedish, not Finnish — and their own network of well-funded independent theatres. This uniqueness perpetuates insularity: there is reassurance in remaining ghettoized, comfort within self-defined group cohesion. But a more practical situation reinforces Finland-Swedish isolation.

Whereas theatres in the Baltics, Russia, and many Western European countries tend to keep plays within their repertory for years, reviving them on a regular schedule, the Finland-Swedish theatre is ephemeral by its nature. With so many independent theatres vying for funds and competing for paying members of an obviously limited audience pool, groups pop up, perform maybe 15 shows, and then disappear. It becomes difficult to sustain an interest in any one production — the buzz that creates excitement around a performance.

The result is a kind of phantom theatre that has a built-in obsolescence.

Even in their desire to attract a younger, hipper audience to experimental projects, many companies are gone before they are recognized. This reliance on fly-by-night productions also disrupts the professional draw of a theatre profession. When so many diverse groups share small funding projects, often the only people who actually get paid are the theatres that the groups rent and the technical help without whom there would be no performance, a situation discouraging to writers and actors as it prevents new energetic work from being staged.

This friction between those like af Enehielm, who prefer to destabilize the ideological underpinnings of a language-based cultural-identity tag inherent in institutionalized theatre, and those dedicated to the preservation of the Finland-Swedish language is neatly illustrated by an anecdote by Fabian Silén, an actor and student of af Enehielm. He remembers studying Shakespeare with Kristin Olsoni, founder of Klockrike Theatre and a former professor at the Academy. She worked incessantly to perfect the students' enunciation, stressing the importance of precision in the spoken language. The exercise soon became absurd. First, the language of the Swedish text was not Shakespeare's; after all, the play had been translated from its original English. Second, the essence of the play was not contained in the Swedish text, and especially not in the precise enunciation of that particular rendering. Because the play had already been translated, and thus was not "true" in any linguistic sense, the essence might be more faithfully rendered if the play were further translated into a physical language that expressed the intent of the playwright outside of the artificiality of the linguistic construct.

The "old school" represented by Olsoni and others who prefer to maintain a classical faithfulness to the text and language continues to exert a strong influence on the teaching methods at the Academy, and this "old school" mentality is what af Enehielm has tried to remedy. Her targets, in what resembles a crusade, are fledgling actors like Fabian Silén, who reject the psychological realism favored by the mainstream theatres and prefer a more "European" style, especially the more radical performances resonating in the Baltics, Berlin and the Russian avant-garde.

Silén represents a new breed of Finland-Swedish actors that have, as it were, internationalized their approach to acting. (Among his various postgraduate studies in the United States and on the continent was a stint with the renowned Lithuanian director Eimuntas Nekrošius.) Silén notes that in 1999, the Finland-Swedish theatre community was like an island, isolated in a sort of self-exile, a closed network of predictable trends and restrictive expectations. The institute's idea of international interaction was to arrange for the students to visit Sweden to study the style and language of what was considered basically the preferred and requisite technique of theatre art.

But Silén's generation marked a change in emphasis, a renaissance he attributes not only to the eclectic methods of af Enehielm but also to the influence of Erik Söderblom, a director associated with both Finnish and Swedish theatre who was hired to teach on the Swedish-speaking course at the Academy. One of the original founders of Q Theatre, Söderblom was instrumental in internationalizing the curricula at the Swedish Institute. As one of the early principals involved in the Baltic Circle international theatre organization, he was intent on exposing his students to the dynamic styles of performance originating in Eastern Europe, stressing (as in her own way does af Enehielm) anti-textual, metaphorical and physical theatre as opposed to the psychological realism still dominating the education system and the expectations of the mainstream theatre establishment.

Söderblom's mother tongue is Swedish, but partly because of his extensive work both in Finnish and Swedish theatre he was chosen while teaching at the Swedish Institute to serve as rector of the Theatre Academy. One of his priorities at the academy was to integrate the various disciplines like dance and music into the theatre program, creating a holistic unity, or at least allowing various elements of performance to interact in a hybrid form of cross-genre productions. Silén is convinced that the positive changes Söderblom brought to the education of actors at the Institute is directly related to the fact that Söderblom is a director, whereas his predecessor, Dick Idman, was an actor groomed in the classic Swedish tradition. Söderblom does not shy away from Silén's view. "Actors who direct their colleagues act like stage managers," he says, "just moving people around on stage."

According to Silén, Idman promoted a collective sense of cultural values, discouraging individualism and what Silén refers to as "star power" that allows dominant personalities to shape a performance. Söderblom, on the other hand, associates the collective approach with the kind of bureaucratic thinking that chokes off innovation.

To implement his initiatives, fueled by a sense of a theatre in crisis, Söderblom organized a committee called Lust, the purpose of which is three-fold. The first task is to change critical perception of how to discuss theatre. Silén bluntly accuses the popular press of lacking the critical acumen to understand — much less to appraise — trends in progressive theatre, especially regarding Finland-Swedish productions. Second, the committee hopes to educate the theatre audience so that they might better appreciate contemporary performances that challenge instead of conform to the expectations of a theatre-going public comfortable in their bourgeois cultural habits. Finally, Lust would like to internationalize Finland-Swedish theatre, actively working to export their performances and to widen the influence of foreign styles of performances on the local writers, actors and directors, which in turn will enlighten audiences to appreciate diverse styles and force theatre critics to respond accordingly.

Trumping the enthusiasm for innovative theatre, the issue of Finland-Swedish identity continues to simmer beneath the psychological surface of the community. Annika Tudeer, artistic director and founder of Oblivia, resists the idea that her work can be defined or limited to a cultural base. She describes the milieu of her theatre as "Swedish, Finnish, Icelandic, Great Britain," implying that her theatre artistically and thematically transcends the pedestrian concerns of national or cultural identity politics. She is not exactly dismissive of the issue, but her remark, along with those of others whose work is as a genre more performance based than traditional, indicates an aloofness that belies her compatriots' passion and sensitivity to their minority status. The nature of Tudeer's work, more than any over-arching ideological concern, lends itself to a trans-cultural expression, as it is not language specific and deals with more abstract, universal themes embodied in the semiotics of mixed media.

Others, more prosaic, like Dan Henriksson, artistic director of Klockrike Theatre, point to actual threats to the language, which are necessarily threats to the culture. He cites movements generated by a pernicious populist movement to eliminate the bi-lingual aspects of the Finnish and Finland-Swedish culture that have long been the norm in Finland. Not only are all street signs and traffic directions in both languages, but the Finland-Swedes enjoy the privilege of conducting business, including matters of law enforcement, medicine, education and government in their own language. Finland-Swedes, for instance, are guaranteed to be able to answer to an offense or consult a doctor in their mother tongue. Henriksson finds a parallel with the Canadian situation in Quebec, minus the militancy.

But militancy might be provoked if recent trends continue. As recently as the spring of 2009, an article in *Helsinki News* (*Helsingin Sanomat*) pointed out a worrying trend in which fewer students were including Swedish in their baccalaureate programs. In 2005, 90 percent of students included Swedish. In 2009, that percentage had dropped to 68 percent.

The paper noted that many Finnish students refer to their having to learn Swedish as "forced Swedish," a play on the phrase "forced labor." A recent Finnish graduate vehemently resented having to study Swedish. "It's a waste of time," she said. "The Swedish speak English. When I go to Sweden, I speak English. We have nearly as many Russians in Finland, but there is no talk of students being forced to learn Russian. And Russian would be much more practical because the Russians don't usually speak English."

As the *Helsinki News* makes clear, there is more than anecdotal evidence to suggest a new, marked negativity toward learning Swedish, when other languages would prove to be more practical and even necessary. The immediate implication of this trend suggests that services that are now guaranteed by law to be provided in their native tongue will be denied the Finland-Swedish community. Further, this hostility toward Swedish in Finnish schools, aligned with and promoted by this surge in populism, indicates a gap between the well educated and the ill educated. Being able to speak Swedish is often seen not just as a sign of respect for the culture of the five percent minority, but also as demonstrating an understanding of their role in the history and culture of Finnish society.

No matter how much younger members of the theatre community like Fabian Silén hope to internationalize the performances and erase practical distinctions between Finnish and Finland-Swedish theatre, or how much idealists like Annika Tudeer suppose their work artistically elevates aesthetics beyond political and cultural conflicts, the issue festers. How seriously people think the situation has become depends on whom you ask. Many Finns simply think the relationship between the two camps is fine, suggesting, with no hint of condescension, that "they" have been beneficial to the overall cultural context of Finland. Some of the most radical of the Finland-Swedes, not so easily pacified, find parallels not with the Québécois but with the Palestinians. Not that anyone equates the suffering of the Palestinians to the minor deprivations within the otherwise sumptuous life enjoyed by the Finland-Swedes, but the analogy is meant to point out the fact that both cultures are distinct, stateless, and discriminated against. One director involved with the Finland-Swedish theatre festival at Hanko, summed up the prevailing attitude, curtly, but without malice, saying, regarding theatre productions, "The Finns don't mention us. We don't mention them."

One new theatre group that is not shy about confronting the cultural situation with atypical in-your-face frankness is New Ramp. A true ensemble, the company consists of three recent graduates of the Swedish Institute at the Theatre Academy, Jakob Öhrman, Elmer Bäck and Rasmus Slätis. New Ramp offers exactly what a small theatre company should: freedom to explore themes and styles without restrictions. Their aim is self-consciously avant-garde, as they talk of "post-dramatic explorations" and "new ways to enter the theatre space." But this posturing is less artsy than it sounds; actually, it is refreshing, given the new vogue in much of Finland-Swedish theatre for social realism. The members of New Ramp also prefer alternatives to text-based theatre and want "to alter the preconceived notion that many people share" about the meaning of theatre.

Funding, as usual with any small company, remains a problem, but so far New Ramp has overcome the money issue by aligning itself with larger, government-sponsored theatres like Wasa and Viirus that offer space and financing without interfering in their work. While the principals are writers, directors and actors themselves, they often use other actors and guest directors when necessary.

Their history dates back to before the university, which explains why they named their theatre New Ramp. The "old" original Ramp, an amateur project popular in the 1970s, was founded by Saija Metsärinne, a friend of their families and later the artistic director at Wasa. The three aspiring theatre aficionados convinced their friend to direct them in a few shows; during their university years they continued to perform as self-described "happy amateurs" until they decided after graduating to form a "new and improved" version, New Ramp. The term means the same in Swedish as English, implying access or a route into, but for Öhrman, Bäck and Slätis, the meaning is clear: a focus on theatre as an aesthetic window into contemporary culture in Finland.

Their play *What Is Being a Swede in Finland?* (*Finland/svensk?*) is indicative of both their approach to dramatic performances and their unhesitating enthusiasm for hot, controversial themes. The title, in Swedish, plays with the term Finlandssvensk, which means Finland-Swede, a Swedish-speaking person born in Finland. The term is normally written as one word, so the slash in the title is a violent indication of the ambiguous cultural division: the mark simultaneously divides and unites. Finland is a country in which a member of the Swedish minority resides as both an insider — born into it as a full citizen — and an outsider — not accepted as fully Finnish.

Exemplifying the company's philosophy, the play is a trilogy. Each of the three parts was written by one of the members, and each is staged in a different area of the performance space, performed as the audience moves from one set to the next. The team worked separately while developing the individual components, maintaining artistic autonomy by intentionally not commenting on each other's work, not even reading what the others had written until the day before rehearsals began.

The first of the trilogy, by Öhrman, is *Sushi Geisha Boy*, titled in English. The action centers around two elderly upper-class Swedish women at a resort where they indulge in golf, massage therapy, fine wine and gourmet food. Their servant at the spa, an old ill-educated Finnish country bumpkin who has lost his land and family, drinks too much and is generally soured on life, facilitates these luxurious amenities. While the women represent the impossibly exaggerated stereotype propagated by prejudiced Finns, the servant represents the equally ridiculous caricature the prejudiced Swedes have of Finnish men. Significantly, the characters speak their own language, further allowing Öhrman to explore how the language differences exacerbate the dichotomy in Finnish culture.

Though a synopsis of the play suggests a text-based script grounded in psychological realism and drawing-room humor, the action actually unfolds through a series of abstract, physical and metaphorical scenes of visual theatre. The symbolism for Öhrman is enhanced by the title. It refers to a fad in Japan in which a man eats sushi off the body of a naked woman, a geisha. In Öhrman's view, the skewed attitude of the Finns toward the Finland-Swedes embodies what he considers a false perspective: Finns see the Finland-Swedes as privileged blue-bloods, men at the sushi bar, while the Finns stew in a self-deprecating view of themselves as geishas serving up sushi off their naked bodies. Öhrman understands that his presentation of this cultural hierarchy is an exaggeration, but he also knows that extremes in theatrical language work. This explains his use of the Finnish servant as a barometer of the absurd bigotry subtly expressed but always denied in both populations. At the opening, he is a rabid Finnish nationalist with fascist leanings espousing hatred toward the Finland-Swedes; by the end, he has been "converted" but not changed, expressing fascistic violence and hatred directed at Finns as a nationalistic Finland-Swede. Öhrman's play is like a funhouse mirror that reflects the distorted views Finns have of Finland-Swedes, and vice-versa. The image is ridiculous, bizarre, comical, and, finally, as scary as it is true.

The second play, by Bäck, is more abstract, featuring three boxes on stage from which emerge characters who engage in an absurd investigation into the meaning of identity — thus the title, *Camouflage (Kamouflage)*. For Bäck, the niceties of political correctness and the notion of "belonging" to a certain group masks — camouflages — the competitive truth and harshness or identity politics. He echoes Freud, especially in *Civilization and Its Discontents*, wherein Freud ironically espouses the genius of St. Paul's tactic of organizing a brotherhood of like-minded Christians so that they could satisfy two of the most basic human drives: love and hate. The Christians could love one another and hate those who were different. (Although it is now fashionable for Christians to "love the sinner and hate the sin," this homily has not proven realistic or true.)

Bäck's play is oblique, but his inquisition is refreshingly straightforward. "We define ourselves not by what we are," he says, "but by what we are not." The function of the "Other" is to solidify the group. Bäck's position again has philosophical grounding, including De Beauvoir when she posits the necessity of the "Other" as a political tool justifying racism, sexism, xenophobia and other manifestations of Us vs. Them thinking. As for what Bäck identifies as identity politics in Finland, he admits that it is difficult to defend any sense of persecution within Finland-Swedish experience as a minority. After all, on paper the Finland-Swedes are integrated in their segregation, with equal citizenship, and their language is preserved through their own education system, cultural network, and legal institutions, rights that do not seem so fragile and threatened in the eyes of most of the citizenry, regardless of the saber rattling of the radical populists. Even so, Bäck recalls as a child being ashamed of speaking his mother tongue, and of being attacked and beaten at school when he would speak Finnish (episodes shared by Öhrman and Slätis). All three agree that the situation is not as bad as it has been in the past because other immigrants — "real immigrants" — from outside of Finland have taken their place as convenient scapegoats. Still, the situation for Finland-Swedes — as historical leftovers — remains awkward. They are always sensitive about their minority status, and yet their feeling of being oppressed — at least, thought of by Finns as not Finnish enough — seems false. They are not actually oppressed, but it is a feeling they cannot entirely shake off, and the result is frustratingly complex. Faced with unfounded envy, even hatred, their response is a sense of unfounded guilt and shame. An honest ontological reality seems to have been displaced by posturing that even acknowledgment and understanding cannot eradicate.

The third play, by Slätis, is a camp extravaganza called *Battle of the Country* (*Landets Kamp*). Inspired by the carnival antics of American "professional" wrestling, Slätis cites one particular episode from *Monday Night Raw* as the basis for his storyline. Edge, a particularly vain wrestler, planned to marry a female wrester (and real life love interest) named Lita, but the ceremony — performed in the wrestling ring — was interrupted when Lita's ex-husband, another wrestler named Kane, crawled from beneath the ring and started a freewheeling melee. Using this "raw" material, Slätis developed a scenario in which four competitors square off in a perverse battle of the sexes.

In one corner, representing the Finland-Swedes, are two authoritarian figures, a priest and a military commander. In the other corner, a virginal woman — Suomineito, or The Finnish Maiden, the visual image of Finland — symbolizes a pure, chaste, beautiful traditional and mythical Finland, while her teammate is the exact opposite, a modern, vulgar bimbo, a washed-up celebrity who continues to dominate the tabloids with her inane escapades (a la Johanna Tukiainen).

The plot involves the intrigue of the military man's efforts to marry the virginal image of a pristine Finland, but the wedding ceremony — like the Edge and Lita fiasco — is interrupted and ruined by the celebrity. The situation devolves into a free-for-all until the teams unite along sexist allegiances, the men against the women. In a twist on Brecht's alienation effect, just as the women are about to defeat the men, the play ends, but the action continues, even as the lights come up. The fight continues, as if in real life outside the fiction of the play. The men, desperate to regain and maintain control of the women, beat them mercilessly as the audience watches uncomfortably without the distancing or softening effects created by the actual performance.

While it lacks an overt commentary about the Finland-Swedish experience in Finland — there are allusions and connotations of imperialism, patriarchal attitudes and the exploitation of stereotypes associated with a mythical pristine Finland spoiled by colonialism and its own naïveté— Slätis's play is ripe with philosophical implications. Beneath the absurdity of the surface action and the framework of Finnish and Swedish historical prejudices, Slätis creates a subtext exploring the nature of how electronic media — especially television — mitigate depictions of violence and inures the viewers to the consequences of aggressive behavior and brutality. A corollary theme for Slätis is how audiences tend to accept flagrant and demeaning chauvinism when it is expressed in popular media, while in the theatre they find the same language and action disturbing and unacceptable.

Theatre, according to Slätis, has become too tame, too timid, a victim of political correctness and hypocrisy. In this context, the play becomes an essay on the differences between television images and theatrical performances, and how audience interaction and their expectations with each medium condition their responses. With television, the action remains in a tightly controlled frame, a small world limited by the size of the screen and negated with a click of the remote control. In theatre space, the action is close, and the risk of live action spilling into the audience is threatening. Performed in an area where the possibility of participation is real, where no remote or distant framing of electronic signals can reinforce the safe sense of unreality that keeps the television viewer in a secure comfort zone, Slätis's play is amusing until it becomes unsettling.

Another provocative New Ramp production is *Exception*, their adaptation of Brecht's 1930 play *The Exception and the Rule* (*Die Ausnahme und die Regel*). Brecht's original story tells of a wealthy oil merchant who, under duress in a trek across the desert, kills his porter when he mistakes the man's offer of kindness as a threat. Later, a jury acquits him of murder on the grounds that the merchant was justified because he was right to fear his porter based on class differences that imply implicit threats from the underprivileged against those in power. In this sense, the play embodies a classic Marxist ideology of power relationships based on wealth and social status. The critical response was mixed, with Söderblom praising its ambition and style, Lundström complaining that it was too intellectual and ironical, and af Enehielm suggesting that Brecht "did it better." The play was, however, honored with an invitation to the 2009 Tampere Theatre Festival, and its production galvanized the reputation of New Ramp as an important independent company.

New Ramp's decision to stage *Exception* has less to do with the political

(Left to right) Jakob Öhrman, Rasmus Slätis, Lidia Bäck and Elmer Bäck in New Ramp's production *Exception*. Their take on Brecht's *The Exception and the Rule* combines metaphor with dance, nonverbal performance with physical theatre, to interrogate Brecht's alienation effect (photograph by Chris Erlbeck).

angle than the chance to experiment with Brecht's "alienation effect." True, the play deals with issues that still resonate in geo-political contexts: imperialism, exploitation, class conflicts and so-called exceptionalism — especially regarding the foreign policy of the United States under George W. Bush. But the real interest for New Ramp — evident from their opening sequence — is to experiment with the framing aspects of performance. The actors greet the audience and discuss why they chose to perform the play, explaining that they could not secure the rights to perform Brecht's play, so they improvised, creating a new text based on the original, but in essence there is little difference between the two stories.

The actors then dress in the costumes of their characters, all the while reciting moral platitudes. The idea is to mock so-called political theatre, the kind in which characters, like lay preachers pounding their pulpits, exhort the audience into self-righteous action. In one curious sequence, an actor leaps back and forth between an imaginary "performance line" and his position downstage, where he addresses the audience. When he crosses the line upstage, he triggers music from the production. When he jumps downstage, the music stops. He is basically moving between actor and character, between

(Left to right) Robert Enckell, Lidia Bäck, Jakob Öhrman, Elmer Bäck and Rasmus Slätis in *Exception*. The play deals with issues that still resonate in geopolitical contexts: imperialism, exploitation, class conflicts and so-called exceptionalism. But the real interest for New Ramp is to investigate the framing aspect of performance (photograph by Chris Erlbeck).

stage reality and the "real" life of the audience outside the performance space. This strategy of breaking the frame continues as the actors deliver the action through a series of dance review skits and physical theatre, accompanied by a sort of voice-over narration and continual dialogue with the audience. Less successful is a coda in which the actors don masks of their own faces and conduct a seminar on political issues, sexual arcana and the death of a fly that might symbolize their deaths as characters, signaling the end of the performance.

The renewed interest in political theatre on the part of young writers and directors in Finland represents an attempt to return a sense of relevance to performances. Brecht's original play was, after all, considered one of his "teaching plays" (Lehrstücke), designed to tour through school systems, spreading the gospel of socialist principles. This desire to rehabilitate political theatre might be an attempt to correct a trend in contemporary theatre that has certainly left theatre-goers alienated, but not in the Brechtian sense; they have become actually uninterested in theatre because, in the recent past, performances have become so heavy with obscure metaphorical structures that the themes for many ordinary audiences seem unrecognizable. They cannot connect the action to any ameliorative experience in their lives. By foregrounding the style of the production, while maintaining the pretense of serious political commentary, New Ramp avoids what would otherwise be an exercise in nostalgia, a sentimental return to the political style of the 1970s. To avoid obscurity, they ground the action in socio-political issues of interest, but they release the performance from its issue-oriented fetters into a lively showcase. The play is more of a variety show with political overtones than a political play couched in variety acts. The result is a hybrid model for a new style of "theatre engage" or "committed theatre."

A prime example of this new energy and artistic vision in Finland-Swedish theatre is Maria Lundström's adaptation of P.O. Enquist's 1985 novel *Downfall: a love story* (*Nedstörtad ängel*), the title translated in Lundström's version more literally as *Fallen Angel*. The performance was created in conjunction with Sirius Theatre and performed at the Stora Mekans site during the 2009 Hanko Theatre Festival.

Ostensibly, the novel is an essay on perspective, what separates humans from monsters, love from madness, and normalcy from perversion, but the plot presents three bizarre and freakish stories in which love morphs into obsession. One recounts Bertolt Brecht's third wife, Ruth Berlau, who, after Brecht's death, carried around a plaster cast of the playwright's head in a box. Another explores a psychiatrist who befriends a serial killer who murdered his daughter. A third delves into a true account of Pasqual Pinon, who grew a second, female head with whom he claimed to correspond telepathically. Throughout the narrative, Enquist discusses his relationship with his father, whom he never knew.

Working within the vacant, empty space of the warehouse, Lundström centers the small audience of less than 50 spectators on stools among drapes dividing the space into separate rooms. The action develops around and through the audience — an inverted theatre-in-the-round challenging the idea of a performance space and demolishing any pretense of a "fourth wall" experience. The audience is situated figuratively inside the writer's mind but literally inside the action. The scrim separates not only physical space but, more significantly, mental space. (Setting the scenes in rooms representing interiority echoes Keats' curious conceit of the mind as a mansion of many rooms.) Lundström concedes that this effect was not unintentional, pointing out that the use of space stems from the text itself. At one point in the original story, the narrator undergoes a gastronomic exam with a camera. On the video screen, he literally watches himself from the inside out. The audience is situated in the same position, watching from inside while all the characters come together.

In the tradition of Fellini in *8½* and Beckett in *Malone Dies*, this dramatic pastiche presents an artist driven mad by his inventions, conflating his actual life with that of his imagination as his characters resist control and clamor for independent lives. The artist speaks directly to the audience, directing their attention to this scene or that, rearranging their stools, arguing with the actors, shouting advice. At times, he pleads his case like a man on trial, appealing to the audience to sympathize with his plight. An exercise in perspective, the play shifts points-of-view from one room to the next, one episode to another, as the writer tries to control his three-ring circus, interacting between the audience and his characters like a master-of-ceremonies in Bedlam. The approach marries Grotowski with Thornton Wilder while maintaining a classical sheen of polished restraint.

As well as its mélange of directing styles, the play also offers a virtual clinic on acting, combining the nuanced and seductive precision of the Stanislavski method with overtly stylized caricatures. To showcase the talent of her actors, Lundström exploits a mélange of styles, mixing absurdist antics and surrealism with psychological realism, creating a surprisingly eclectic performance of controlled intensity. Pinon unfurls a bandage to expose his brain. Musicians play actual amplified guy wires — which Lundström calls "sky harps" — like cellos. A nurse writhes in a masturbatory fantasy as a colleague drones on about a diagnosis. All the while the writer, fighting a bout of alcoholism, broods in his studio, tormented by his visions that implacably draw him back into the action with the audience and the escapades of his rebellious characters.

Lundström's preoccupation with dramatic space is evident in another of her productions, *Hit* (*Drabbad*), from a text by Satu Rasila, also staged at the Stora Mekans site at the 2009 Hanko Festival. The title implies being hit with something, like an event, in this case the impact of murder on the survivors. The play tells the stories of four different murders. One involves the abduction and killing of a young girl and the grieving parents as they negotiate the purchase of a casket for their daughter. Another recounts a woman who has been involved in murder and cannibalism with her boyfriend, her confrontation with her mother in prison and her subsequent attempt at suicide. A third depicts a grisly murder based on a true story of a young Finn and his girlfriend; having abused her for years, he involves her in the senseless mass murder of a family over a stolen bicycle. The fourth episode describes an elderly woman who asphyxiates her invalid daughter.

While the individual stories are not as tightly interwoven as, say, Arthur Schnitzler's *The Ring* (*Der Reingen*), which Rasila's structural ploy seems to emulate (without Schnitzler's success), Lundström connects the chapters with her directorial style, creating an eerie mood of dim, haunting memories from

(Left to right) Rebecca Viitala, Niklas Groundstraem and Maria Ahlroth in Satu Rasila's *Hit*. Director Maria Lundström's preoccupation with dramatic space creates a subjective perspective that allows the audience access to the raw emotions and private world of the characters. She elevates a voyeuristic narrative of macabre tabloid newspaper items into a challenging aesthetic experience (photograph by Otto Väätäinen).

the landscape of her performance space, her minimalist set, and the unsparing intensity of her actors. The seating for the performance was strictly fourthwall, but Lundström managed to create the sense that the audience occupies a privileged vantage, a subjective perspective that allowed the viewers access to the raw emotions and private world of the characters. Lundström's emphasis on how the story was staged elevates the performance from a mere voyeuristic narrative of macabre tabloid newspaper items into an aesthetic experience that tests the subjective possibilities of dramatic presentation.

To hear the director of *Fallen Angel* suggest that the problem with much of the new theatre in Finland is that the plays are too ironic seems counterintuitive. But as the director of *Hit*, Lundström speaks with conviction. Her complaint accuses new actors and writers, but especially directors, of selfconsciously devising new ways to distance themselves from the theatre experience, trying too hard in their need to "make it new" to remove the illusions that frame and define theatrical performances. The result is a clinical, mechanistic performance that might be intellectually stimulating but is too often emotionally cold. In the final analysis, she says, to be truly successful a play must engage the viewer's feelings. These new dramaturges, enthralled by alienation techniques, metaphorical and physical theatre, ignore at their peril one of the basic tenets of theatre: telling the story in a way that welcomes the audience into it.

As for what is best about the new theatre, Lundström appreciates the way actors are beginning to stress body language, exploring the possibilities of physicality. Old-style actors are comfortable "just standing and talking," she says. She attributes this new interest in dance, rhythm and motion as alternative tools of expression to the fact that performances from the former Eastern Bloc countries have recently been made available to students and young directors. She specifically cites the efforts of Baltic Circle and other theatre organizations intent on internationalizing the Finnish theatre scene. She also cites the influence of teacher/directors like Cris af Enehielm and Erik Söderblom who incorporate foreign influences into their actor training courses.

To complement this new turn away from straight naturalistic styles of acting, Lundström notes that new writers, as well as directors, are developing fresh ways of approaching drama. The best are eschewing traditional storytelling based on literary texts and experimenting instead with poetic, associative narratives, using fragmented storylines and collage. One of the problems with realizing in practice the new theories in dramatic performances is that there is no training in Swedish; Finland-Swedes interested in training as directors can only study in Finnish. This means that most of the Swedish-speaking directors at the Academy have been trained as actors. Another related difficulty is that the major institutions, including the Swedish Theatre in Helsinki and all the other major city theatres throughout the country, do not like to take chances with experimental productions. Instead, they rely on dependable standards that reinforce rather than challenge the audience's expectations to keep their houses full. And though there is a wealth of independent theatres, most of these must find ways to fund their productions. Often, depending on support from the major institutions leads to a cycle of compromises that disrupts the aesthetic balance between the sponsors and the independent theatres dedicated to experimentation.

For Lundström, they key is collaboration. She recalls an anecdote to illustrate the dilemma she faced moving from her independent work with Theatre 90⁰ to The Swedish National. One of the principals at the theatre asked her what she thought the set would look like, and she responded that she had no idea because she had not spoken to the set designer. The theatre official, obviously an old-school repertory player, assumed that Lundström as director would dictate everything from costumes to choreography. Her taking the job, she hopes, is not an example of "selling out" but a necessary step toward realizing her goal of bringing a new, progressive style to the major theatres and the larger audiences they attract.

For the time being, collaboration between the small, independents and the institutional theatres serves the purpose of keeping the new theatre alive. Of the several independent Finnish companies performing in Swedish, Lundström points to Blaue Fraue as the most dynamic. According to Lundström, not only do they consistently turn out high-quality performances, but they also tackle difficult, controversial issues. As a self-described feminist theatre group, Blaue Fraue often focuses on the theme of violence against women, a timely topic about a problem only tacitly acknowledged in Finland.

"In 2006," she points out, "the leaders of all the major theatres in Finland were men. Blaue Frau was the first theatre group to address this issue and ask difficult questions that most prefer to ignore." Lundström does not, for now, advocate the kind of quota system used in Sweden, but she does believe that involving more women in upper-level management positions — whether in theatre, business corporations, or government — would help prevent violence against women.

About other independents, Lundström is circumspect, allowing her aesthetics to override her politics. Of Viirus, for instance, she complains that while their theatre is dynamic, their tendency to produce ironical theatre too often "misses the mark." On the Groth brothers from Mars Theatre, she appreciates their style of realism, although she sees it as is fairly traditional, as they work to create what she calls "their own style of realism." That approach, incorporating the innovative use of Gestalt theory, allows the actors to feel relaxed and comfortable, so it suits their kind of productions. She calls it "safe, good institutional theatre" without sounding dismissive. New Ramp, however, seems to provoke a more political response, even as she tries to stick to an aesthetical context. She finds their work interesting but "too intellectual," accusing them of employing irony at the expense of sympathy for their characters, but she cannot resist assessing them from a feminist perspective. "They are a familiar constellation," she says. "Three men."

While a turn from the polemical to the aesthetical seems as though it would liberate theatre from the proselytizing associated with issue-oriented work, this is not necessarily the case. In practice, the phrase "turn to the aesthetical" is imprecise. Performances like *What Is Being a Swede in Finland?* and *Fallen Angel* could not be more thematically different. One is a scathing depiction of a Finland-Swedish identity crisis, the other an absurdist portrait of an artist in the throes of poetic fever. But these seemingly dissimilar plays actually have more in common than either has with straightforward family comedy-dramas like *For Sheer Love of Me* (*Av ren kärlek till mig*), directed by

Mats Hulmquist and Ann-Luise Bertell in *Unnecessary People* by Reko Lundán, a Finnish writer who came to fame in the 1990s with gritty plays about social issues. The play has a very different tenor under the guidance of the Swedish-Finland director Joakim Groth. Typical of the best of this kind of Finland-Swedish productions, the light style and subtle acting mitigates the melodramatic scenes of domestic violence (photograph by Gunnar Bäckman).

Marcus Groth at the 2009 Hanko Festival and sponsored by the Swedish Theatre of Helsinki, or with household tragedies like *Unnecessary People* (*Onödiga mänskor*), directed by Joakim Groth, Marcus' brother.

The Groth brothers are classic old-school dramaturges (Marcus the actor, Joakim the writer and director). They have been associated for decades with both Finnish and Swedish national theatres, and together in 1985 they founded Mars Theatre. *For Sheer Love of Me*, written by Anna Krogerus, is a typical fourth-wall production about a yuppie couple whose self-love causes emotional problems for their pre-teenage daughter. Despite fine performances from the actors — especially Anna Hultin as the wife and mother — the performance plays like a television sit-com, complete with sight gags, clever double-entendres — all the trappings of the genre minus only the canned laugh track. (Actually Groth brings levity to Krogerus' play, alleviating the strained sense of importance in an otherwise mediocre dramatic piece.) *Unnecessary People*, written by Reko Lundán, a Finnish writer who came to fame in the

1990s with plays about social issues, has an equally made-for-television feel. The plot involves scenes of domestic violence, tawdry affairs, career crises; it even ends with one of the "evil" characters paralyzed in a wheelchair. Typical of the best of this kind of Finland-Swedish production, however, a light style and subtle acting — especially by Johan Fagerudd — mitigates the melodrama.

Of course, *For Sheer Love of Me* and *Unnecessary People* can also be appraised aesthetically. The acting is crisp, the characters convincing. Their emotional life is expressed with precision. These types of issue-oriented plays dealing with inter-personal relationships, social ills, dysfunctional families — the sundry maladies of ordinary life — can be framed in realistic structures heavy on plot, psychology and exposition. The plays demand their own aesthetic considerations. So, while what seems to differentiate the classic approach preferred by the national theatres and a more experimental style adopted by progressive theatres could be described as a turn from the polemical to the aesthetical, it is more accurate to say that it is an intentional focus on the framing itself on the part of the playwright or director — not the facts within the case — that identifies "progressive" in Finland-Swedish theatre.

The Groths' embrace of social realism — especially for writer/director Joakim — designed to raise social consciousness about specific issues ailing society is perhaps not surprising, even if early in both brothers' careers they were associated with the experimental postmodern theatre of the 1980s. This reputation of being avant-garde began with Joakim's version of Beckett's *Waiting for Godot* (*En attendant Godot*) in which he famously took exceptional liberty with the text. Their experiments with integrating psycho-dramatic processes like Gestalt theory into their theatre work (and developing the Nordic Training Program for Actors and Directors of Theatre as part of the Gestalt Institute of Scandinavia) have also earned them the moniker "postmodern" from sympathetic critics. But their collective hearts have always been in studies of family social drama. One of Joakim's most successful plays, for instance, *Strangers* (*Främlingen*), staged at The Little Theatre in 1987, deals with a family consumed by mental illness, alcoholism and struggles with homosexuality.

At first glance, the efforts of Groth and other Finland-Swedish directors to stage plays by Finnish writers like Lundán, Rasila and others seem indicative of producers in search of an issue. Given the general social status of the Finland-Swedish community, it seems trendy that Finland-Swedish directors would look outside the "duck pond" for material that certainly highlights social inequities and the underside of the socialist welfare state but which are foreign to the director's (and their audiences') actual experience. One reason might have less to do with social consciousness than exposure, as some critics from within the community complain that Finland-Swedish theatres cannot have a major "hit" production because they are not writing in Finnish and they are not writing about Finnish social realities. Lundström admits that, in her view, the story in a play like *Hit* does not conform to the Swedish experience of life in Finland. There is, in general, not a strong tradition of gritty social realism in the Swedish theatre. Suitably, she describes *Hit* as "a bit Finnish" and makes a point of having the characters speak both Swedish and Finnish (typically, with the criminals and misfits speaking Finnish).

Lundán, for instance, wrote within a strong Finnish social context (as in *Can You Hear the Howling?*), and many critics from the Finnish community question whether these themes are actually a part of the Finland-Swedish reality. Domestic violence, addictions of various flavors, alcoholism and the general coarsening of society certainly make up fragments of the social fabric of Finland. But the systemic abuse seems more active in the Finnish community and seems somehow foreign to the solidly middle-class, successful, relatively affluent minority of 300,000 Finland-Swedes. The stereotype of the drunken, disenfranchised, unemployed, emasculated and finally violent Finnish male is not operative in the Finland-Swede context, historically or currently.

Unsympathetic critics find this new appreciation of social theatre problematic, claiming it neatly illustrates the schism that defines the separate cultures. Some concede that the concern is genuine, but the experience is manufactured. One Finnish researcher participating in a discussion on the subject among Finland-Swedish writers and directors implied that these artists had not lived this life; they had researched it, visiting prisons, talking to police, interviewing victims. To some, the performances were not realized from real life but from a vicarious, intellectual experience. For the Finns in the audience, these plays might be well crafted, but they seem generated from a culture outside of the reality they intend to depict. After all, the stereotype of the "criminal Finn" is well established in popular Swedish fiction. In Henning Mankell's *Faceless Killers* (*Mördare utan ansikte*, 1991), for one example, Kurt Wallander, the Swedish detective at the center of the mystery, quips, "'When we don't have a lead, we usually say it's Finns'" (70).

Of course, the reality falls somewhere in the middle between disingenuousness and authenticity. Social crises occur in all strata of society, rich and poor, educated, ill educated, no matter the ethnic backgrounds or geo-political persuasions. Even the Finland-Swedes, who might easily (and with some justification) dismiss this sort of Finnish criticism as so much ethnocentric carping, agree that the social problems highlighted in *Unnecessary People* and similar plays are less prevalent and less visible in the Finland-Swedish community than in the Finnish.

To explain their exceptionalism, Finland-Swedes point out that their community — because of its minority status — promotes a kind of cohesion that is perhaps lacking in the Finnish model. The Finland-Swedes resemble an extended family, which after World War II maintained a community spirit that was lost by the Finns. While the Finnish seemed unsettled by the various crises that ripped into Finland over the post-war years and broke up their natural family units, the Finland-Swedes enjoyed exclusive access to Swedish-speaking schools and universities (in Wasa and Turku), which helped stabilize the social disruptions and mitigated the impact of these social traumas. Even their military units are segregated, and Finland-Swedish politicians vehemently resist any suggestion that this program be scrapped. Obviously, the kind of cohesion established by a language-based minority as small as that of the Swedish-speaking Finns reduces violent antisocial behavior usually associated with disenfranchisement, poverty, ignorance and lack of self-identity.

Another, even less sympathetic view of this trend, might detect a condescending empathy on the part of the Swedish-speaking writers, a motive that might explain the trend of Finland-Swedes appropriating work by Lundán and others writing out of the Finnish experience. Lundström seems to approach the situation from a position of civic duty. She wonders if, as an artist and a citizen participating in the collective social contract, she can ignore the headlines? If not, what form does the material take to prevent it from becoming sensationalistic, shocking but titillating, perhaps even inadvertently promoting the very action she is trying to discourage? It's as if, after years of being inundated with heavily metaphorical theatre from Berlin and the Baltics, often self-referential to the point of onanistic navel gazing, or exhausted by plays built around the notion of a middle-class materialistic wet dream turning into a debt-ridden nightmare, directors are desperate to once again make social contact with their audiences. Postmodern challenges to the nature of theatre have reached a level of saturation, in which meta-theatrical gymnastics and similarly esoteric games of genre politics have emptied the soul of theatre, as well as the heart of its audience. To reestablish some meaningful connection between the performance and the audience directors are reconsidering plays that forefront social relevancy.

Along with this sudden interest in socially relevant theatre and the corollary new appreciation for the political activism alive in the theatres circa 1970, another — some might characterize as cynical — motive for staging these types of plays is funding. Education programs addressing hot-button items like domestic violence, drug addiction and broken families are in vogue, and funding opportunities abound. The idea is to increase awareness of these issues in schools, using theatre as a tool to expose these abuses but also to provide hope for a younger generation traumatized by their present and fearful of their future. This kind of theatre experience, the thinking goes, consoles people. It offers the public a place to mourn, openly and collectively, to bond with their fellow citizens.

Another consideration is that this type of socially sensitive theatre presents disturbing trends that upset audiences. To ease the violence of the shows, the programs include discussions after the performances that allow the audiences to decompress, to express their feelings regarding the issues and — in a truly Aristotelian moment — to feel purged, more complete, aesthetically and psychologically satisfied, healthier, and, in a sense, tamed.

Even the most adventurous theatre companies seem unable to resist the trend toward social realism. Blaue Frau, for instance, was formed by Academy graduates Sonja Ahlfors and Joanna Wingren in 2005. Their aim, according to their artistic policy, is to question gender roles and power structures in society. Blaue Frau is technically a branch of Subfrau, a theatre group of eight women from Finland, Sweden, Norway and Iceland whose performances have been described in their promotional material as "a theatre-drama-dance-movement-concert-performance-entertainment-show" designed to challenge gender roles and relationships between the sexes. Adhering to this philosophy, Blaue Frau's productions tend to subvert gender expectations and challenge conventional notions of femininity and masculinity.

Accordingly, one of the early shows by Blaue Frau was *Teena*, based on the life of Brandon Teena as documented in the 1999 film *Boys Don't Cry*. Brandon was a transgendered teen who lived as a boy until it was discovered that he was actually born biologically female. Brandon is subsequently raped and murdered. The controversial film addresses questions of sexuality and the general public's confusion regarding gender identity, including the often-violent responses when codified gender certainties are challenged.

Produced in collaboration with the Swedish Theatre and performed on the mini-stage there in 2007, Blaue Frau's adaptation was fairly straightforward social realism. Directed by Arn-Henrik Blomquist, the play relies on story and theme — basically the content — to provide the subversive element. In this case, the frame merely acts as a vehicle to deliver the message. The form itself is neutral without informing, commenting on or reinforcing the theme. Ideally, to paraphrase the American poet Robert Creeley, the form should be an extension of content. Because popular media tends to reinforce socially defined, acceptable gender identity, to employ a conventional form to destabilize an entrenched value system is counter-productive, even contradictory.

The play was criticized because the storyline so closely resembled the movie version. Other critics pointed out that it would be impossible to stage a story based on real events without echoing some of the scenes from the film. The complaints about episodes in the play mirroring the events depicted in the film do, however, point out the problem with narrative-driven drama: What separates the theatre experience from the cinematic one? The play certainly draws attention to the narrow-minded bigotry rampant in small-town America, and it achieves a nicely calculated shock when Brandon is found to be a girl — a scene of stark violence when Brandon, played in a cross-gendered role by Wingren, is stripped, revealing a woman's body beneath the boy's costume.

Arguably more effective at undermining rigid and comfortable notions of gender roles, sexual identity and media complicity in defining and preserving this value system is Blaue Frau's *I Am Your Girlfriend Now* (*Jag är din flickvän nu*). Produced jointly with Viirus, directed by Anders Larsson and performed at the 2009 Hanko Festival, the show is a macabre cabaret based on comics by Liv Strömquist and Nina Hemmingsson, including music composed by Helen Willberg and poems by Kristina Lugn. Mixing irony with

(Left to right) Marika Parkkomäki, Sonja Ahlfors and Joanna Wingren of Blaue Frau in *I Am Your Girlfriend Now*. The women resemble paper dolls dressed in garish '60s fashion. Their actions are stiff and stylized, as if they had just been brought to life by a demented Gepetto. The performance, parodying paternalistic ideology, targets the media's obsession with images of pop icons (photograph by Henri Sinisalmi).

self-deprecation, caricature with parody, the performance manages to celebrate and lacerate contemporary pop culture. It is a self-referential satire exposing not only media reinforcement of sexual determinants and gender exploitation, but also the underlying paternalistic ideology at the root of cultural values.

The three main women performers — Ahlfors, Joanna Wingren and Marika Parkkomäki — resemble paper dolls dressed in ridiculous, garish parodies of sixties' fashion — bright mini-skirts and tights — with their faces

In *I Am Your Girlfriend Now*, Sonja Ahlfors of Blaue Frau mirrors a scary stereotype, evoking media sensations from Shirley Temple to Britney Spears as she deconstructs a weird mixture of innocence and sexuality (photograph by Henri Sinisalmi).

painted like grotesque clowns. Their actions are stiff and stylized, as if they had just been brought to life by a demented Gepetto — horny drag versions of Pinocchio, stoned on aphrodisiacs and teenage angst, unsure of their movements but determined to talk dirty, mimic vulgar sex acts, and assert their feminine freedom. In their doll-like simplicity, they flaunt a stereotype popularized and exploited by titillating media sensations ranging from Shirley Temple to Britney Spears, that of an alluring virgin-whore, a weird mixture of innocence and sexuality, of acceptance and defiance, a femme fatale vamping as a cookie-cutter ingénue.

Billed as "a feminist class-awareness variety show," the performance is designed as a contest to determine who among the pop icons throughout modern history would make the worst or most irritating boyfriend. Accompanied by two musicians, the women run through an iconoclastic series of skits and songs designed to debunk the reputations of male media darlings. A related competition tries to decide which of the men is the most hypocritical toward prostitutes. The eclectic list of candidates includes Karl Marx, whom the women accuse of not giving his wife credit for her contribution to his Manifesto; Einstein, who mistreated his wife; John Lennon, who relied on Yoko Ono to keep his career on track as he assumed the role of child to her mothering guidance; David Beckham, whom they accused of infidelity; and Sting, who won the contest for his song "I'll Be Watching You," which the women conclude is the confession of a stalker. Figuring in the top echelon of men who have most disparaged prostitutes is Charles Bukowski, whose unflattering depictions of prostitutes belies his habit of frequently availing himself of their services, and Sting again for his song "Roxanne," performed, as the women point out, by a band called The Police, indicative of the paternalistic control of women's sexuality reinforced by popular culture.

I Am Your Girlfriend Now illustrates a freedom and resilience that denotes a major difference between Finland-Swedish productions and those of the Finnish theatre. Finns tend not to make fun of themselves. Their theatre history, dating from the nineteenth century, is grounded in performance as an expression and assertion of independence and national identity, a tool for educating the masses and dealing with prominent social issues. The Finland-Swedish theatres, on the other hand, are much more comfortable with subtle self-deprecating humor. "Revue and satire of the Scandinavian of Anglo-Saxon type have their recognized place on the Swedish stage, but are rare in Finnish" (Ahlfors 8). *I Am Your Girlfriend Now* is successful as politically edgy theatre because it discards all pretense of social realism.

The play has an obvious polemical slant, which irritates critics like Söderblom, who describes the theme as "worn out." But unlike the political theatre that gained so much notoriety in the 1970s, the performance in no way resembles agit-prop, soapbox or kitchen-sink theatre. Söderblom dismisses the form as "kitsch," preferring "in-your-face punk to "a prolonged joke." The revue, nevertheless, offers a scathing indictment (and lampoon) of media's obsession with manipulating images to create pop icons while reinforcing an artificial and outmoded paternalistic ideology.

While many of the so-called independent theatres like Blaue Frau and others in both the Finnish and the Finland-Swedish communities have achieved a modicum of success — some even a certain cachet of notoriety — few will be able to remain true to their professed principles. Some will simply not survive. Others will join or be absorbed by larger companies. Many will morph into entities that no longer reflect the original intent of their founders. Almost all of them begin as post-graduate projects that allow the actors, writers and directors to continue working while they mature as artists until they decide to try a different, more practical and profitable career, or until these people join one of the repertories at the national theatres and settle into a professional acting life.

But the refrain from the independents in the Finland-Swedish theatre scene is similar and familiar, reflecting either youthful idealism or sophomoric naiveté, depending on one's perspective. New Ramp offers "an alternative to the traditional text-based theatre." Skunk Theatre (Skunkteatern) proposes "to create work that fuses high and low forms of culture deconstructing everyday phenomena." Theatre 90° creates "groundbreaking performances based on current affairs and social issues." Even the more established independents often sound impenetrably highbrow. Mars Theatre has "developed a kind of artistic praxis." Sirius "specializes in experimental and alternative theatre." Viirus "aims to provide an alternative to the traditional theatres." These are worthy artistic principles, but they are decidedly not the formulae for drawing in the sort of audience that can sustain a theatre — which is why these "alternative" theatres are so heavily dependent on subsidies, arts funding and collaboration with larger institutional theatres. The inconsistency of this situation, if not the paradox, is painfully self-evident.

One cautionary tale is that of The Little Theatre (Lilla Teatern). Established in 1940 as a light entertainment venue, by the 1950s it had become transformed by Vivica Bandler into a radical avant-garde powerhouse producing some of the most experimental work in Finland and launching the careers of some of the most talented writers to emerge from the 1960s. It was also known for its international connections, especially French and Italian theatres. Throughout the 1980s it continued to attract innovative work, most notably premiering *Are There Tigers in the Congo?* (*Finns det tigrar i Kongo?*) by the Finland-Swedish writer Bengt Ahlfors, one of the most exported plays by a Finnish writer. But as if a victim of its success, The Little Theatre merged with Helsinki City Theatre, the municipal flagship of mediocrity. This tragedy — which some describe as a farce — appears to be case of poetic justice. Like The Little Theatre, Helsinki City Theatre was once associated with controversial productions by Kalle Holmberg and Jouko Turkka, but now both theatres have settled for financial security at the expense of artistic integrity. Both will survive, but each is compromised.

One theatre that has managed to survive while minimizing compromises is The Klockrike Theatre. Founded by Kristin Olsoni and Martin Kurtén, the performances from the beginning were less visually experimental than they were radical ethical, driven by Olsoni's old-school '60s activism. She was a vegetarian, an anti-nuke activist, and a peace advocate. But her style of political theatre, though always message-oriented, never slipped into the sort of invective-laden harangues usually associated with soapbox theatre. Olsoni's mix of styles — she studied theatre in Chinese, with Grotowski in Poland — combined with Kurtén's expertise in Stanislavski allowed the performances to experiment, not so much with form but with what artistic director Dan Henriksson describes as "ethical depth."

The name derives from *The Road to Klockrike* (*Vägen till Klockrike*), a 1948 novel by the 1974 Nobel Prize–winning author Harry Marinson. The story follows the travails of bums and other social outcasts as they pursue a drifter's life on the road through the Nordic regions in the 1800s. Marinson exposes the prejudice and contempt society shows towards misfits. An adaptation of the novel by Olsoni in 1991 became the first production at the theatre, and the name stuck. The theatre was formed in 1994 and moved into its present space on Skillnadsgaten in 1996. Olsoni left in 2004 and began to focus more on dramaturgy as an independent artist but she still directs shows there occasionally, as when she premiered Tua Forsström's *The Snow Dress* (*En klänning av snö*) at Klockrike in 2007.

In many ways, *The Snow Dress* is both typical and atypical of the kind of theatre Henriksson is developing at Klockrike. The story involves a female guard at The National Gallery who becomes overly fond of a statue of a simian creature. What happens when the director of the museum threatens to remove the statue of the creature to make room for a new exhibition is the basis for the comedy of manners that follows, a dreamlike sequence of songs, dancing and surreal encounters among a strange group of characters mingling in the museum. The virtues of the "Swedish style"— the lightness, subtlety, humor and finesse incorporating dance and music into stylized performance — are prominent. The attempt to mix genres is ambitious, the presentation slick. But there is no metaphorical framework to elevate the action out of the particular, nothing dramatic seems to be a risk, and there is something quaint, predictable and precious about the performance.

Another performance that demonstrates Klockrike's ambition and diversity is *Swim Naked* (*Simma Näck*), written by Susanne Ringell and directed by Ulrika Bengts. The title derives from a folk tradition that would more literally translate as "do it with the death." It is a classic tale of Death coming for a woman in the guise of a man, not dissimilar to Edward Albee's 1960 play *The Sandbox*, in which The Angel of Death takes the form of a buff young calisthenics enthusiast from southern California who comes for the grandmother. In Ringell's version, the woman expects her death to be a major event of metaphysical depth and gravity, something with the weightiness perhaps of a Bergman movie. But instead of a philosophical demon with a scythe and hood, Death shows up as a crass young punk who drinks his way through her liquor cabinet and is clearly not an expert at "reaping" the living. The woman, attracted to the young man, seeks to explore the ultimate meaning of her life, and expects to engage Death in the big questions. The young man, ironical and aloof, prefers acrobatics and diversions, mocking the woman with sarcasm and gamesmanship. The strength of the performance lies in the poetry of their absurd *pas de deux*, in which the couple performs songs and plays various musical instruments, complemented by the bizarre physicality of the young man's shenanigans.

The rap around Helsinki's Finland-Swedish theatre scene against Klockrike is that it is "old-fashioned," an epithet indicating the lingering influence

Ylva Ekblad and Jakob Höglund in *Swim Naked*, written by Susanne Ringell and directed by Ulrika Bengts, performed at Klockrike. The strength of the performance lies in the physical poetry and acrobatics, complemented by the bizarre physicality of the young man's shenanigans as he mocks the woman with sarcasm and gamesmanship (photograph by Hector Hernandez).

of Olsoni and Kurtén on Henriksson. But even the detractors are quick to praise Henriksson's attempts to internationalize the theatre and co-produce new groups. Henriksson readily admits his main influence comes from his association — closer to an apprenticeship — with Olsoni and Kurtén, which some perceive as being more of a curse than a blessing. Henriksson graduated from the Swedish Acting Academy in 1985 and did postgraduate work exploring the possibilities of applying Stanislavski's principles to performances of ancient Greek theatre. Having been intimately involved in opera in several countries, including the United States, Russia and Chile, and having taught theatre studies while also working in film and television, he did not began directing until 2005.

Kurtén's knowledge of Stanislavski is enviable, and Henriksson certainly benefited from his experience. Olsoni's eclecticism and early activism gave Henriksson an ethical context that continues to inform his work. But Henriksson has found it difficult to move away from their influences, which seem perversely stuck in a 1970s aesthetic. He admits most of his work is text-based, and prefers mainly Scandinavian plays, which are notoriously focused on the literary word. He still employs Stanislavski's techniques, but only as "a tool," he says, "not a religion" as he consciously tries to free the performance from the written script — a positive sign of his efforts to internationalize Klockrike.

If his reliance on a seventies' aesthetic, his use of text-based plays, and his use of a directing approach grounded in Stanislavski have earned him the reputation among some critics — no matter how unfairly — of creating predictable, stale performances, outmoded and out of step with contemporary trends, the saving grace of the Klockrike portfolio under Henriksson's guidance is his passion for using Klockrike as a performance space for small and experimental local theatres as well as international groups. Henriksson promotes co-productions, guest appearances and staged readings of new drama. He produced, for instance, local plays by Paula Rehn-Sirén's Pure Theatre. He also allowed established houses like Viirus to pursue new productions using Klockrike facilities. He has planned collaborative efforts with Estonia's Von Krahl Theatre and is pursuing projects with the Ukrainian director Andriy Zholdak. Recent plays staged at Klockrike have experimented with mixed media, combining music, dance, video and poetry to create solid cross-genre performances.

Perhaps his most ambitious project to date — still to be concretized — is based on Naomi Klein's *The Shock Doctrine* (2007) and her theory of catastrophe capitalism, in which neo-liberal governmental and economic policies are enacted during times of stress on a vulnerable, "shocked" populace. Henriksson envisions tracing the "doctrine" back to the exploits of Ulysses during and after the Greeks' invasion of Troy, when the Greeks used a tragic, arguably unnecessary war as a means to profit. His proposed plotline then moves forward through a series of events in history that further illustrate Klein's theory, concluding with George W. Bush's war-profiteering during his invasion of Iraq, which Henriksson equates with Ulysses' actions against the Trojans. The show includes a mixed media spectacle of dance, acrobatics, epic sets and physical theatre. The most interesting aspect from Henriksson's point of view as the producer is the collaboration between various performance artists and theatre impresarios, including actors, set designers and the director from Von Krahl, Peeter Jalakas.

One of the most innovative of Henriksson's ideas involves not performance but audience development, which is a key concern for any theatre that faces a difficult economic environment and a shrinking audience pool. His plan is to host *Soup Theatre*, during which the audience shares a simple lunch while watching a performance. Most importantly, the audience mingles with the actors as they all eat together and discuss aspects of the production. This intimacy eliminates the divide between consumer and producer, as it were, and creates a more casual experience for the viewers. Having a nice meal, watching a performance and discussing it afterwards is specially designed to attract a new audience outside of the regular theatre-going public, which consists mostly of older, well-educated professionals, university students and the typical culture vultures. Henriksson knows that small theatres must draw on the ordinary working citizens who might otherwise be hesitant to go to a play, whether because of busy schedules or ignorance, as well as younger viewers looking for a different kind of theatre experience.

Afterword

Making generalizations about the nature of a country's theatre, even in a community as compact as that of Finland, is problematic. Even Finnish critics hesitate to characterize the general "state of the art" as they try to come to terms with what exactly does define the essence of Finnish theatre.

To simply reiterate homilies that apply to any literature of quality, as Satu Rasila does in her unequivocally titled essay, "The Finnish Play Today," written when she was chairperson of the Finnish Dramatists' Union, is not much help. But after stating some obvious notes about "well-written" plays — suggesting, for instance, that "[a] good play tells a recognizable story about someone with whom I can directly or indirectly identify. The language in a good play is rich...." (4), etc.— she homes in on the traits that she thinks make a play specifically Finnish.

Because "Finland is a geographically large country which is sparsely inhabited," she writes, with an increasingly cosmopolitan population divorced from its rural roots, many themes common to Finnish theatre deal with "communality and selfishness" (4). Both situations, people living in remote rural locales and those residing in the isolated anonymity of urban environs, contribute to one thing that new Finnish plays, according to Rasila, do have in common: "some kind of theme of loneliness" (4). Concomitant with themes of anomie, displacement and estrangement, she identifies typical Finnish plays as dealing with "the lack of communication between different generations" (4).

The trouble with Rasila's attempt to define a typical Finnish play is that stories dealing with lonely people unable to share community values, to live satisfied, productive lives, to feel empathy for their fellow citizens or even to communicate with others in their lives in meaningful ways have been the definitive stuff of literature throughout history. Her attempt at taxonomy is equally unhelpful. She suggests that New Finnish plays "can at least be divided into the following groups: 1) those dealing with historical themes, 2) family plays, 3) sports plays, 4) those portraying identity crises and human growth, 5) those set in the business world, 6) new political plays and 7) communal plays" (4). Again, with the odd and potentially intriguing exception of "sports plays" and the curious grouping of "communal plays," her categories are familiar and generic.

Identifying the defining characteristics of a nation's theatre in the contemporary world is not made easier by the notion of Western Europe envisioned by the European Union. Faceless bureaucrats in Brussels tend to collapse national customs and languages into a shared reality that erases cultural differences. In a homogeneous political entity like the European Union, where open borders, rampant migration, the lingua franca of Euro-English and an interfused mass media dissolve cultural identities, singling out the distinctive characteristics that define a national type can be tricky, if not futile.

One resolution would be to focus on the process, not the themes of contemporary Finnish theatre. Granted, cultural tidbits peculiar to Finland crop up in popular songs, jokes, film, television and all sorts of literature. Most of them involve stereotypes constructed around *Koskenkorva* and saunas, pickled herring, and (in the prevalent masculine paradigm) the schizophrenic nature of a technologically advanced nation (read: Nokia) comprised of male country bumpkins displaced to the city and preyed upon by emasculating harridans bent on establishing a matriarchal republic.

Caricatures are, after all, constructed from fundamental historical truths, no matter how reductive the practice of national typecasting seems.

But there is something essential to the Finnish character outside the formal aspects of Finnish theatre. For instance, the concept of a "Northern Man" has been a constant in art criticism since John Ruskin's *The Seven Lamps of Architecture* (1849). Most famously, Wilhelm Worringer popularized the idea in 1912 with his influential *Form in Gothic* (*Formprobleme der Gotik*), and Herbert Read later integrated it into his definition of Expressionism representing a Transalpine "*metaphysical* anxiety" (220). As late as 2009, Michael Duncan, paraphrasing Hans Belting, author of the 1998 study *The Germans and Their Art*, evoked the stereotype in his review of the "Art of Two Germanys/Cold War Cold War Cultures" at the Los Angeles County Museum of Art by describing the Northern character as exhibiting "neurotic self-doubt, ponderous theorizing, Lutheran restraint and compensatory nationalistic fervor" (160).

Although these art historians are distinguishing between the art of Gothic and Expressionist traditions — especially as these styles are realized in Germany — and the classical style associated with Mediterranean Europe, the essence of Finnish theatre can be situated and understood within this context. The primitiveness, the distrust of complexity and metaphor, the raw, crude visceral expressiveness of the performances all comply with the psychological profile known as "northern man."

Historically, Finnish theatre displays an introspective, psychological depth that reflects the natural landscape in which the works were produced. The "northern" character, "conscious of his isolation, his separateness" (Read 56), is represented as a brooding subject whose heaviness and expressive manner, coupled with a lack of refinement, exists in marked contrast to the classical refinement of the Renaissance tradition of the European "south." The rough Nordic style also contrasts with the polished excess of the German romantic tradition, although the German influence is without doubt more pronounced than the boulevard plays and the rigidity of Neo-Classicism popular in the countries below the Rhine, the Alps and Bohemia.

Commedia dell'arte was not a natural outgrowth of the Nordic landscape.

While the Swedish-speaking minority theatre in Finland maintained the tradition of naturalism and the psychological method of Stanislavski, expressionism was the preferred style of the Finnish-speaking theatres. "Expressionism had a long-lasting effect on the style of acting: the stylized, strong outbursts of emotion typical of expressionism were very popular on stage" (Suur-Kujala 251).

This trend continues today. The Finland-Swedish theatre celebrates its sophistication, its light touch, its ironical deftness with situation comedy and conventional family dramas. But it too is a theatre in transition. While the new writers and directors are eager to try out more international styles, incorporating physicality and metaphor into their performances, playing with frames and questioning traditional boundaries between spectators and performers, the major theatres stick to the tried and true psychological realism and the so-called "well made play." Most interesting, perhaps, regarding the situation of the Swedish-speaking theatre in Finland is the recent trend of appropriating themes and translating plays from Finnish writers dealing with the gritty underside of Finnish society. Aside from the argument that the Finland-Swedish life experience is removed from the reality the Finnish writers bring to stage, the other problem is that, when translating Finnish plays into Swedish, the result is often like an American rock 'n' roll song performed in French.

A case in point is the staging of Reko Lundán's *Unnecessary People* at the 2009 Hanko Festival, in Swedish, and a couple of months later at the 2009 Tampere Festival, in Finnish. In Swedish, the acting was subtle, precise, the action almost precious. In Finnish it was loud, brash, verging on violent.

Just as the difference between Swedish-speaking Finnish theatre and Finnish theatre can be demarcated not by the themes of the individual plays but by the technique, the process, the formal qualities of the production, so too can Finnish theatre be distinguished from other theatres in the European community. Of course, just as the incidental tiles that make up the mosaic of Finnish life can be distorted by caricature and satire — about beer and saunas and emasculated rubes dominated by liberated fishwives — the style of performances can be reduced to cliché too.

Ask anyone intimately involved in Finnish theatre to characterize Finnish acting, and the response usually includes the observation that Finns on stage tend to shout a lot and take off their clothes. Naked emoting (which is decidedly not a trait in the Finland-Swedish acting community) seems to sum up Finnish dramatic talent. This critique, not so much of a joke as it seems, is front and center in assessments of Finnish acting, even from someone as invested in Finnish theatre as playwright and Director of Espoo City Theatre Jussi Helminen. In a left-handed compliment, Helminen writes, "Physical expression that 'comes from the boots' is better in Finland" (18). Helminen's comment might explain what he means when he claims "Finnish actors, both men and women, are not as sexy on the stage as their counterparts in Sweden and Denmark" (18). He accuses the artistic directors of most city theatres in Finland of "provincial mentality [...] and lazy thinking" (18). He asks, rhetorically, "It isn't a sin to belong to the cultured elite in other Nordic countries, so why should it be in Finland?" (18).

With a rich recent tradition in experimental, non-dramatic forms of theatre, and given the excess of spectacle in work by Klemola and Smeds, the question is: What accounts for a virtual crop of "targeted" translations all dealing with a particular dissatisfaction rooted in a confused middle-class adjusting to a new materialism, bemoaning a loss of spirituality and the disruption of the common purpose promised in the welfare state ideal?

Some dramaturges attribute this sudden proliferation of so many generic plays to a shift in focus at the Theatre Academy away from acting and directing and toward writing. Maria Kilpi, one writer critical of this new style, lays much of the blame on writing workshops — like KOM's "text-hatchery" — that tend to favor plays remarkable mainly in their similarities. Many of the writers, in Kilpi's view, pattern their scripts on television shows, filled with skits and gags and clever characters discussing their collective foibles. These scripts are reworked by the playwrights' mentors until they seem fit to become, in a word, mainstream, popular in a negative sense, clones of the internationally popular American television series *Seinfeld* and *Friends*.

Maybe Finland has achieved a middle-class status that is reflected in these types of plays — homogenous, easy to digest — in which the themes reflect the values of the consumers. These plays have quit smoking and joined the gym. They prefer white wine to heavy spirits. In short, they have become domesticated, made safe for moderate consumption.

Gentle sniping aside (criticisms based more in truth than many like to admit), there are an abundance of promising dissidents. They produce plays that still swim in ice, lie drunk in a smoldering sauna, preen off key and half-naked against the karaoke microphone....

These plays seem to be evolving in three directions.

The first is a return to the Lutheran tradition of using theatre as a pulpit, mixing a sermon with a dramatization of the action. Juha Jokela's *The Fundamentalist* is a good example of this tendency, not only in its style but also ironically in its subject matter. The narrative, often delivered straight to the audience, is didactic. The action, used to dramatize the moral point explicit in the sermon, exemplifies the moral dilemma of the characters like an illustrated Bible storybook. Appropriately, the theme of the play concerns religious piety and moral rectitude. The same impulse is evident in Anna Krogerus, when in *As If for the First Day* Ritva preaches to the audience about the inequities in the "reformed" Finnish welfare system. And while Mika Myllyaho's approach is refreshingly oblique, his themes are no less didactic. Behind the humor and the existential antics is a moralist warning of a narcissistic, materialistic, dog-eat-dog society spinning out of control in a Finland that is becoming more and more Darwinian and less altruistic. Heikki Kujanpää, closer to Myllyaho than to Jokela or Krogerus with his emphasis on the spectacle of a total theatre experience, is an unrepentant humanist animated in his moral indignation at the "new" Finland succumbing to a business ethic that threatens the social contract many progressives consider sacrosanct. Without sounding tautological, it is probably safe to say that a moralistic urge runs deep in Finnish theatre, often at the expense of aesthetic values.

The second movement is toward the international style represented by Kristian Smeds. It is significant, for instance, that his new play after *The Unknown Soldier* premiered not in Helsinki but at the Royal Flemish Theatre in Brussels. The idea is to situate the nexus of Smeds' influence squarely in the center of the European Union, not in the parochial outback of Finland. Smeds' self-conscious attempts to distance himself from his Finnish roots by appropriating styles from Lithuania and Berlin seem overly derivative and lacking originality to some, but many critics as well as his colleagues find Smeds' use of pastiche inspiring. Reinforcing Smeds' trans-national style, the publicity material for the new play, entitled *Mental Finland*, claims it "examines and challenges national identities, Europe and European identity." Paradoxically, given his penchant for internationalizing Finnish theatre, Smeds anchors the play in his home turf by having only one nation — Finland — resist allowing its cultural quirks to be subsumed into the generic entity of the European Union. The Finnish natives, adrift in a huge cargo container, cling to — what else? — their beer, saunas and crass sense of humor.

A third direction is the punk cabaret of Leea Klemola, exemplified in

Top: Kristian Smeds' *Mental Finland* continues his attempts to achieve a trans-national style. Smeds still manages to anchor his play in Finnish jingoism by having only one nation — Finland — resist allowing its cultural quirks to be subsumed into the generic entity of the European Union. Dancer on the floor is Ana Velasquez. On the right is Stefan Baier. Kicking in the middle is Juhan Ulfsak. *Right: Mental Finland*: The Finnish natives, adrift in a huge cargo container, cling to their identity, defined by their passion for beer, saunas, heavy metal and crude humor. Sniffing glue is Juhan Ulfsak. In the background from left are Tommi Korpela and Hannu-Pekka Björkman (both photographs by Bart Grietens).

In a self-conscious attempt to distance himself from his Finnish roots, and to resituate his influence squarely in the center of the European Union, Smeds held the premiere of *Mental Finland* in Brussels, Belgium. Janne Reinikainen, Tommi Korpela and Eva Klemets contemplate their situation as radical Finnish ex-pats in a world of Homogenized Europhiles (photograph by Ville Hyvönen).

her plays *Kokkola* and *Into Colder Climates*. While introducing new elements into these performances, she maintains a strong sense of traditional Finnish theatre. The language is abrasive. The jokes are irreverent and crude. The characters are miscreants, whores, drunks, shiftless con men, half-wits, derelicts and loveless idealists. The actors shout a lot. They get naked. The acting style is comically bombastic, the actors willfully reduce their characters to caricatures, and the storyline is outrageous. The performances embody exactly what Worringer described in his analysis of the essential Northern man: "Everything becomes weird and fantastic. Behind the visible appearance of a thing lurks its caricature, behind the lifelessness of a thing an uncanny, ghostly life, and so actual things become grotesque" (qtd. in Read 54).

Into this expressionistic chaos, Klemola blends issue-oriented themes such as global warming, the welfare state, religious piety, the plight of the elderly, and family values lost in a culture that worships youth and technology, all while simultaneously mocking the very issues she highlights. Klemola is an equal-opportunity offender. But the result is a delightful, faithful allegiance to the Finnish tradition, with its roots in amateur theatre.

Anu Komsi (center), Hannu Niemelä (in cage) and Mati Turi (in trailer) in *Lulu*. Leea Klemola maintains a strong sense of traditional Finnish theatre. As in much of her other work, the language is abrasive. The jokes are irreverent and crude. The characters are miscreants, whores, drunks, shiftless con men, half-wits, derelicts and loveless idealists. The actors shout a lot. They get naked. Klemola epitomizes the essence of the Finnish acting style (photograph by Maarit Kytöharju).

Klemola continues to create in this mode, to critical and popular acclaim. While democratically satirizing political posturing, hypocrisy and outworn traditions, she maintains a militant, post-feminist paradigm in which the women are the tough, two-fisted drinkers, aggressive survivors refusing to comply with the conventional role of sexual objects for male fantasies. Her 2009 opera *Lulu*, based on Frank Wedekind's 1895 *Earth Spirit* (*Erdgeist*) and his 1902 sequel *Pandora's Box* (*Die Büchse der Pandora*) presents Lulu not as the alluring *femme fatale* but as a hairy ape woman. She is, says Klemola in a March 2009 interview with *Helsinki News* (*Helsingin Sanomat*), "'an opportunist who does not calculate'" (Sirén). She has always objected to "productions of 'Lulu' in which the main character is coquetting as an object of the male gaze, frequently wearing sado-masochistic outfits." Her Lulu "does not expect candlelit suppers, she is a willing sex partner. No boys in the backseat have ever called her a whore, nor has she been shaped by any images of the Virgin Mary."

Outrageous. Brutish. Violent. Uncomplicated. Irreverent. The actors shout. They get naked.

Maybe Klemola is the avatar of Finnish theatre.

Works Cited

Aaltonen, Sirkku. "Retranslation in the Finnish Theatre." *Cadernos de Tradução* 11 (2004). Universidad Federal de Santa Caterina, Brazil. 141–159.

_____. "Targeting in Drama Translation: Laura Ruohonen's Plays in English Translation." VAKKI. University of Vaasa.

Ahlfors, Bengt. "Theatre in Finland-Swedish." *Finnish Theatre* 52 (1998): 4–8.

Alftan, Maija. "Poet Sees Her Own Life Onstage: Aila Meriluoto Visits Q Theatre Before Premiere to See Final Act of Play on Her Life." *Helsinki News*, February 26, 2005.

Arens, Katherine. "Robert Wilson: Is Postmodern Performance Possible?" *Theatre Journal* vol. 43, no. 1 (March 1991): 14–40.

Arhinmäki, Paavo. "The Masses Against the Quarter Economy." *Helsinki Times*, February 15, 2008.

Barskova, Polina. Rev. of *Master i Magarita*. KinoKultura. <http://KinoKultura.com/2006/13r-master.shtml>.

Bruckner, D.J.R. "Drama in Review." *New York Times,* June 1, 1993.

Bult, Jeroen. "Finland Debates Its Ties with NATO." Worldpress.org. <http://wwwWorldpress.org/Europe/2279.cfm>.

Carroll, Denis, and Elsa Carroll. "Contemporary Finnish Theatre: National Myths and Beyond." *The Drama Review: TDR* vol. 26, no. 3 (Autumn 1982): 35–50.

_____. "KOM-teatteri: Finland's Theatre of Socialist Action." *Educational Theatre Journal* vol. 30, no. 3 (October 1978): 376–86.

"Dragonfly nymph." Buglopedia. <http://www.busurvey.nsw.gov.au/html/popups/bpedia_08_tol_dr-ny-a.html>.

Duncan, Michael. "How German Is It?" *Art in America* (June/July 2009): 160–169.

Halonen, Tarja. "Second Inauguration Speech, 2006." The President of the Republic of Finland press release. <http://www.presidentti.fi/netcomm/news/showarticle.asp?intNWSAID=48430&intSubArtID=20196>.

Helavuori, Hanna-Leena. "Weak Dramaturgy as Performative Resistance." *On the Theatresruin*s. Helisnki: Kiasma, 2005. 65–86.

Helminen, Jussi. "What Can Finland Learn from Theatre in Other Nordic Countries?" *Finnish Theatre* 62 (2008): 16–19.

Honko, Lauri. "The Kalevala: The Birth of Finland's National Epic." *UNESCO Courier*. <http://findarticles.com/p/articles/mi_1985_August/ai_3877965>.

Hotakainen, Kari. "Border Crossing." Trans. Marja Wilmer and Steve Wilmer. *Humour and Humanity: Contemporary Plays from Finland*. Helsinki: Like, 2006. 13–109.

Hyvärinen, Teija. "Laura Ruohonen: Does the Soul Have a Gender?" *Finnish Theatre* 54 (2000): 24–27.

Introduction to "The Finnhorse." Trans. Eva Buchwald. Helsinki: Lasipalatsi, 2005. 6–7.

Jansson, Tomas. "Finland-Swedish Theatre on the Border Between Finnish and Swedish Tradition." *Finnish Theatre* 52 (1998): 20–25.

_____. "The Hunt for Plays." *Finnish Theatre* 52 (1998): 26–27.

Johnson, Ken. "Cool, Hot and Finnish, With a Dose of Mythic Imagination." *New York Times,* June 6, 2008, natl. ed., B30.

Jokela, Juha. "Mobile Horror." Trans. David Hackston. *Humour and Humanity: Contemporary Plays from Finland.* Helsinki: Like, 2006. 111–197.

"Jouko Turkka."<http://en.wikipedia.org/wiki/Jouko_Turkka>.

Kaiku, Jan-Peter. "The Swedish Institute of Acting." *Finnish Theatre* 52 (1998): 34–39.

Katz, Jonathan D. "Cold War and Hot Art." *Art in America* (June/July 2008): 83–88.

Kelloniemi, Toivo. "Keta laitostunut taide kiinnostaa?" *Helsinki News,* August 2, 2009, B5.

Kermode, Frank. "Literary Ficiton and Reality." *Essentials of the Theory of Fiction.* Eds. Michael Hoffman and Patrick Murphy. Durham: Duke University Press, 1988. 218–237.

Kirby, David. *A Concise History of Finland.* London: Cambridge University Press, 2006.

Korpela, Salla. "The Church in Finland Today." *Virtual Finland.* Ministry of Foreign Affairs of Finland. May 2005.

Kujanpää, Heikki, Sami Parkkinen and Heikki Huttu-Hiltunen. *Falling Angels* (*Putoavia enkeleitä*). Trans. Anselm Hollo. Helsinki: Lasipalatsi, 2006.

Kurki, Anneli. "*Kokkola*: A Portrait of Arctic Finland." *Finnish Theatre* 59 (2005): 24.

_____. "Text-Hatchery to the Aid of New Plays." *Finnish Theatre* 54 (2000): 36.

Kuyl, Ivo. "Theatre Is a Public Sauna." Trans. Dan Frett. Etcetera. September 2, 2009. <http://www.e-tcetera.be/index.php?upnr=-9&newsnr=47>.

Kylätasku, Jussi. "Oven." *Stages of Chaos: The Drama of Post-War Finland.* Helsinki: Finnish Literary Society, 2005. 250–274.

Lago, Don. *On the Viking Trail: Travels in Scandinavian America.* Iowa City: University of Iowa Press, 2004.

Lavery, Jason. "The Branding of a Nation." *Helsinki Times,* August 15, 2009.

Lonergan, Patrick. "Globalisation and Irish Theatre." Critical Interventions. <http://www.writerscentre.ie/centre/anthology/plonergan.html>.

Lukács, Georg. "Marxist Aesthetics and Literary Realism." *Essentials of the Theory of Fiction.* Eds. Michael Hoffman and Patrick Murphy. Durham: Duke University Press, 1988. 203–217.

Lundán, Reko. "Can You Hear the Howling?" Trans. David Hackston. *Humour and Humanity: Contemporary Plays from Finland.* Helsinki: Like, 2006. 199–321.

Mahoney, Elisabeth. Rev. of "Olga." *The Guardian,* December 6, 2001.

Mankell, Henning. *Faceless Killers.* Trans. Steven T. Murray. London: Vintage, 2000.

Manner, Eeva-Liisa. "Burnt Orange." *Stages of Chaos: The Drama of Post-War Finland.* Helsinki: Finnish Literary Society, 2005. 156–244.

Maukola, Riina. "Anna Vielalainen: Towards Complete Theatre." *Finnish Theatre* 58 (2004): 20–22.

McMillan, Joyce. "A Kind of Love in a Cold Climate." *The Scotsman,* December 12, 2001.

Meri, Veijo. "Private Jokinen's Wedding Leave." *Stages of Chaos: The Drama of Post-War Finland.* Helsinki: Finnish Literary Society, 2005. 16–150.

Myllyaho, Mika. "Panic." Trans. Sarka Hantula. *Humour and Humanity: Contemporary Plays from Finland.* Helsinki: Like, 2006. 323–395.

Peltola, Sirkku. "The Finnhorse." Trans. Eva Buchwald. Helsinki: Lasipalatsi, 2005.

Rantala, Raija-Sinikka. "A Happy Union of Languages." *Finnish Theatre* 52 (1998): 2.

Rasila, Satu. "The Finnish Play Today." *Finnish Theatre* 62 (2008): 4–6.

Read, Herbert. *A Concise History of Modern Painting.* New York: Praeger, 1959.

Ruohonen, Laura. "Queen C." Trans. David Hackston. *The Dynamic World of Finnish Theatre.* Helsinki: Like, 2006. 397–441.

Ruuskanen, Annukka. Introduction to "Queen C." *The Dynamic World of Finnish Theatre*. Helsinki: Like, 2006. 399–402.

_____. "Outlaws." *Finnish Theatre* 61 (2006): 4–6.

_____. "The Reality Research Centre." *Finnish Theatre* 60 (2006): 11–12.

_____. "The Whole of Europe Is Kristian Smed's Theatre Home." *Finnish Theatre* 61 (2007): 4–8.

Sandler, Irving. "Abstract Expressionism and the Cold War." *Art in America* (June/July 2008): 65–74.

Seppälä, Mikko-Olavi. Dissertation abstract, "Workers' Theatres in Finland Until 1922" ("Teatteri liikkeessä: Työväenteatterit Suomen teatterikentällä ja työväenliikkeessä kaksiteatterijärjestelmän syntyyn asti vuonna 1922"). May 12, 2007. University of Helsinki, Faculty of Arts, Institute for Art Research. <https://oa.doria.fi/handle/10024/5337>.

Seppälä, Riitta. "Theatre for All." *Theatre People — People's Theatre*. Eds. Kaisa Korhonen and Katri Tanskanen. Helsinki: Like, 2006. 9–11.

Silde, Marja. "New Performance Art: Physicality and Technology." *Finnish Theatre* 60 (2006): 13–17.

Sirén, Vesa. "Director Leea Klemola's Lulu Is a Hairy Apewoman." *Helsinki News*, March 5, 2009.

Sutinen, Virve. "Memo: On Vanishing Performers — An Attempt to Remember and Let Go." *On the Theatresruins*. Helisnki: Kiasma, 2005. 27–46.

Suur-Kujala, Anneli. "Finland." *The World Encyclopedia of Contemporary Theatre*. Ed. Don Rubin. London: Routledge, 1997. 250–253.

Upton, Anthony. "National History and Identity." *Studia Fennica Ethnologica* no. 6 (1999): 153–165.

Valo, Vesa Tapio. "The Boys." *Stages of Chaos: The Drama of Post-War Finland*. Helsinki: Finnish Literary Society, 2005. 282–425.

Wilmer, S.E., and Pirkko Koski. *The Dynamic World of Finnish Theatre*. Helsinki: Like, 2006.

_____. Foreword. *Humour and Humanity: Contemporary Plays from Finland*. Helsinki: Like, 2006. 9–11.

_____. Foreword. *Portraits of Courage: Plays by Finnish Women*. Helsinki: Helsinki University Press, 1997. 1–3.

_____. Foreword. *Stages of Chaos: The Drama of Post-War Finland*. Helsinki: Finnish Literary Society, 2005. 8–10.

_____. Introduction to "The Boys." *Stages of Chaos: The Drama of Post-War Finland*. Helsinki: Finnish Literary Society, 2005. 277–281.

_____. Introduction to "Burnt Orange." *Stages of Chaos: The Drama of Post-War Finland*. Helsinki: Finnish Literary Society, 2005. 153–155.

_____. Introduction to "Can You Hear the Howling?" *Humour and Humanity: Contemporary Plays from Finland*. Helsinki: Like, 2006. 201–321.

_____. Introduction to "Law and Order." *Portraits of Courage: Plays by Finnish Women*. Helsinki: Helsinki University Press, 1997. 219–225.

_____. Introduction to "The Oven." *Stages of Chaos: The Drama of Post-War Finland*. Helsinki: Finnish Literary Society, 2005. 247–249.

_____. Introduction to "Panic." *Humour and Humanity: Contemporary Plays from Finland*. Helsinki: Like, 2006. 325–326.

Index

Aaltonen, Sirkku 20, 22, 59
absurdism 46
af Enehielm, Cris 153–57, 163, 169
Agarth, Marika 80, 81
Ageev, Vladimir 74, 77
Ahlfors, Bengt 18, 147, 179
Ahlfors, Sonja 147, 152, 175–77
Aho, Irene 57, 72
Ähtäriin 83, 84
Aitta, Tuomo 80
Albee, Edward 180
All the Love That Belongs to You 100, 101
Alter Ego 42
Alternate Spaces Group 4
amateur theatres 30, 31
Amoralia 61, 66
Anglo-American topics 49
The Apprentice 88
Are There Tigers in the Congo? 179
Arhinmäki, Paavo 126
Arkadia Theatre 29
Aron, Geraldine 51
"Art of Two Germanys/Cold War Cold War Cultures" 185
art theatre 51
Artaud, Antonin 47
As If for the First Day 13, 59, 60, 188
Attempts on Her Life 124
Austria 37
avant-garde 10
avanto 5, 9

Bäck, Elmer 146, 159–62
Bacon, Francis 126
Bahne, Martin 146
Baltic Sea 9, 25
Baltic Theatre 9–11, 66; directors 74
Baltics (and Baltic Circle) 9, 10, 29,

46–49, 51, 62, 64, 79, 82, 84, 97, 98, 102, 126, 137, 155–57, 169, 174; Festival 10, 52; theatre conference 101
Bandler, Vivica 179
The Barn Keeper 104
Barskova, Polina 75
Battle of the Country 162
Bausch, Pina 117
Beckett, Samuel 167, 172
Beckham, David 177
Belarus 11
Belting, Hans 185
Bengts, Ulrika 180,181
Bergius, Niina 14
Bergman 180
Berlau, Ruth 166
Berlin 48, 51, 55, 64, 69, 71, 77, 97, 109, 110, 156, 174, 188
Berlin Alexanderplatz 109, 110
Between Dead People 115
Bible 188
bildungsroman 83
Birth of a Salesman 52, 70, 85, 87
The Black Rose Trick Hotel 48
Blasted 51, 106
Blaue Frau 147, 152, 170, 175–78
Blomquist, Arn-Henrik 175
Border Crossing 39, 40, 45, 65, 85
Bortko, Vladimir 75
bourgeois theatres 30, 33
bourgeoisie 47
The Boys 38, 39
Boys Don't Cry 175
Brecht, Bertolt 10, 71, 79, 131, 142, 162–66
Brezhnev, Leonid 23
Bruckner, D.J.R. 75
Brussels 47, 120, 188, 190
Buchwald, Eva 23

Bukowski, Charles 178
Bulgakov, Michail 74, 75, 77–79, 125
Bult, Jeroen 18, 19
Burnt Orange 37, 38
Bush, George H.W. 126
Bush, George W. 164, 182

Čakare, Valda 49
Calvinism 23, 25
Camouflage 161
Can You Hear the Howling? 44, 45, 85, 173
Canada 158
Candid Camera 127
Candide 73
Canterbury, England 132
capitalism 27, 37, 47, 51
Carroll, Dennis 27, 46, 68, 80, 97
Carroll, Elsa 27, 46, 68, 80, 97
Cassandra 37
Castle Theatre 8
Castorf, Frank 52, 69, 70, 132
Catchment Area—Memos of Freedom 63
chamber theatre 8
Chaos 14, 71, 72
Chekhov, Anton Pavlovich 105
Chicken 105, 106
The Children of Baikal 2
Chile 181
The Chosen Ones 2
Christianity 161
The City 49
Civil War of 1918 30
Civilization and Its Discontents 161
Cleansed 51
Cobain, Kurt 83
A Coin in the Hat of Love 111
Cold War 9, 18, 19, 65, 67, 107, 126
Cologne 8
Communism 46, 109, 125
Communist Party 80
A Concise History of Finland 17
Contains Violence 53
"Contemporary Finnish Theatre: National
    Myths and Beyond" 27
Continuation War of 1941–1944 31, 39,
    126, 129
Creeley, Robert 175
Crimps, Martin 124

Danzig 93, 95
Darwinian capitalism 23, 188
De Beauvoir 161
Death, Angel of 180
Death of a Salesman 87

deconstruction 52
Denmark 11, 187; actors 49; theatre 48
Descartes, Rene 43
Döblin, Alfred 109
Dr. Phil 58
documentary cabaret 50
Don Quixote 88, 151
Donald Duck 126
The Donkey Hot Show 151
Dostoyevsky, Fyodor 70
Downfall: a love story 166
Dragonfly 103, 104
Drama Academy 147
Drevitski, Viktor 105
Dubrovnik club 11
"duck pond" 144, 155, 172
Duncan, Michael 185
The Dynamic World of Finnish Theatre 29

Earth Spirit 191
Eastern Bloc 169
Eastern Europe 84, 146, 157
eco-anarchism 4
economic terrorism 106
Edinburgh, Scotland 20, 21, 54
8½ 167
Einstein 177
Eliot, T.S. 57
"Emotions" 5
England 23; language 158, 160
Enquist, P.O. 166
epic effects 131
Epilogue 54
Eskola, Hanno 110–12, 115–117, 123
Eskolin, Masi 5
Espoo 25; City Theatre 187
Estonia 8, 11, 28, 46, 50, 103–06, 126, 182;
    critics 49; performance art 50; theatre 10,
    49, 66
Etiquette 53
Europe (and European Union) 15, 19, 37,
    46, 51, 98, 101, 119, 120, 137, 154,
    185–190; post-war 94
Eurovision Song Contest 9
Evita 145
Exception 163, 165
The Exception and the Rule 163, 164
Expressionism 185, 186

Faceless Killers 173
Fagerudd, Johan 172
Fallen Angel 166, 168, 170
Falling Angels 90–92
Fascism 67

Fellini 167
feminist humanism 44
"feministic theatre" 152
Fennomans 28, 29
Fever 2
Finland-Swedes 12, 13, 18, 123, 186, 187; theatre 144–83
The Finland-Swedish Theatre 146; festival 159
Finnair 9
The Finnhorse 117–119
Finnish Civil War 138
Finnish Critics' Association Award 57
Finnish Diet 28
Finnish Dramatists' Union 184
Finnish National Theatre 5, 20, 32, 61, 125
"The Finnish Play Today" 184
Finnish Theatre Academy 84, 150
Finnish Theatre Centre 144
Finnish Theatre Information Centre 9, 12
Finnish Theatre magazine 53, 68, 144
Folk Theatre 31
folklore: Finnish 29; Karelian 29
For Sheer Love of Me 13, 14, 57–59, 170–72
Forge Theatre 8, 61, 62
Form in Gothic 185
Formula One 8
Forsman, Fiikka 70, 93–96, 124
Forsström, Tua 180
France 27
free theatres 99
Freud, Sigmund 4, 37, 161
Freundlich, Johanna 81, 82
Friends 187
The Fundamentalist 14, 112, 113, 117, 188

Gandhi 41, 42
Germany 14, 27, 31, 37, 52, 69, 93–95, 117, 125, 142, 144, 155, 185, 186; actors 49
The Germans and Their Art 185
Gestalt Institute of Scandinavia 172
Gestalt theory 170, 172
Getting Out 90
globalization 47
Gogol 6
The Golden Calf 30
The Government Inspector 6
Grass, Günther 93, 95, 124
Grauzinis, Cesaris 102
Great Britain 14, 16, 27, 158
Greece 182
Greenland 3; Nuuk 121, 122
Groth, Joakim 146, 148, 149, 170–72

Groth, Marcus 146, 155, 170, 171
Grotowski 167, 179
The Group Theatre 12, 48, 64, 69, 70, 74, 112, 116
The Guardian 21
Guilbaut, Serge 67
Gustafsson, Kim 146

Hafrén, Mia 148
Hakaniemi Square 33
Halonen, Tarja 70
Halttunen, Iira 83, 84
Hamlet 63
Hammarberg, Johanna 9
Hampton, Anthony 53
Hanko 7; Theatre Festival 13, 159, 166, 167, 170, 176, 186
Hanseatic League 28, 144
Harmin paikka 65
Hauptmann 70
Heidegger 62
Helavuori, Hanna-Leena 59, 63, 107
Helminen, Jussi 187
Helsinki 4, 8, 10, 11, 19, 25, 29, 31–35, 52, 54, 56, 59, 61, 62, 69, 80, 84, 98, 99, 101, 107, 111, 115, 127, 130, 144, 145, 147, 169, 171, 180, 188
Helsinki by Night 52
Helsinki City Theatre 179
Helsinki News 32, 158, 191
Helsinki School of Economics 25
Helsinki Students' Theater 3
Helsinki Swedish Acting School 150
Helsinki Theatre Academy 124
Helsinki Times 19
Helsinki University: Acting Academy 33; Department of Theatre Research 11
Hemingway, Ernest 8
Hemmingsson, Nina 176
Henriksson, Dan 13, 124, 158, 179–83
Hermanis, Alvis 13, 49, 52, 99,102
Hietala, Antti 97, 108–11
"Hills Like White Elephants" 8
"History and National Identity" 18
Hit 167, 168, 173
Holmberg, Kalle 10, 179
Honko, Lauri 17
Hot Estonian Guys 50
Hotakainen, Kari 39, 65
Hotinen, Juha-Pekka 61, 62
How New York Stole the Idea of Modern Art 67
Hughes, Ted 90
Hukkinen, Nina 151

Hulkko, Paulina 61, 66
Hume, David 128
Humour and Humanity 39, 45
Hunger Theatre 62
Hurme, Juha 5, 62
Huttu-Hiltunen, Heikki 90
hybrid style 48
Hytti, Jukka 9, 10, 98

I Ain't Taking Mama in My One-Room Place
  117
I Am Your Girlfriend Now 176–78
Ibsen, Henrik 28, 29
Iceland 158, 175
*An Ideological Karaoke Night in the Non-
  Ideological Finland* 137, 138
Idman, Dick 146, 148, 157
"I'll Be Watching You" 177, 178
In Alternate Spaces 62
independent workers' theatres 30
Insensitivity 2
Inspector Clouseau 27
International Theatre Project 9
Into Colder Climates 121–123, 190
Iraq 182
Ireland 51, 52, 70; Dublin 137
Irish Art Center 53
Iron Curtain 98
Itkonen, Juha 81

Jalakas, Peeter 182
James Bond 27
Jansson, Tomas 148
Japan 161
Jarovojs, Andrejs 49, 52
Jarry, Alfred 117
Jerusalem 77, 78
Jesus 78, 114
Johnson, Ken 28
Jokela, Juha 14, 22, 41, 64, 112–14, 188
Jooseppi from Ryysyranta 124
Jotuni, Maria 30
Joyce, James 136
Jung, Carl 55
Jurkka Theatre 8

Kafka, Franz 4
Kajaani City Theatre 59
Kajava, Jukka 116
Kallinene, Aune 62
Kane, Sarah 51, 106
Kanerva, Ilkka 129
Kantor 142
Kapteeninkatu 80

Karelian region (and Karelia) 3, 38, 65,
  125, 127
Kaukolampi, Mikko 104
Kaunas, Lithuania 50
Kaurismäki, Aki 8, 15
Kavén, Outi 95
Keats, John 115, 166
Kermode, Frank 64
Kianto, Ilmari 124, 137–141
Kiasma Theatre 5, 61–63
Kilpi, Maria 14, 54, 55, 57, 65, 187
Kinnunen, Heikki 121
Kirby, David 17
Kirkkopelto, Esa 4, 62
Kiseliov, Oleg 66
kitchen-sink drama 23, 36, 45
Kivarähk, Andrus 49, 50
Kivastik, Mart 49, 50
Kivi, Aleksis 28, 132–137
Kivierähk, Andrus 103,104
Klein, Naomi 73, 182
Klemola, Leea 3, 120, 123, 124, 187, 188,
  190, 191
Klivis, Edgaras 50
Klockrike Theatre 13, 124, 146, 147, 156,
  158, 179–82
Koitto Theatre 31
Kokkola 3, 121, 122, 190
Kokkonen 63
Koko Theatre 11, 12, 33, 48, 51, 81, 101,
  103, 104
Koljada, Nikolai 105
KOM Theatre 12, 45, 46, 48, 51, 68, 70,
  80, 81, 83, 84, 112, 116
Kommersant 129
KOMtext 51, 187
Koršunovas, Oskaras 50
Koski, Pirkko 9, 29, 36, 44–46, 64, 65
Kristian Smeds' Ensemble 5
Krogerus, Anna 13, 14, 22, 57–61, 171, 188
Kujanpää, Heikki 52, 66, 70, 85, 87–92,
  96, 188
Kumpulainen, Pekka 28
Kuritan Company 8
Kurtén, Martin 146, 179, 181
Kylätasku, Jussi 38, 39
Kylián, Jiri 48

The Laboratory 152
Lada 127
Ladies and Gents 53
Lago, Dan 17
Lahti, Ari-Pekka 8, 80
Lahtinen, Outi 51, 64

Laitala, Marja 117
Lampela, Pasi 22, 24
Långbacka, Ralf 10
Lappeenranta City Theatre 139
Lapps 28
Larsson, Anders 176
Latvia 9, 11, 28, 46, 102, 120; theatre 66
Latvian National Theatre Union 9
Lauri Viita 91
Lavery, Jason 19
Law and Order 31
The Left Alliance 126
Lehtonen, Jussi 66
Lenin 117; Museum 117
Lennon, John 177
Leskinen, Esa 52, 69, 70, 74–79, 125, 126
liberal capitalism 82, 85, 88, 89
liberalism 17, 71
The Lieutenant of Inishmore 70
Life Like 62
Linkola, Pentti 139
Linna, Väinö 125, 126, 128–132
Linnavuori, Matti 27
Lit Moon theatre 16
Lithuania 9, 11, 28, 46, 64, 77, 97, 99, 101, 102, 132, 142, 149, 156, 188; theatre 50, 66; Vilnius 66
The Little Theatre 147, 172, 179
Local Council 3
Local Government Act 35
London 48, 53
The Lonely Rider — A Performance About Depression 5
Longinus 14
Lönnrot, Elias 29
Look Back in Anger 23
Los Angeles County Museum of Art 185
The Lost Colony 130
Lotäs Wife 61
Lovers Theatre 8, 54
Lugn, Kristina 176
Lukács, George 67
Lulu 191
Lundán, Reko 13, 44, 45, 80, 171, 172, 174, 186
Lundström, Maria 147, 152, 163, 166–70, 173, 174
Lust committee 157
Lutheran 16, 29, 46, 89, 112, 185; Church 17; Evangelical 40; tradition 32, 66, 188
Luukkonen, Juha 137–141
Lyric Theatre 53

macho culture 16
Mahoney, Elisabeth 21, 22
Mail to Eva Dahlgren 62
Malmö 49
Malone Dies 167
Mankell, Henning 173
Manner, Eeva-Liisa 37
Mannerheim 126
Mannerheim Boulevard 145
Marinson, Harry 179
The Marlboro Man 27
Mars Theatre 13, 146, 170, 171, 179
Marti, Martina 132, 134, 136, 137
Marxism 50, 67, 82, 177
Master and Margarita 74, 75
matryoshka 128
McDonagh, Martin 51, 70
McDonald's 145
McMillan, Joyce 21
McPherson 51
Medea 61
Mekans, Stora 167
Memo I 63
Memo II 63
Memo III 63
Mental Finland 5, 188–190
Mercuriali, Silvia 53
Meri, Veijo 36
Meriluoto, Aila 90–92
message plays 14
Mestola Theatre 146
metaphorical theatre 96
Metsärinne, Saija 160
Meyerhold 117, 142
Midsummer Dances 108
Mill Theatre 61
Milonoff, Pekka 52, 80–82, 84
Ministry of Education 19
Ministry of Trade and Commerce 19
Mr. Nilson 4
Mobile Horror 40, 41, 45, 64, 65, 85
Modernism 67
Monday Night Raw 162
Moscow 48, 75, 77, 78
Moscow Theatre 143
municipal theaters 2
Museum of Contemporary Art 61
Myllyaho, Mika 14, 15, 22, 41, 64, 69–72, 129–132, 188

Napoleonic Wars 28
National Awakening 29
National Theatre 30, 32, 33, 56, 57, 68, 112, 129

nationalism 17, 97
NATO 19, 26
naturalistic theatre 71
Nazism 93–95
Nekrošius, Eimuntas 13, 50, 74, 101, 156
Neo-Classicism 186
neo-liberalism 22, 69
New Ramp Theatre 146, 147, 159, 160, 163–66, 170, 178
New Riga Theatre 49
The New Theatre of the Baltics 9
"New Theatre on the Baltic Shores" 11
New York 53, 153
New York Times 28
Niemi, Marjo 80
Nikkala, Antti 99, 100, 101, 123
Nikkalä, Jussi 136
Nirvana 83
Nokia 7, 185
Nokialandia 15, 69
Nordic Drama competition 113
Nordic Drama Corner 14, 22, 58
Nordic region 27, 52, 79, 98, 186, 187
Nordic Training Program for Actors and Directors of Theatre 172
Norman, Marsha 90
"Northern Man" 185
Norway 11, 28, 101, 175
Numminen, Katariina 3, 57, 62
Nurmelin, Minna 56

Oblivia 158
Odradek 4
The Odyssey 136
Öhrman, Jakob 146, 159–62
Ojasoo, Tiit 49, 50
Oksanen, Sofi 50
Old Juko Theatre 8
Olga 20–22
Olsoni, Kristin 149, 156, 179–81
On the Viking Trail: Travels in Scandinavian America 17
Ono, Yoko 177
Orlando 5
Osborne, John 23
Ostrobothnia 145
Oulu 39
Our Town 114
outlaw theatre 9, 11, 12, 16, 35, 99, 102, 112, 145
The Oven 38, 39

Palestine 159
Pandora's Box 191

Panic 14, 15, 41, 42, 43, 45, 70, 71, 85
Paris 78
Parker, Lynne 20, 21
Parkkinen, Sami 90
Parkkinen, Seppo 93
Parkkomäki, Marika 176, 177
Partnership for Peace Program 19
people's theatres 31
Peasant Estate 28
Peltola, Sirkku 117–120
perestroika 105
performance art 10, 13
A Performance with an Ocean View 4
Pilate, Pontius 75–78
Pinon, Pasqual 166, 167
Pinter, Harold 51, 57
A Place to Worry 65
Plath, Sylvia 58, 90
Poland 11, 179
The Police 178
Politkovskaya, Anna 106
The Popular Theatre 147
Pori 8
Portraits of Courage: Plays by Finnish Women 44, 46
postmodernism 10, 67, 146, 172
post–Reformation period 43
postwar era 36
Pöyhönen, Emilia 2
precariats 5
preservationism 15
primitivism 107
Private Jokinen's Wedding Leave 36, 37
Prufrock 57
psychological realism 29, 48, 77, 81, 96, 100, 144
Punahukka 65
Pure Theatre 146, 147, 151, 182
Purging the Cathedral 114
Putin, Vladimir 49, 76, 78, 106, 126
Putin's Russia 106

Q Theatre 11, 48, 66, 68, 70, 81, 84, 85, 90, 92, 96–98, 108, 111, 112, 115, 116, 132, 157
Quebec 158, 159
Queen C 43, 45
Queen Christina 43, 44

racism 70
radicalism 46, 71
Rage Cabaret 2
Rantala, Raija-Sinikka 144
Räsänen, Heidi 5

Rashomon 53
Rasila, Satu 167, 168, 172, 184
Ravenhill, Mark 51
Read, Herbert 185
The Reality Research Center 4, 5, 8, 53–55
The Red Line 137, 139–141
Reds 30, 31
reformists 71
Rehn-Sirén, Paula 146, 150–52, 182
Reich, Wilhelm 154
Renaissance 115, 186
"Renan" 151
Repin, Ilya 120
Rhymäteatteri 69
Riga, Latvia 9, 49
The Ring 167
Ringell, Susanne 180, 181
Rintala, Paavo 39
Ritva 188
The Road to Klockrike 179
Roiha, Mikko 134–136
Romanticism 18
Rome 77
Romeo and Julia 103, 104
Romeo and Juliet 104
Rosenberg, David 53
Rosendahl, Hanna 13
Rotozaza 54
"Roxanne" 178
Royal Danish Theatre 48
Royal Flemish Theatre 188
Ruikka, Maarit 61
Ruohonen, Laura 20, 21, 43, 44, 51
Ruskin, John 185
Russia 11, 12, 17, 18, 28, 29, 39, 40, 65, 76, 78, 82, 98, 106, 126, 128, 129, 131, 155, 158, 181; avant-garde 156; directors 74, 77; writers 105
Russification programs 29
Rytmi Bar 33

St. Paul 161
Saisio, Pirkko 2
Salama, Hannu 108, 109
Salminen, Arto 22–24
The Sandbox 180
Santa Barbara, California 15
Santa Claus 9
Sarkola, Milja 62
Saro, Anneli 49, 50
Sartre 73
Satan 76
Satan Comes to Moscow 52, 74–76, 126

Savonia literary award 59, 60
Scandinavia 84, 98, 101, 102, 144, 182; theatre 148
Schnitzler, Arthur 167
The Scotsman 21
Seinfeld 187
Seppälä, Riitta 9
The Seven Brothers 132, 135–137
The Seven Lamps of Architecture 185
7/1 132, 136
Shakespeare, William 63, 70, 104, 137, 156
Shepard, Sam 118
Shipyard Theatre 12, 110, 111, 115, 117, 118
The Shock Doctrine: The Rise of Disaster Capitalism 73, 182
Silén, Fabian 156, 157, 159
Silk and Knife 48
Siltanen, Juha 2, 5
Simberg, Anna 152
Sippola, Miira 61
Sirén, Mitja 152
Sirius Theatre 13, 146, 166, 179
Skunk Theatre 178
Slätis, Rasmus 146, 159, 160, 162, 163
Slovenia 11
Smeds, Kristian 5, 8, 50, 52, 61, 62, 112, 125–130, 132, 187–190
Smeds' Ensemble 62
Snellman, J.V. 17
The Snow Dress 180
social democrats 31, 33
social realism 45, 50, 80, 175, 178
socialism 17, 30–32, 80, 138, 165
Söderblom, Erik 34, 98, 146, 148, 150, 157, 163, 169, 178
Sore Spot 55–57, 65
Sørensen, Signa 48
The Sound of Music 145
Soup Theatre 182
Soviet Union 9, 19, 23, 31, 37–41, 49, 50, 65, 74, 76, 78, 98, 109, 117, 125, 126, 128, 129, 131, 132, 138, 141; army 95; economy 85, 88; occupation 46, 50
Spēlmaņu Nakts 9
Stages of Chaos: The Drama of Post-war Finland 36
Stalinism 10, 75, 76, 78, 79, 117
Stanislavski 144, 146, 154, 167, 179, 181, 182, 186
Stein, Peter 52
Sting 177, 178
Stockholm 43
Stockroom 23, 25
Stoppard, Tom 51

Storgärd, John 152
Strang, Pekka 146
Strangers 172
Strindberg, (Johan) August 28
Strömquist, Liv 176
Stubb, Alexander 19
Stückemarket prize 56
Subfrau 175
Such As—Supplementary Writings on Good
  5
Suomenlinna 69, 130
Sushi Geisha Boy 160
Suzuki, Tadashi 61, 66
Sweden 11, 12, 17, 18, 28, 29, 43, 69, 144,
  156, 158, 175, 187; Acting Academy 181;
  actors 49; Indigenous Theatre 147; lan-
  guage 80, 158, 170, 186; theatre 144
Swedish Institute (at the Theatre Academy)
  146, 150, 153–59; see also Theatre Acad-
  emy
Swedish National Theatre of Finland 147,
  169
Swedish-speaking (and Swedish-language)
  community 144–83; theatres 28, 46,
  102, 112, 124, 144–83, 186
The Swedish Theatre 80, 144, 145, 150, 151,
  169, 170, 175
Swim Naked 180, 181
Switzerland 132

Takomo Theatre 8; see also Forge Theatre
Tallinn 104
Tampere 8, 13, 83, 99, 110, 111, 115–117;
  City Theatre 12, 99, 141; International
  Theatre Festival 12–14, 56, 72, 95, 132,
  134, 163, 186; Worker's Theater 2, 117,
  132, 134
targeting 22, 24
"Targeting in Drama Translation: Laura
  Ruhonen's Plays in English Translation"
  20
Teena 175, 176
Teena, Brandon 175
Telakka 115
Theatre Academy 5, 32, 54, 51, 62, 99, 101,
  107, 111, 148, 155, 169, 187; see also
  Swedish Institute
Theatre Information Centre 19
theatre law 11, 12, 102, 103
Theatre Museum 59
Theatre 90° 147, 152, 169, 179
Theatre of Cruelty 47
Theatre People—People's Theatre 9
Theatre Siberia 12, 99, 101, 123

Theatres and Orchestras Act of 1993 33,
  34
Thirty Years War 43
The 39 Steps 145
This Is Riga Calling 49
The Tin Drum 92–96, 124
Tolstoy, Leo 120
Töölö Bay 33
Toulouse-Lautrec 61
Towards 52, 81, 82, 84
Traverse Theatre 20, 21
Treaty of Hamin 17
Troy 182
Trump, Donald 88
Tudeer, Annika 158, 159
Tukiainen, Johanna 162
"Tulips" 58
Tuomisto, Tuire 5
Turhapuro, Uuno 118, 124
Turkka, Jouko 10, 107–10, 124, 150, 179
Turku 147, 174
Turku Swedish Theatre 144, 145, 151

Ubu Roi 117, 118
Ukraine 182
Ulysses 182
The Umbrella 152
Uncle Sam 26
Uncle Vanya 105
United States 10, 14, 16, 27, 126, 127, 143,
  156, 176, 181; foreign policy 164
Universe 146
University of Helsinki 9, 64
University of Tampere 51, 115
University of Vaasa 20
The Unknown Soldier 52, 61, 112, 125, 128,
  129, 137, 188
Unnecessary People 13, 171–73, 186
Unto These Hills 130
Upton, Anthony 18, 30, 32

Valo, Vesa Tapio 38, 39
Vanhanen, Matti 129
van Itallie, Jean-Claude 75
Varnas, Gintaras 50, 51
Vedel, Karen 48
Veijalainen, Anna 33, 51, 101–06
Venus Theatre 146
Vesta, Grabstaitė 66
Viherjuuri, Mikko 123, 141–43
Viipuri Artistic Theater 3
Viirus 102, 112, 146, 152, 159, 170, 176, 179,
  182
Viita, Lauri 90, 91

Viitala, Anna 5, 136
Virgin Mary 191
Volga River 105
Von Krahl Theatre 182
Vuori, Eero-Tapio 52, 53
Vytautas Magnus University 50

Waiting for Godot 172
Walker, Paul 53
War of Lapland 31
Wasa 174; Theatre 144, 145, 159, 160
Watercolored 151
Wedekind, Frank 191
West Germany 78, 95
Westend 24
Western Europe 10, 146, 155, 185
What Is Being a Swede in Finland? 160, 170
Where There's a Watcher, There's a Doer 108, 110
Whites 30, 31
Wilder, Thornton 114, 167
Willberg, Helen 176
Wilmer, S.E. 29, 36, 41, 44–46

Wilson, Robert 52
Wilson, William 28
Wingren, Joanna 147, 152, 175–77
Winter War of 1939–1940 31
With Love from Pori 54
Woland 78, 79
Wollstonecraft, Mary 44
women's issues 30
Woolf, Virginia 5
workers' rights 30
workers' theatres 31, 33
World War I 37
World War II 23, 89, 93, 99, 109, 110, 125, 126, 174
Worringer, Wilhelm 185
Wuolijoki, Hella 31

xenophobia 70

Yoldia Sea 4
youth movements 30

Zholdak, Andriy 182